AF104152

Pseudo Ecotourism

In the Shadow of the Bengal Tiger

Arnab Basu

Ukiyoto Publishing

All global publishing rights are held by
Ukiyoto Publishing
Published in 2024

Content Copyright © Arnab Basu
Cover Photo Courtesy Arnab Basu
ISBN 9789362690210

All rights reserved.
No part of this publication may be reproduced, transmitted, or stored in a retrieval system, in any form by any means, electronic, mechanical, photocopying, recording or otherwise, without the prior permission of the publisher.

The moral rights of the author have been asserted.

This book is sold subject to the condition that it shall not by way of trade or otherwise, be lent, resold, hired out or otherwise circulated, without the publisher's prior consent, in any form of binding or cover other than that in which it is published.

www.ukiyoto.com

This book is dedicated to all the forest dwellers and forest guards of this subcontinent who risk and sacrifice their lives for the protection and conservation of forest and wildlife.

Few words for the book

Brinda Nair, two decades as a systems and management consultant, a theatre artist, and a recent masters degree in English literature.

"Arnab offers a compelling and insightful analysis of tourism practices foregrounding commodity fetishism and the phenomenon of greening capitalism. He weaves together captivating narratives through different wildlife sanctuaries and national parks across the subcontinent, with vivid storytelling and inspiring anecdotes often blending humour with moments of suspense. His thoughtful suggestions for combating pseudo-ecotourism make this book an invaluable resource for both seasoned travellers and eco-conscious adventurers seeking to make a positive impact on the environment while experiencing the wonders of the world."

Pooja Uthappa, a nature enthusiast and Managing Consultant at Global Sustainability Consulting firm, ERM

"For those who complement our busy corporate lives with hobbies in the natural landscape, this book shares some interesting reflections. Are we carrying our city mindset and corporate culture into the natural world? Can we let our guard down, let nature show us the way, to dwell in the beauty of the natural world."

Gauri Noolkar – Oak, Operation Manager at GetFresh Ventures, Vancouver and a Hydro-Geo Policy expert, Founder and Chief Editor at Lokmanya,

"Good transition from personal story to a larger issue. Narration style keeps readers hooked and makes them want to know more"

R. P. Nair, Principal Executive Officer at TATA Hitachi, CEO at Hydrolines and President at Welspun

"I hope mankind will recognize the danger and risk of pseudo-ecotourism. I believe the book, a very readable one, will contribute substantially to make the earth a better place."

Anupam Bhattacharyya, an avid traveller, a sustainability consultant, a singer and Associate Director at KPMG India

"This book is a thriller, a page turner, a wonderful melange where science, hobby and wanderlust confluence. With a stunning sense of wildlife photography and vivid storytelling, Arnab brings to life the diverse ecosystems and inhabitants of our planet, especially the Big Cat. Each page is a window into the wild, showcasing the beauty and complexity of the natural world. Whether you're a seasoned wildlife enthusiast or someone looking to reconnect with the wild, this book can be an indispensable companion. It's a testament to the awe-inspiring diversity of life on Earth and a rallying cry for conservation action. So, embark on this

exhilarating adventure and let this novel awaken the ecologist in you."

Chubzang Tangbi, a wildlife photographer, Managing Director at Langur Eco Travels, Bhutan, and a Photojournalist from University of Wales

"I extend my sincere gratitude to the author for his insightful book, "Pseudo Ecotourism: in the Shadow of the Bengal Tiger". Through engaging storytelling, he explores human desires for fame and glory within the context of wildlife photography and ecotourism. The book sheds light on nature's commodification and the importance of inclusive ecotourism for sustainable development. I commend the author for his dedication to raising awareness about these issues and offering valuable insights into conservation practices. This book serves as a timely reminder of the need for responsible tourism. Thank you, Arnab, for your contribution to the discourse on ecotourism and conservation."

Contents

Preamble	1
CHAPTER ONE: The Hobby for Fame	6
CHAPTER TWO: We Have a Unique Hobby!	20
CHAPTER THREE: Desperation for Fame	47
CHAPTER FOUR: Fame Breeds Arrogance	79
CHAPTER FIVE: Non-human Shatters Human Arrogance	119
CHAPTER SIX: The Tiger Economy	172
CHAPTER SEVEN: The Great Indian Tiger Show	194
CHAPTER EIGHT: The Under(-Rated-) Story!	251
CHAPTER NINE: The Silver Lining	291
CHAPTER TEN: The Wonder Wasteland	306
CHAPTER ELEVEN: The Wise Use of Wetland	324
CHAPTER TWELVE: Other Areas Are the New Hope	348
CHAPTER THIRTEEN: The Climate that is Changing.	393
CHAPTER FOURTEEN: When Human Culture Merges with Non-Human Nature	426
The Epilogue	446
Acknowledgements	473
Bibliography	477
About the Author	*482*

Preamble

"The History of Life on earth has been a history of interaction between living things and their surroundings. To a large extent, the physical form and the habits of the earth's vegetation and its animal life have been moulded by the environment. Considering the whole span of earthly time, the opposite effect, in which life actually modifies the surroundings, has been relatively slight. Only within the moment of time represented by the present century has one species – man – acquired significant power to alter the nature of his world." - Rachel Carson, Silent Spring

The "ecosystem integrity" of the planet is compromised, as Carson states in 1962, and this single book of hers *("Silent Spring")* was instrumental in launching the environmental movement of the Western world. It forced the ban of the extremely harmful chemical – DDT, and spurred revolutionary changes in the laws affecting air, water, and land.

But who knew that the "springs would be even more silent" with the onset of a new millennium?

When I started writing the final manuscript of this book, it was January 2021. Two years in, the battle of human versus microbe was still on. The COVID 19

Global pandemic caused by the recently discovered coronavirus, originated in December of 2019 from Wuhan, the sprawling capital of Central China's Hubei province, and spread rapidly across the world by early 2020. India was one of the worst hit nations. As a sustainability consultant who must travel to various sites and industries to make his living, I was hit financially by this pandemic. But as a hobbyist nature explorer I saw the worst effect of this pandemic on my ecotourism and wildlife photography tour organizer friends, as well as nature guides, gypsy drivers and staff who work at eco-lodges located in the fringes of various forests and sanctuaries of this subcontinent. Scientists claim that this pandemic is also an outcome of compromised ecosystem integrity, which makes Carson's philosophy so relevant even after 60 years of her legendary *Deep Ecological* publication.

I believe, the pandemic, forest cover loss, or climate change, any environmental crisis which has affected ecotourism business across the subcontinent, can be countered by ecotourism itself. However, it needs to be more wholistic, inclusive and regenerative.

More than a decade ago, I started my active ecotourism journey with a focus on a single species – the Bengal Tiger. During this time, I explored forty-five reserves, protected habitats and territories of Bengal Tiger, in four tiger range countries of this subcontinent. These include twenty-nine tiger reserves of India, twelve of Bhutan, three of Nepal, and one of Bangladesh. However, besides these tiger reserves and habitats I also explored more than 200 important ecotourism destinations in eight countries of three continents. On this journey I met numerous ecotour operators, local nature guides, wildlife photographers, biodiversity experts, and general ecotourists. In this book, I have used the real names of the people I met except for three people. The real identity of the three people whose personal life is integral to the context of this book was kept discreet and pseudonyms were used. As my interaction with the people I met on this journey went deeper, so did my perception towards ecotourism.

Besides Bengal Tigers, in the places I explored, I saw around 700 bird species, 125 mammals, 50 reptiles, and around 40 amphibian species. Clearly, nature's bounty has plenty of jewels and not just a single species called the Bengal Tiger. After all these explorations, sightings and interactions, my intention to continue this ecotourism journey and eventually write this book is to uphold the concept of an inclusive ecotourism against a single species focused, tiger centric ecotourism - the *"Pseudo-Ecotourism"*.

Inclusive ecotourism is not just about non-human life forms. As I was concluding writing the manuscript of this book, I had the opportunity to interact with various indigenous people of this subcontinent. I was amazed to see their level of sustainability consciousness and how they lived harmoniously with non-human life forms. I was particularly astonished by the empowerment among their womenfolk, which plays a crucial role in protecting nature. When the Global Leaders are breaking their heads to find an amicable path to implement "Sustainable Development" to combat climate change, these indigenous people have already embraced the sustainable way of life for centuries. Their way of life reminded me of the principles of Deep Ecology which was introduced by Norwegian philosopher ecologist Arne Naes in 1973. On this journey I was also amazed to see how age-old Buddhist philosophy of compassion and loving-kindness brings a spiritual connection with this scientific theory.

Thus, I realized the core value of inclusive ecotourism. An integrated concept and interlinkage between regenerative ecotourism, which encompasses and learns from community and indigenous people; the nature-based solution, which paves path towards 'sustainable development'; deep ecology which recognizes equality of every living life form; and the Buddhist philosophy of compassion and kindness, that takes the human to eternal happiness.

An ordinary human who takes part in ecotourism or clicks pictures of nature and her rare flora and fauna, despite not being a wildlife expert, helps in dispersing the splendors of nature and wildlife among many other ordinary humans who haven't yet experienced these. This makes the hobbies of ecotourism and wildlife photography powerful influencers in promoting the concept of nature-based solution. The solution to save the planet, which is hidden within nature herself. All we need is, to let such hobbies become inclusive. So that the beneficial impacts are bestowed equally upon all living life forms, not just on one single species.

Let us together embrace an inclusive ecotourism, where every human and non-human life form have equal place and let us discard the pseudo-ecotourism from this beautiful planet, we call home.

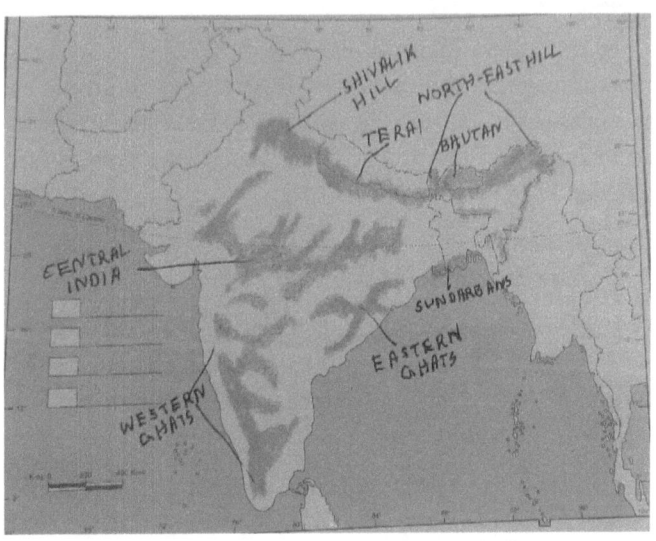

Map of subcontinental tiger landscape explored by me

CHAPTER ONE: The Hobby for Fame

The Oxford English dictionary defines hobby as an activity done regularly in one's leisure time for pleasure.

This dictionary definition of hobby, however, does not tell us what drives people to take up something as a hobby. For children these drivers could be curiosity, an urge to try new things. For adults these drivers, are perhaps, not as straightforward.

Circumstances were such, that I chose to re-write the dictionary definition of what hobby meant to me.

For thirty-seven years, I had no plan or fascination to pick up wildlife photography as a hobby. It happened rather abruptly, as an outcome of another activity which I intended to pick up for pleasure.

After living for nearly a decade in Delhi, at the age of thirty-five, I officially walked out of my marriage and moved to Bangalore. I was obese with a sedentary lifestyle and no sense of healthy eating and fitness. No, that's not why my marriage fell apart. However, that's not the aspect of my life that I intend to cover in this book. The intent is to tell you how I was attracted to a hobby.

Living alone in a new city required that I think of different ways to keep myself occupied. Focussing on health and fitness was certainly one way of doing that.

Feeling rejected and neglected was natural during that period of my life. It stirred within me a desire to be noticed and to become famous. Presenting myself as a fitness enthusiast, to a large extent, served to get the much-needed attention I was seeking. At times, unwanted too.

Thus began my journey of active sports and fitness and eventually I became a long-distance runner and Mixed Martial Arts (MMA) fighter. The obsession with these two sports was so strong, that following a flurry of my social media postings people around me were convinced that fitness was my serious hobby.

I was suddenly the most interesting guy in the room. As my social circle expanded though, the number of 'most' interesting guys also increased. And suddenly, from the most interesting guy I became a regular guy with a penchant for long distance running and MMA to stay fit. Like many other people do many other things for the same purpose.

Although I am trained in science of environment, my professional activities in this discipline have always been centred around providing advisory services to corporates on institutional environmental management and environmental law. In today's capitalist world such services are known as Sustainability Consultancy. Though I am a Sustainability Consultant, biodiversity or aspects related to wildlife have never been my core area of professional work. In my teen age days, I nurtured the idea of pursuing a career in nature and life science - a dream of dealing with flora and fauna in the wild had always excited me. What one may call the romanticism of a teenager - deeply engrossed in the idea of having a career in nature and life science. During the final phase of my Post Graduation in Environment Management, the neo-liberal concept of integrating environment and economics (termed as Sustainable Development) shifted my focus towards materialistic aspects of environment science. Thus, I became an environmental professional, specializing in sustainability, i.e., advising polluters to be "less problematic" for this planet.

Nevertheless, somewhere deep within my heart, the romanticism for nature stayed alive.

With this dormant romanticism and a single man's urge to become the most interesting person in the room, I re-discovered one of my childhood friends - Vedavyasa.

I met him in Bhopal. We had lost touch for over a decade. Vedavyasa is an electrical and power engineer by training and profession and was working in various power station installation projects. He was on a journey to establish himself as a Wildlife Photographer. I, on the other hand, was exploring various options of establishing myself as someone different from other regular guys.

Essentially, we both had the same objective but we were on different paths to arrive at the same destination.

Thus, I tagged along with him on his wildlife photography tour of Gir National Park in Gujarat, the only home on Earth of the Asiatic Lion.

After an overnight train journey from Bhopal to Junagarh, followed by an hour and a half drive by road, we arrived at Maneland Jungle Lodge, located about three kilometres away from the main entrance of Gir National Park. Vedavyasa had arranged for us to stay there for two days.

The lodge matched the aesthetics of the Saurashtra Peninsula. The stylizing by using local material and construction techniques appealed to me.

"Why bother with a safari. If you are lucky, you may see a lion in our backyard". Pointing his finger towards a water tank, the lodge manager announced. The water tank was right behind our room, clearly visible from our window. In the scorching summer of Gujarat, apparently the lion pride occasionally made their way to the water tank.

Wildlife photography aside, this trip was my first ever safari experience in wild. Just about anything was sufficient to get me excited. The ethnic design of the lodge and the possibility of a lion sighting right in the backyard of this lodge was enough to get my adrenalin rushing.

I promptly captured images of the lodge and the surroundings in my humble mobile phone. Who needed long distance running or MMA? With the wild stories that my new adventure was sure to provide I knew I would soon establish myself as the most interesting person in the room. Any room.

The following morning, a driver accompanied by a nature guide drove up to our lodge in a safari gypsy. Vedavyasa was ready with two Canon DSLR cameras, mounted with 600 mm and 500 mm canon lenses, respectively. We were set.

I wondered what magic the DSLR could do, that my smartphone couldn't. What is the difference between a 600 mm and a 500 mm lens, besides the obvious 100 mm that is?

Camouflaged in a printed cap, t-shirt, and safari track pants, Vedavyasa looked like a soldier armed with an automated light machine gun in each hand.

Looking at us, or perhaps at Vedavyasa, our friendly nature-guide Abu bhai (*bhai* in Hindi and Gujarati means brother) enquired,

"What subject are you working on…. Lion?"

Work? So, aren't we on vacation?

I concluded it was Vedavyasa's attire and gears. Professional photographers. That's what Abu bhai was thinking.

Vedavyasa nodded with a certain seriousness on his face. I mimicked him.

Abu bhai and our driver, Mehboob, took us to route number six of the national park. This route had been pre-allocated to us by the forest department. Soon as we entered the forest, both Abu bhai and Vedavyasa simultaneously exclaimed with equal energy – *'Look!! Pugmarks!'*

The pugmarks of the Asiatic lion on the soil were fresh, which was soft due to the early morning dew. We followed the footprints. Abu bhai and Mehboob pointed out the prominent male and female pugmarks, along with those of their cubs. They suggested that the small pride was probably shifting from one location to another. We smelled carcass, but found no vultures or other scavengers. After two hours of trailing and covering around twenty to twenty-five kilometres, at a distance of fifty metres from us, under the shade of trees at the crossing point between route number five and six, we caught sight of two male lions. Abu bhai surmised that they were about three to four years old – the subadult males

We were super excited. Although Vedavyasa had been roaming the Indian forests for a while, it was his first ever sighting of the big cats in the wild.

The lions were lying in the shade beneath the trees, guarded by the forest guide and other forest officials. I was amazed at their courage, as they were on their foot and precariously close to wild Asiatic lion of Gir.

The forest officials explained that the two cats went hunting early in the morning, and after a good meal had settled under the cool shade of the tree to rest for the day.

We came back victorious. Both Vedavyasa and I. For Vedavyasa it was being able to shoot his first big cat images in wild; and as for me - it was being able to do something that I had never done.

Our second safari of the day began in another exclusive gypsy with a fresh pair of driver and guide.

In the scorching heat of mid-summer Gujarat, I could see no other tourists with high-end photography gears like Vedavyasa's. However, there were plenty of Gujarati tourists with kids and large extended family out on summer vacation trips.

They noticed us, and I saw a mix of respect and curiosity in their eyes. One young boy walked up to Vedavyasa and enquired if we were wildlife photographers. Vedavyasa made a similar expression that he had given that morning to Abu bhai in response to *"What subject are you working on"*

Our ninja-looking attire, confident body posture and the impressive gadgets we wielded captured the attention of intrigued tourists, who looked at us in admiration and curiosity. I felt very special indeed.

The first two hours of our second safari were far from productive. We did not spot any big cat. No fresh pugmarks were noticed. Our fortune changed at around 5:00 pm, on route number five, at around 5:00

pm, on route number five, when we saw a female lion lying in the shrubs at a distance of about 200 metres from us. She was lying on her back sleeping in a bizarre posture with both her hind legs lifted in air.

Vedavyasa started shooting. In a gypsy close by, were a few young Gujarati women, who took more interest in sighting us than the lioness.

I could feel the adrenaline rush through my veins. *"Perhaps next time I too will come with a DSLR and lens and do photography.",* I told Vedavyasa who was busy shooting the lioness.

"Pick up the other camera and start clicking. What is stopping you?", he replied.

The moment I had waited for. Instantaneously I picked up the camera – the one mounted with a 500 mm lens. That was the beginning of my wildlife photography.

I had never used DSLR before, but I had a basic idea of photography. As a student of Botany and Environment Management, photography was required as part of my academic curricula. All the knowledge that I had gained, served well at Gir that day. Between our safaris, as we travelled from one location to another, Vedavyasa took it on himself to teach me the basics of DSLR usage. I learned how to control and play around with exposure, ISO (sensitivity of the camera's sensor, essentially its light gathering ability) and shutter speed.

For the rest of the safari, I was a "shutter-happy" wildlife photographer.

We continued on our safari along the same route. Fifteen minutes later, about ten kilometres from the spot the lioness was sighted, at a distance of forty-fifty meters from our gypsy, we found an adult male resting under the trees. He seemed quite exhausted in the scorching summer heat. The local weather report indicated it was 35-40°C. As the sun went down, the heat eased up.

We continued further on the pre-defined track. In the summer afternoon the forest smelt woody, much like a wooden cupboard with old and stale millets.

About five kilometres from the previous sighting, at about half past five, we spotted a female lion resting in the shade of a tree next to a water tank built by the forest department. We were merely 20-30 meters from the lioness.

The cool breeze, flowing from the direction of water tank added an earthy smell. The diffused light of early evening cast a grey shade in the bright yellow-green foliage of the dry deciduous semi-arid western Indian forest. Vedavyasa called it the "golden light". Anything that you shoot in the forest in that light is "gold", he declared!

Abu bhai explained that the Asiatic lion typically hunts and eats at night, and subsequently moves early morning to find a cool shaded place. They go to sleep at dawn, resting the entire day. Towards evening, right before dusk, usually between 5:00 to 6:00 pm, they prepare for the upcoming night. The best time to spot lions in Gir, he explained, was thus between 5:00 and 6:00 pm, the last hour of the last safari of the day.

While the safari for the day was almost over, the climax was yet to be. About ten kilometres down, almost at the end of route five, sat another fully grown adult lioness in a relatively less dense patch of the forest. At a distance of just fifteen meters from us. To our surprise, she got up, started moving towards our parked gypsy.

Unbelievable luck! And that too on my first ever safari in the wild. In my excitement, I sprang from my seat.

The forest department officials, keeping eyes on lioness and tourists, warned our driver to move the vehicle further away. They indicated that the lioness was going to drink water at a waterbody close by. Within a few minutes the lioness came out in the open. I could feel my heart racing as she walked just at five meters from the gypsy completely indifferent and oblivious to our presence, with a royal, strong, and fierce gait as she made her way to the waterbody.

We were the only gypsy enjoying this grand show. Soon after, another gypsy arrived with tourists, a young couple. The lady ignoring us while also pointing at our gypsy, loudly professed her wish,

"We want to be in that spot."

How dare you! Asking two wildlife photographers to make way for you. You, who are not even equipped with a point and shoot camera?

I gave her the cold shoulder. Taking a cue from my indifference, Vedavyasa decided to ignore her too.

Drivers and guides of both gypsies were visibly helpless.

The lioness quenched her thirst and resumed walking back to her original place. We captured the entire show of catwalk, both in our camera and etched into our memories, and then mercifully decided to leave the place to allow the other gypsy to enjoy what remained of the show.

The Safari ended with a feeling of great respect, fear, and adoration for the king and queen of the jungle, as I had known them since I had been a child. In spite of an exhausting day, we were filled with happiness and a sense of achievement at a successful exploration.

The feeling of being special and different from other mortals was, of course, prominent among all the feelings engulfing my heart and soul.

Nurturing the idea of picking up wildlife photography as a hobby and its potential to establish myself as the most interesting guy in the room, I returned from Gir.

The dictionary meaning of hobby is an activity to be done regularly for pleasure in one's leisure time. However, that day, I concluded that this definition was insufficient and needed some important corrections. If you do it only in your leisure time, then how can it help you in establishing yourself as the most interesting guy in the room? Especially when you are hard pressed for leisure in your corporate profession.

If it is meant only for pleasure, then how come the experienced safari guide asked us, *"What subject are you working on?"*. Hobby is indeed work and not merely means for pleasure or enjoyment.

That day I wrote my own definition of hobby. *A hobby is a regular activity that is done as many times as possible in one's lifetime to fulfil the desire for fame and glory.*

Author Amir Yawari in his article titled, *Why Everyone Wants to Be Famous (and why it's a problem)*, published in the online journal *Illumination,* states, *"You might feel ashamed to admit it to your friends or anyone you know but at some level, you too want to become famous. It's not just a few people who want fame, everyone does (most people just don't admit it)."*

In this article, he also mentions, *"Apparently, famous people seem to get many benefits that everyday people don't. This makes people believe that life is a lot easier for a famous person, they believe that being famous solves all problems, poverty, neglect, rejection, lack, and so on. All these benefits make the idea of being famous very appealing to the anonymous one; this is also why most people think they would like to become famous.".*

Today's commodity market sees this human desire for fame as an opportunity to create another lucrative commodity for which a large consumer base is readily available.

This commodity market was struggling with 1960-1970s social movement against capitalism, such as anti-Vietnam war campaign, the civil rights movement, women's liberation, the student movement, and last, but not least, the counterculture.

During this period, environmentalism also became a part of mass social movement. Drawing on a culture of political activism inspired in part by the civil rights and anti-war movements, thousands of citizens, particularly young middle-class Western men, and women, became involved with environmental politics.

This socio-environmental movement embraced radical ecology, which demands nature and ecology to be placed at the centre of any developmental decision. This radical ecology criticises capitalism's expansionist logic. Therefore, capitalist force turned this radicalism on its head. The first and foremost step in this process was to make ecology and economy equivalent and integrate them to make a new commodity called sustainability. This sustainability, which was created to deal with radical ecology is often termed as neo-liberal sustainability.

Being part of anything radical (including radical environmentalism) always helps in achieving fame and glory. A trend emerged among urban affluent class to become radical. To deal with this alarming trend of being part of radical environmentalism, capitalism started selling the commodity called neo-liberal sustainability to humans desperate for fame, eventually, to use them against radicalization of ecology.

Wildlife photography and ecotourism as hobbies are integral parts of that commodity, sellable to fame-hungry humans.

CHAPTER TWO: We Have a Unique Hobby!

Sometime ago I read a famous Bengali novel by renowned Bengali novelist Buddhadeb Guha titled *Madhukari* (Art of Honey-gathering). The protagonist of the novel, Prithu, is a sensitive man who struggles to find the purpose of his existence in a material world.

Prithu, of Guha's novel, is confused about the nature of his independence. He believes that in exchange for temporary protection, he forfeited his essential liberties. The liberty of choosing food, shelter, and mating partner. The liberty of living in harmony with nature. The liberty, that all other non-human life forms enjoy.

This temporary protection provided for by a materialistic lifestyle appears as an essential need for the weak and frightened human. Civilized human of today's world embraces this protection, that comes in the form of family, conventional job in urban areas and access to a technology enabled elite community.

The privilege to have a family, conventional urban job and access to such elite community also comes with certain demands. These demands determine what to eat; where and how to live; and with whom to make love. These demands force the human to partake in the process of creating a comfortable life and living that life. Prithu, of Guha's novel, was convinced that to live that comfortable life humans had sacrificed their essential liberties.

Prithu is left with no choice but to live this life, because exercising essential liberty is forbidden in the elite community to which he belongs. Leaving this community to enjoy essential liberty is beyond the threshold of his courage, as that would cause him to lose the privilege of temporary protection.

Every other human, like Prithu, lives with this dilemma, which perhaps makes them envious of non-human life forms.

Guha's Prithu desires to be like the protagonist from another world-famous fiction – Mowgli, from Rudyard Kipling's *The Jungle Book*.

In Kipling's novel, despite Mowgli's right to access the essential liberties, he encountered significant opposition from the main antagonist, the non-human Sher Khan- a Bengal Tiger, when attempting to exercise these rights.

Here, the non-human Bengal Tiger harboured insecurities regarding the perceived supremacy of the human, Mowgli, in the forest. Unlike his human counterparts, Mowgli never expressed his desire to establish his supremacy in the forest. Rather he sought to coexist in harmony with others, as just another life form. Nevertheless, the other non-human life forms were suspicious of his true intentions.

Prithu's desire for living the life of Mowgli is the hidden expression of human's desire to live like just another life form. However, the materialistic lifestyle inculcated in the human society does not allow them to experience life as yet another life form in nature.

Therefore, this lack of essential liberty in civilized human society necessitates the pursuit of escapades. As an outcome, the human embraces nature exploration, ecotourism, and wildlife photography as the closest possible way to experience life as just another life form.

The urban dwelling human with substantial disposable income, embraces these activities. They also discover that these activities can make them the most interesting person in the room. These activities are their means of achieving the much-desired fame and glory.

Stricken by the desire of being the most interesting person in the room, after my Gir trip, I decided to further strengthen my newly developed hobby of wildlife photography and create another opportunity to live in proximity with nature. Therefore, I bought my own DSLR (a second-hand Nikon D3100 mounted with a 70-300 mm Sigma lens) as I planned my next trip to undertake in winter.

I signed up for and completed online courses on Photography and also attended a workshop

Pseudo Ecotourism 23

conducted by famous wildlife photographer and film maker Kalyan Verma, to prepare myself for the next trip with Vedavyasa in the forests of Western Ghats.

This time I took the lead in planning. I charted out the itinerary that included Bandipur - India's oldest tiger reserve; Nagarhole - a controversial tiger reserve owing to tribal resettlement issues; and Periyar – one of the few tiger reserves of India where trekking and camping inside the forest is allowed.

The reason I chose these three tiger reserves and national parks, was proximity to Bangalore, where I lived then.

As I planned this trip for my newly developed hobby, I had little idea that new dimensions would be added to the definition of hobby I had outlined.

And one winter morning, with our base camp at Jungle Inn resort, Vedavyasa and I with our driver cum "Man Friday" Purushottam, set out for the Veeranahosahalli range of Nagrahole National Park.

At 6:30 in the morning the sky was overcast. The temperature was around 20-22°C. The security and safari arrangement at Nagarhole National Park did not appear very impressive. We booked a canter (twelve-seater bus used by general tourists) safari. On arrival for our safari, we were told that the canter would not start unless there were at least ten passengers.

We then asked for a gypsy. A senior forest guard explained that there was presently only one gypsy and that the driver was currently unavailable. He added that the gypsy would cost Rs. 3000/- for a single exclusive safari, compared to Rs. 300/- per person for a canter safari. We waited until 8:00 am for the gypsy, a gypsy returning from its previous safari. We finally began our first safari at Nagarhole. Also, the first in a Bengal Tiger habitat.

A local Kannadiga couple also waited for a safari gypsy. Instead of hiring an exclusive gypsy though, they wanted to share a gypsy with others.

Gypsy driver cum nature guide Adinarayan, after noticing we were equipped with photography gears, commented on the couple, *"These people are not fit for wildlife tourism, they only look for opportunity to save money"*.

The couple's only hope was us. Equipped, as we were, with photography gears and fuelled by ego-gratifying comments from the gypsy driver we completely ignored the couple and headed for the forest.

Purushottam accompanied us as well. After driving about three to four kilometres through the teak forest of the park, and spotting a lot of spotted deer and jungle fowl *en route*, Purushottam suddenly let out a scream. He claimed he had spotted an elephant on the right side. Adinarayan was not interested to stop initially as he was unsure about the presence of the animal. Vedavyasa, though, asked him to stop. He spotted the elephant too, and then the rest of us did too. They were a good ten-twelve kilometres away from the vehicle but their huge heads were visible through dense bushes. There certainly was more than a couple of elephants. Perhaps a herd. I was excited.

I was also mighty impressed with Vedavyasa and Purushottam, and proud to be in the company of two humans who appeared to be ace wildlife tourists. Tropical evergreen forest of Western Ghats is very different from Gir, as it is moist, cool, and much darker due to a high canopy. The huge elephants can easily get engulfed in the vastness of such a forest.

We arrived at a watchtower that was fifteen feet high, and we climbed up to the top to get a better view. We spotted three female elephants distinctly and one huge bull further away from them.

We continued on the safari till half past ten. Other than spotting a bunch of spotted deer, sambar, southwest langur, and a lot of birds like jungle mayna, wagtail, peacock, green bee-eater, red wattle lapwing, and egrets - we did not spot any other more significant species such as any big cats, particularly Bengal Tigers, that we were looking for. The overcast sky and intermittent rain kept big animals in their hideouts in the dense forest of Nagarhole. This overcast sky and intermittent heavy and light rain followed us throughout this trip except for the first day at Ranganathittu bird sanctuary. That day was exceptionally sunny.

Before arriving at Nagarhole, *en route*, we visited the largest bird sanctuary of Karnataka, situated on the bank of Cauvery River. On a bright and sunny winter morning, we were delighted to sight spot-billed pelican, darters, cormorant, black headed ibis, common river tern, Tickell's blue flycatcher, Eurasian think-knee, Asian open bill stork, grey heron, black crowned night heron, and many other water birds. We also spotted flying fox (or fruit bats, as they are popularly known) and plenty of marsh crocodiles in water.

Throughout this trip, I never stopped making notes of what I was seeing. Publication of this list of species sighting in social media would, after all, help me in establishing myself as that most interesting guy in the room.

We went on two safaris at Nagarhole. In the second safari we saw a parade of elephants near a big pond, created by rainwater accumulation. We saw a tusker and herds of gaur (Indian bison, as popularly known) on the highway that cuts across Nagarhole forest towards Kerala.

The most satisfactory part though, was that, we two were the only tourists with high-end cameras and big lenses. That gave us ample opportunity to show-off in front of other non-photographer tourists. That was to change at our next destination – Bandipur.

When we started our first safari early in the morning at Bandipur, there was already news that a male tiger had killed a gaur the previous night. This news brought in many wildlife photographers and enthusiasts from Bangalore and other parts of India.

At Gir, I did not have the opportunity to interact with other wildlife photographers besides Vedavyasa. Bandipur, however, was a conglomeration of wildlife photographers.

At around 6:45 am, as we entered the safari zone of the park, besides the driver cum guide Boma, we were accompanied by four other companions in our safari gypsy – two wildlife photographers from Bangalore and a Gujarati couple on honeymoon. The wildlife photographers had obviously landed to spot the gaur-killer tiger.

As we proceeded, at around 7:15 am, we heard the first warning call let out by a southern grey or black-footed grey langur from the southeast direction of the forest. A couple of gypsies began tracing the call. After driving about two to three kilometres both the gypsies came to a halt. Big cats, the most elusive creatures of the forest, a pair of leopards, were spotted. Leopards always make their presence highly imperceptible. By the way, that was the first time in my life that I had heard warning calls by an animal. In fact, if Vedavyasa hadn't told me, I would have never recognized it as a warning call.

The mating pair was sitting on the open land to our left. The langur, that continued giving the warning call, was perched atop a teakwood tree right next to the female leopard. The pair was moving on from the spot, after having mated, presumably a short while ago, explained Boma. At first the pair was baffled, and they quickly sunk into the bushy scrubs. A few minutes later, the male leopard came out into the open and boldly lay down. The female followed. The lady was shy and unsure about being in the open. After a while, she headed for the thicket nearby and settled down.

I was still a novice in wildlife photography and yet to decipher the mysteries of light and camera settings. As a result, I was unable to capture any sharp or clear images of the leopards.

After about two to three minutes, the pair stood up and walked slowly into the undergrowth. We could hear them growling in the bush. What we witnessed was a partial courtship behaviour which is hardly ever seen live. Given that leopards are very discreet about their presence, they become even more elusive during the mating period. We could hardly believe our luck in witnessing such a rare moment. We continued to wait for another ten-fifteen minutes but the pair did not come out.

We resumed looking for any trace of the tiger that had killed a gaur the previous night. A photographer from Bangalore said that the tiger was spotted the previous evening near a waterbody. The gypsies made their way to the said waterbody, and sure enough, the carcass of the gaur was found hidden inside a dense bush. The lower part of the carcass was half eaten. Probably the intermittent light and heavy shower of the intervening night kept the tiger away from it. It was certain that the tiger would return to finish eating.

Pseudo Ecotourism

We waited for a while, making a few rounds in the gypsy around the area, but found nothing that indicated the presence of the tiger in the area. A sloth bear, however, made a sudden appearance. It was crossing over from one side of the forest to the other. One of the photographers from Bangalore, seated in the front seat spotted it and alerted others. All four wildlife photographers with hi-end cameras were caught by surprise at this sudden appearance of another elusive animal. None of us were adequately prepared to capture the rare sight and gradually the sloth bear disappeared into the dense forests of Bandipur National Park.

We explored until 9:00 am. Significant sightings included a few bird species – long tailed shrike, streak throated woodpecker, Malabar parakeet, brown fish owl, brahminy sterling, spot bill duck etc. No sight of any big animals.

The feeling of disappointment due to non-sighting of tiger, was overridden by the pride I felt in identifying the birds (of course with the help of Boma and Vedavyasa) and uttering their fancy names, particularly in front of the Gujarati couple, who appeared very impressed. I smiled to myself.

Although Vedavyasa was more experienced in tiger habitat explorations, he was taking equal pride and bragging, albeit covertly, how he was different from others.

We returned to the base, and after a good lunch and a short siesta, we set out for the next round of exploration at about 4:00 pm, a little later than originally scheduled.

Three gypsies and two canters proceeded to the forest. We later realized that the late start was planned so as to stay back late in the forest in an attempt to spot the gaur killer tiger. The photographers in different gypsies and their companion forest guides and drivers were eager to sight the tiger. For over two hours, the gypsies and other vehicles circled the fifteen square kilometres area around the bush where the carcass was hidden. We were no longer on a safari, instead we had transformed into watch guards for the carcass. The intermittent rain throughout the day suggested that the sighting of the tiger in the afternoon was unlikely.

At 5:00 pm, towards the northwest direction from the carcass, approximately three kilometres away, a male leopard lay on the branch of a teakwood tree. Another rare sight.

Once it noticed the presence of gypsies, the shy animal jumped down from the tree and disappeared into the deep forest. So far, in the evening safari, we had seen a few spotted deer, southwest langur, bonnet macaque, herds of gaur, few racket tail drongo, oriental magpie, flame back woodpecker and a pair of yellow footed green pigeon. None of them can really match up to the delight of sighting a Bengal Tiger.

Around 5:15 pm, a strong repeated warning call by a barking deer was heard from the northwest direction to the carcass. Rising excitement and hope gripped us, and other wildlife photographers. On advice from other more experienced wildlife enthusiasts present there and with agreement of forest guides, we concluded that the tiger was going to appear any minute now from the direction where the call bellowed.

I was highly impressed by the confident prediction of the wildlife enthusiasts and forest guides.

The vehicles were segregated into two groups, creating a fifteen-twenty feet corridor between the anticipated point of tiger's appearance and the spot where the carcass was hidden.

We expected the tiger to come through the corridor created by us and eat the remains of the half-eaten gaur in front of the hundred-odd tourists gathered there. The waiting game resumed.

As we waited, Vedavyasa and I were silent. We had accepted that both of us had a long way to go before becoming wildlife experts like the others around us.

After waiting for ten-fifteen minutes, someone mentioned that the call was coming from the direction where the male leopard had disappeared to. At about the same time, it dawned on everyone, that the call was perhaps to alert the presence of the leopard. Disappointed, with no trace of the tiger, it was time to move on.

My respect for and high expectations from the wildlife photographers gathered at that national park received a minor setback.

"It was alright. Good effort by the experienced wildlife enthusiasts in predicting the appearance of the tiger. It didn't yield any result. But that is normal I suppose. Even Jim Corbett was not always accurate!". I told Vedavyasa and myself.

He nodded in agreement.

We exited the forest at around 6:00 pm. Again, we spotted a sloth bear in the dark. Perhaps the same one that we had spotted in the morning. But it was too dark to be certain, and ethically capture (without camera flash) any image of that creature.

Next morning, at 6:30 am, we started our last safari in Bandipur National Park in a forest department canter. The forest was unusually quiet compared to the previous day. It had stopped raining and the sun was out. All the wise wildlife enthusiasts had apparently gone back to their respective homes after several unsuccessful attempts in sighting the tiger.

Vedavyasa and I were however very pleased as we were the only wildlife photographers in our canter.

Equipped with DSLR and bazooka telephoto lenses, it was a golden opportunity for us to prove we were different and unique achievers, being the only "elite" passengers in the canter.

The driver of the canter too paid us more attention, stopping the vehicle whenever we requested, allowing us to take pictures.

Apart from the regular bird species we spotted a pair of happy stripe-necked mongoose.

The real opportunity to demonstrate to everybody in our circle, that we have a unique hobby, was waiting for us just around the corner, at our next destination.

On completing our exploration in Bandipur, the same afternoon, we returned to Bangalore and took an overnight bus to Munnar, arriving next morning. We spent the entire day exploring Eravikulam National Park. In the evening, we arrived at the forest rest house at Thekkady.

Exploration in the park and taking images of endangered Nilgiri tahr in the presence of a crowd of non-photographer tourists, were immensely joyful few hours of our life.

Everyone was taking notice of us, or rather our photography gears. Vedavyasa was wearing a jacket with the logo of *National Geographic*, which he received for being an annual subscriber of their magazine. A group of young college students approached him and requested a selfie. They perhaps assumed that he was a professional wildlife photographer from *National Geographic*.

We were now convinced that we were different from others, expressed partly by our raised chins and gratifying smiles.

The following morning at 9:00 am, we arrived at the check post of Periyar Tiger Reserve to embark on one of the most adventurous and challenging forest hiking in our country - the Periyar Tiger Trail. We hoped to get a real opportunity to live like non-human life forms. Periyar did not disappoint us.

Three Spanish hikers – Sichov, Fernando and Anna, and a French hiker Juliet, accompanied us. Sichov and Anna came from Madrid, while Fernando and Juliet had been living in Delhi for the past year. There were four forest guides with us – C. C. Thomas, S. Pandya, N. S. Kunjumon and C. Armugam – all of them were rehabilitated ex-poachers with thirty-forty years of experience in dealing with forest and wildlife. A forest official cum gun man, Ajimon, also accompanied us.

I was feeling glorious at the thought that I was going to be part of something similar to Bear Grylls's adventure in the wild. The upbeat feeling was soon challenged by reality.

At 10:00 am, the whole contingent, armed with cameras, survival kit and three days' worth ration in 25-30 kg heavy rucksack, began the trek from the forest department's check post. The initial trek was roughly four kilometres to the bamboo rafting point at the edge of Periyar Lake. Along this stretch of four kilometres, the key species spotted were male sambar, Nilgiri langur, bonnet macaque, grey-headed fish eagle, wag tail and common drongo, among others.

After a two-hundred-meter bamboo raft ride on the Periyar lake, we arrived at what was to be the most difficult stretch of the trek - the final five kilometres through dense bush and teak wood forests. We began walking enthusiastically.

The forest was full of leeches and to prevent leech attack we applied tobacco powder over our trekking shoes and leech guard socks. The sky was overcast, and the temperature 30°C. Intermittently we noticed fresh pugmarks on the muddy forestland. Guide Thomas announced that the pugmarks belonged to a big male tiger.

Studying and understanding tiger pugmarks when on its trail is no less fun than seeing the elusive animal itself. Trying to speculate where it went, decipher the direction and how long ago it had passed this way – adds an unparalleled dimension to a safari. Particularly when recognizing and following the tiger pugmarks leads one to spot the animal. One experiences a 'pro' feeling. We decided it was apt to pretend to be "pro". Afterall, we had spotted the pug marks. If the forward most points of the two middle toes are almost at the same level; this implies that they are perhaps made by the front limbs. When the shape of the toes is rounded, when there is more space between the toes, and the pugmark almost fits into a square, in all probability, it is a male tiger.

A valuable lesson from Thomas. He also pointed to a scratch mark of a tiger's claw on a tree trunk.

It wasn't the leeches or even a possible tiger attack that caused me to panic, but the crossing of the river streams over loosely placed tree trunks.

With the rucksack on my back and Vedavyasa's 500 mm lens mounted on the Canon camera body in hand, on several occasions I thought I was going to fall into the river. I must confess I was looking forward to the end of the trek. I was certain Vedavyasa was having similar thoughts, as was evident from his stressed-out body language.

Finally, the trail ended. We arrived at the edge of the forest and at the bank of Periyar Lake. From that point on, just another kilometre of bamboo rafting and we would arrive in the core area of the forest, where our tents were pitched for the following three days and two nights.

We arrived at our camp at 1:00 pm, and for the next hour we were busy cooking.

There were three tents for six hikers. The guides decided to stay at the area designated for cooking. The meal for the day was *cappa kodi* or tapioca. Source of drinking water was Periyar Lake, and the bushes in the southeast corner of the forest, around two hundred meters from our tents, was our "toilet". The camp was protected by a meter high bio fencing, and ten-twelve feet deep Elephant Protecting Trench (EPT).

We were anxious at the thought of crossing the EPT on a makeshift bamboo bridge each time we needed to use the toilet.

After lunch, at about 3:30 pm, we resumed walking through the bushes in the northeast direction. Ten minutes into the walk, we heard the distinct warning call of a barking deer. We came to a halt and watched, our eyes darting. There was no movement of any big cat. We continued walking. An old skeleton of a gaur was found on open land; apparently, killed by a tiger.

At around 4:30 pm, after a five-kilometre bush walk in the same (northeast) direction, guide C. C. Thomas noticed elephant footprints. The team followed the trail and lo and behold - through dense bushes a tusker appeared right in front of us. We were rooted to our spots, perplexed and clueless. Gun man Ajimon took position with his rifle.

Vedavyasa exclaimed, *"Don't Panic!"*. I am unsure as to whom that was meant for, but the elephant ran away and disappeared as quickly as it had appeared. We realized later that the Spanish hiker Anna had adorned a pink rain cover and that, perhaps, caused the tusker to panic and retreat into the forest. Guide Thomas was furious at us. He admonished us saying that when in a forest everyone should know how to camouflage. Wearing pink rain cover was suicidal. The elephant could have charged at us.

Ironically, in Malayalam (the official language of the state of Kerala, where Periyar is located) "Aana" stands for elephant. The joke during the rest of the exploration was "Anna scared Aana".

Needless to say, such behaviour from western hikers in the dense forests of Western Ghats, reinforced our belief that we had better understanding of forest and wildlife. Another opportunity to brag.

The night was windy and cold, accompanied by heavy rain, and the fear that the strong winds could possibly blow the tents away. Forest guides created a small campfire with dry woods collected from the forest. We placed our wet shoes and socks next to the fire hoping it would dry by morning. For dinner we had fried fish bought from the local tribal people, who caught it from the Periyar Lake, at a cost of Rs. 200/- per kg.

That night, around 9:00 pm, we were surprised and delighted by the arrival of guests at our camp – Raja and Rani - a porcupine pair. Guide Kunjumon informed us that whenever they camped, Raja and Rani always paid a visit, searching for food.

It was the first time I was spending a night in a tent in a dense forest, and with no access to technology. The stormy night caused me to wonder if this trip and the ensuing hardship was all a mistake.

Next morning got off to a scary start. I headed for the designated toilet area within the forest for a dump. That was also my first experience of dumping in a core area of any forest, but this one particularly, as it was known for movement of predators and big herbivores like elephants and gaur. I was sceptical about venturing into the forest for 'this' purpose, but I was left with no other option. So, I proceeded and sat inside a bush, counting every second, and trying very hard to keep away thoughts of possible predators lurking in the area.

When I was right in the middle of my morning business, I heard three strong warning calls of sambar deer from what appeared to be close by, in the southeast direction. Before I could decide whether it was an alarm or if I had been mistaken, the call ended.

I then heard Vedavyasa call out my name twice, followed by Thomas screaming, *"Sir, come back to the tent quickly!"* Everybody had heard the call. A big cat was perhaps on the move.

But how could I go back when I was in the middle of something?

I quickly attended to my "nature's call" and ran to the tent. Fortunately, nothing significant happened. Once there, I took a deep breath, particularly because they hadn't seen anything that I may have missed. After all the hardship, I wanted to be part of any and all stories.

The morning walk in the bushes was towards the southwest, after crossing the Periyar Lake on bamboo raft. We climbed almost up to 915 metres, but the rain kept all the big animals away from us. An old skeleton of an elephant that had been killed by a tiger was spotted. The rare bird, Indian great hornbill, flew over us as we reached the highest point of our trail.

I call it a trail, but in reality, we were making our way through thorny shrubs and clearing the branches obstructing our paths with sickles. The several scratch marks on our face and exposed parts of neck and hands stand testimony to this.

More alarmingly, the foliage was so dense that we could barely see through it. It was highly likely that hidden in there was something that could be dangerous to our life. It's no wonder that the forest department officials got us to sign an indemnity letter at the beginning of this trek.

The same afternoon, between 1:45 and 2:00 pm, several strong calls of sambar deer were heard from the northeast direction of the forest. As we looked through the binocular; we saw two sambar deer running from northeast to northwest direction. In the evening, we went bush walking in that direction and chased several herds of gaur. Around 4:00 pm, we again heard warning calls. This time it was a Nilgiri langur but found nothing else that indicated a big cat movement. A serpent eagle was spotted flying above us.

All the hiking in the tiger reserve of Periyar through dense foliage and steep terrain with heavy lenses and delicate cameras in hands often threw us off balance.

While our western counter parts might not possess much knowledge of Indian forest and its wildlife, they were doing much better when it came to hiking. Moreover, they had no pressure of taking photographs, and thus were enjoying the liberty of hiking in the raw landscape of Western Ghats.

Vedavyasa was beginning to appear less confident in dealing with the terrain after our first three bushwalks and decided to stay back at camp for subsequent walks.

In fact, during hiking through and camping at Periyar, several times he lost his cool with me, as if I was responsible for exposing his inability to cope with the forests of Periyar.

The second night was relatively quiet with the porcupine pair making their usual appearance to entertain us.

Our final encounter with an elephant on this trip was on the last morning at 6:30 am, right next to the camp. Guide Thomas and Pandya shouted, *"Ladies and Gentlemen come down to the cooking area, quickly!"*

We all rushed there and caught sight of three elephants swimming through the Periyar Lake. Their trunks and the upper part of their heads were visible; they were coming from the west side of the forest going towards east, where our camp was set up. A few minutes later, a female elephant started walking towards the camp. She walked ten-fifteen meters, grazing as she walked, and reached very close to camp. The only barrier between her and us was the ten feet deep EPT, surrounding the camping area.

The elephant stayed there for not less than half an hour. Several times she raised her trunk towards the camp to catch the scent but continued grazing, and showed no sign of attack. She soon disappeared in the dense forest towards the northeast. The cow elephant's tail was broken; therefore, she could be considered a dangerous animal, as broken tail implied, she had been involved in fighting with other elephants. One of our ex-poacher companions enlightened us. This added a little extra thrill to our morning encounter.

Guide Pandya mentioned that five years ago a female elephant came from the same direction and fell into the trench. At that time there used to be a big tree at the northwest corner of the EPT. She coiled her trunk around the tree and got herself out of the trench.

Next morning at 10:00 am, with a full contingent, we retreated from the camp so as to exit the forest. We followed the same route we took on our onward journey to the camp. First hour was sunny, but soon it began to pour, which made the trek through the bushes and the muddy forestland even more difficult. With the heavy rucksack on our backs, there was always a fear of falling. Couple of makeshift bridges over water streams had been destroyed, either due to heavy rain or by animals. We, thus, had to search for new means of crossing water streams. At one point, we had to cross an eight feet deep trench full of water on a half meter wide and two meters long tree trunk. This was quite scary and dangerous. The moist and slippery trunk was not a suitable thing to try a balancing act on. Particularly with rucksacks weighing 20-30 kgs on our back, and cameras in hand.

I was again beginning to wish I had never planned this Periyar trek. We were neither mentally nor physically ready for such hardship. Shooting wildlife from within the safety of a safari gypsy was a far cry from what we were experiencing.

The last kilometre was the toughest of this entire exploration – the downpour became heavier and the mud became thicker and sloppier. We struggled to find firm places to put our feet to maintain balance as we moved. At one point, we had to climb a slanting slope of ten meters, and with every step forward we were sliding down few meters towards the hundred meters deep Periyar Lake, located at the edge of the slope. To add to our worries, throughout this particular stretch fresh tiger pugmarks were spotted towards the southwest direction. Fortunately, we were moving towards the northeast. We also noticed fresh mark of tiger's debuckling on a nearby tree trunk.

Just as we were about to hit our tipping point, we saw the edge of the Periyar lake. We managed to reach the edge of the forest in one piece. The trek had, finally, ended.

From there we boarded the bamboo rafts to cross the two hundred-meter stretch of Periyar Lake.

I was glad and relaxed to see the edge of the forest at the bank of Periyer River. Vedavyasa also returned to his jovial self and started cracking meaningless jokes about our trip.

Once we completed the entire hiking in one piece our ego returned immediately. It is also mention-worthy that through this whole exploration, Vedavyasa and I were the only wildlife photographers among all other explorers and tourists. Bandipur was, of course, an exception.

This thought exponentially raised our ego and our sense of elitism as we headed back to the Kochi airport from Thekkady. It was time to re-write, yet again, my own definition of hobby.

A hobby is a regular activity that is done as many times as possible in one's lifetime for the pleasure of establishing one as a unique achiever but at the same time does not expose one's inability to perform any such activities.

If your hobby exposes your inability to pursue it as hobby, then you are a normal and humble human being. But egoist urban dwellers' who desire to be the most interesting guy in the room, cannot afford to let their inability be exposed.

Nevertheless, on this trip I succeeded in making a good repository of content for my social media postings. Therefore, all's well that ends well.

The path to fame and glory is not easy and cannot be achieved with short term effort. The desperation, though, is so intense, that humans often fall for short term success.

As Amir Yawari states in his article, *"Everybody wants some type of fame. Social media is built around this concept; people enjoy their own smaller version of fame on TikTok, Facebook, Instagram, or Twitter. The traditional perception of fame was limited to and associated with only big musicians, politicians, sports stars, and actors — it's no longer the case now since anyone can use social media to get attention and feel like a celebrity."*

The commodity market that was criticised and constrained by environmental movement and activism, was concerned until 1970s about human's inclination towards embracing ecology as a way of living. However, in today's world, human's desire for fame and their desperation to achieve it easily created a new survival strategy for capitalism.

Capitalism's very survival – rather than its radical transformation – becomes an integral and necessary element of neo-liberal sustainability. Capitalism is now viewed as the means to achieve this sustainability. Thus, it has created multiple opportunities and facilities for humans to achieve their fame in easier ways.

In today's world when "Climate Change" is a household terminology, ability to show-case someone's inclination towards this neo-liberal sustainability is an effective way to establish someone as up-market.

Getting involved in wildlife photography and ecotourism is considered as evidence of someone's inclination towards sustainability.

Therefore, wildlife photography and ecotourism have become a unique hobby as an outcome of ecological modernisation (or the greening of capitalism) movement of post 1970.

CHAPTER THREE:
Desperation for Fame

The protagonist Prithu in Guha's novel *Madhukari* (Art of Honey-gathering) depicts the urban educated and affluent class, who is continuously at crossroads between passion and profession. It is this contradiction that creates serious doubt among the urban folks on the purpose of their existence. To escape this uncomfortable self-contradiction, they find solace in the dream of being like or living like Mowgli, or by being involved in radicalism (or radical environmentalism in the context of this book). In their attempt to convert their dream into reality, often, they realize that their comfortable materialistic lifestyle, which they have earned as a consequence of temporary protection, is the biggest barrier between them and radical environmentalism.

Thus, capitalism comes to their rescue with services like wildlife photography and ecotourism.

The hardship of Periyar trip, thereby, becomes a great adventure story to tell others with a desire to project the image of being radical, albeit for a few days. The conscious mind, however, decides not to repeat such adventures again.

As a result, Vedavyasa and I, designed a much calculated and planned exploration, specifically for spotting Bengal Tigers in wild. An easier way.

The gypsy safari in the summer afternoon at Kariya zone of Satpura Tiger Reserve, was largely about sighting the usual herd of sambar, nil gai, northern plain langur and rhesus macaque. I had now learnt to call "monkeys" as either bonnet (as they were called in Western Ghats) or rhesus (as in Northern and Central India) macaque. That learning served to further my sense of elitism.

With the onset of dusk, we headed towards the exit of the forest, when our driver, Deepak, brought the gypsy to a halt. Guide Harilal whispered, *"Leopards"*.

To the left of our gypsy, in the thick bushes, something moved. A few seconds later, we caught sight of a round head with black rosettes on yellow fur, and then another and then another. Three heads of three leopards, camouflaged by the bushes. They wanted to cross the road but stopped after seeing three gypsies. The shy animals were hesitant to reveal themselves.

After a minute or two, one came out and cautiously crossed the road. A cub. Then the other two followed. All three of them were cubs. But where was the mother? Had she left her cubs alone? That was unusual.

Harilal said that the mother was extremely shy and had not been seen for the last couple of days. Did we suspect foul play?

And thus, on the very first day of the ongoing exploration series, we saw big cats. A happy bunch, we returned to our forest resort anticipating a great and fruitful series ahead. Sighting the cute leopard cubs was not the only reason for our happiness. We were happy in the anticipation of tiger sighting in the upcoming days. We considered sighting the leopard as a good omen and an indication of things to come.

Other significant observations that day included Indian monitor lizard, soft-shelled turtle, and birds like rufous treepie, nests and nestlings of woolly-necked stork, crested hawk eagle and crested serpent eagle. None of the fauna is less beautiful or any less significant from other bigger forms from a biodiversity standpoint.

I continued to update my journal of wildlife sighting. That was my way of establishing credibility on my journey in becoming "Mowgli".

At that time, however, in the core of our hearts we had space only for the great Bengal Tiger. There was a self-imposed pressure to announce to the world that we were capable of seeing and taking images of the Bengal Tiger in its natural habitat.

Our luck in Satpura, though, was limited to leopard cubs, a sloth bear family and an adult lone male sloth bear climbing a tree, searching for honey. Other faunal species we spotted were barking deer, marsh crocodile, and lots of birds - long tailed shrike, pied kingfisher, oriental honey buzzard, purple sunbird, ashy crowned sparrow lark and scopes owl.

With a lot of hope, we arrived at our next destination - the forest of Pench - the forests with a direct connection to *The Jungle Book*. Legend has it that, in 1831, Lieutenant Moor witnessed a human child nurtured by the wolves in the forests. The tale of this incident by Sleeman in a booklet titled *'An Account of Wolves Nurturing Children in Their Dens'* together with Strendale's story in Seonee (or Seoni) inspired the fictional genius Sir Rudyard Kipling to pen down his famous novel and the wolf child was commemorated as Mowgli. The real Seoni forest and Pench National Park are separated by a mere twenty kilometres.

Of the three safaris that we did in Pench, the second one started at 4:00 pm that evening, and both driver Shera and guide Vinod expressed confidence in spotting "Collarwali".

It is a custom for the guides and drivers in Central Indian tiger landscape of the Indian subcontinent, to assign humanized pet names to their beloved tigers and tigresses.

Vinod was a trained guide with certification from the prestigious *Indian Institute of Forest Management (IIFM)*, Bhopal. With a lot of enthusiasm, we began the exploration, but suffered an early setback due to heavy down pour, which lasted for an hour between 4:30 and 5:30 pm. All hopes were washed away. The rain cooled down the forest and minimized the possibility of big cats coming out of the dense forest to quench their thirst. However, intermittent warning calls of langurs, sambar and spotted deer were heard throughout the safari from different corners of the forest, confirming movement of big cats within the dense forest. Some of the calls by male spotted deer, although, were suspected to be false calls. Male spotted deer sometimes give false call to scare female spotted deer, so that they come closer to them out of fear and seek protection. Male spotted deer use it as an advantage for mating. Quite an opportunist lover.

We learned this valuable information from IIFM-trained guide Vinod, which in future would immensely help us in proving our credibility to general tourists as experienced wildlife enthusiasts.

Serious and strong warning calls were heard at around 5:45 pm. There were combined calls of peacock, jackal, barking deer and red jungle fowl. Everybody was convinced that the calls were potentially for warning the presence of Bengal Tigers, and their movement was not beyond two-three hundred meters from our location. Vinod said, *"The spotted deer may not be fully trustworthy, but sambar and jackal never give false call."*

Despite strong calls, nothing came out of the dense forest and an hour of waiting did not yield any result. But we did spot a black napped hare, a flying fruit bat and a juvenile crested serpent eagle, which had just finished its meal of an adult peafowl. Now I call peacock as peafowl as a mark of elitism.

Last safari at Pench started at around 7:00 am and was significant as we heard intense warning call of langurs, and thereafter spotted pug marks of big cat. However, the pugmarks did not look fresh, and both driver Shera and Vedavyasa suspected them to be that of a leopard. There was rumour in the forest that a male tiger had been spotted somewhere near route number one. But when we reached there, we found no evidence of the same.

The same afternoon, we left Pench and arrived at Kanha in the evening.

The last segment of the series started at Kanha at 5:45 am the following morning. Guide Shamim first heard a mild warning call of a sambar, near the crossing point of Kanha and Kisli zone of the tiger reserve. The zone was famously known as the territory of tiger Munna. Around 6:20 am, severe warning calls of northern plain langur and spotted deer were heard in the same area. Vedavyasa admitted that was the strongest warning call he had ever heard in any exploration in any forest. Several spotted deer were found running away in the opposite direction to the bellowing call. We waited for an hour or so, but there was no sight of Munna.

By then, there was news from the other side of the forest that a male and female tiger were spotted near the Kanha zone.

We quickly headed for the Kanha zone, and about five to six kilometres ahead of Kisli zone, we found fresh pugmarks and indications of an adult male tiger having sat on soil.

Around 10:30 am, we started retreating from the forest. Driver Raju kept us entertained and enthralled with tales of Munna, the most respected tiger of Kanha, and more famous for being the only male tiger who had not killed his offspring in Kanha's recent history. Tigers are quite careful about preserving their own gene pool. Therefore, not killing their own offspring is not unique or unheard of.

The significant observations for the day included swamp deer, and among birds - king vulture, sirkeer malkoha and jungle owlet. Swamp deer is an important species in the forest of Kanha considering its vulnerable conservation status and that it inhabits only the three states of Madhya Pradesh, Uttar Pradesh and Assam of India.

In the shadow of the Bengal Tiger, however, all other species are relegated to the background.

The remaining three safaris at Kanha were relatively quiet. The forest was lush and cool, with sights of happily grazing herbivores and vibrantly coloured birds. On our last safari, as we were returning, we spotted fresh tiger poop, confirming recent movement of the big cat. But we had no luck sighting it.

On the 21st of April 2021, a twitter note of a twenty-four-year-old Bangalore based technology professional went viral. The young man desperately sought advice to get rid of his boredom and loneliness. His annual income was rupees fifty-eight lakhs ($70,000) and he had a comfortable professional life. His note was titled *"Feeling Saturated in Life"*. It was apparent that despite enjoying a substantial income and work profile, something was amiss. Perhaps a sense of purpose. This is a harsh reality of today's corporate world.

When creative people are stuck in the cycle of materialism through technology enabled jobs, they are more desperate to show-case their creativity. Wildlife photography appears to them as one of the easiest ways to do so. Nature and her elements are by default beautiful. Seemingly, capturing those can easily demonstrate one's creativity, and thus, exhibit their uniqueness and suggest that they are the most captivating individual in the room. The tools for show-casing such creativity is highly technology based such as DSLR camera, Photoshop software etc. People with high income corporate jobs have sufficient *disposable moolah* to access these easily.

Therefore, increasingly enslaved in their corporate job with lack of social and emotional bonding, the urban affluent class inclines towards wildlife photography. The supressed need for social, emotional, and creative connection makes them radical from within. But the fear of losing temporary protection achieved through materialism creates a dilemma in embracing such radicalism.

Capitalism comes to the rescue yet again, offering them ecotourism services to escape and neutralise the radical feeling. After all, radicalism in any form is not good for materialism.

Being blessed by capitalism, technology needed for achieving fame through wildlife photography and ecotourism are now low hanging fruits for the urban dwelling human. All they need now, is an easy subject to use this technology on.

In nature, though, getting an easy subject is not an easy task.

We came to realize this at Satpura, Pench and Kanha. Access to technology and ability to spend are insufficient if we do not encounter Bengal Tigers in wild.

For us Bengal Tiger became a symbol of fame. Therefore, we converted our ecotourism activity into a tiger tourism activity and channelised all our wildlife photography efforts onto a single species.

In Satpura, Pench and Kanha we saw more than ninety different animals including mammals, birds, and reptiles. Some of them were critically endangered such as white rumped and long billed vulture, endangered dhole (Indian wild dog), vulnerable species like swamp deer and sloth bear. Yet, we refrained from calling it a successful exploration.

Not seeing tiger in the wild, and the imagined failure in so-called ecotourism created fear in our minds. Fear of not achieving the desired fame.

Tiger is beyond doubt a sensitive animal and spotting a tiger in the forest is exciting for any nature lover. Vedavyasa and I have been searching for this reclusive and enchanting animal of the forest for a long time now. But why did we become so obsessed with this one species?

In Buddhadeb Guha's novel, Prithu had a beautiful wife. A woman who was desired by most men in their circle in the village of Seoni. Incidentally, the stories of both Mowgli and his admirer Prithu, were based on the village located in the fringes of the central Indian forest.

Prithu was never certain about his love for his wife. He admitted his attraction for other women on multiple occasions. Human's attraction for multiple romantic or sex partners are not an uncommon phenomenon in any civilization, as documented through History.

Although, typically, such phenomena in the contemporary world are termed as adultery. Polygamy or polyandry is animal nature, irrespective of its human and non-human forms. Non-human enjoys it as their right to essential liberty, whereas human envies it as they are forbidden to exercise this right.

This explains the human desire to personify Bengal Tiger as non-human demigod - the striking symbol of this essential liberty. This symbolizing makes the human even more obsessed with the Bengal Tiger.

The relationship between man and tiger dates back to time immemorial. Our ancestors looked upon the tiger as a symbol of power. Many tribes still worship tiger as God. Some of their deities are called Waghjai or Waghdev. In the Sundarbans, a little-known goddess Bon Bibi graces its forests. The story goes that Bon Bibi, the "lady of the jungle", was chosen by God to protect people who worked in the Sundarbans against a greedy man-eating half sage, half tiger-demon named Dokkhin Rai.

After several close and failed attempts, one winter season, Vedavyasa and I, with this fetish for the Bengal Tiger planned our next exploration to the jewel of Vidarbha – Tadoba Andhari Tiger Reserve (TATR).

We started our TATR exploration through Kolara gate. Spotting rare wildlife in the buffer zone was less likely and so the anticipation was not nail-biting. Guide Praveen informed us that animals are generally shy in the buffer zone, as they are not used to human presence and safari gypsy. Therefore, not many tourists visit the buffer zone. The forest is sporadic, with fewer colonies or herds of herbivores in this part. This also reduces the movement of predators in this zone. Therefore, spotting predators is more challenging in the buffer zone than in the core area.

Praveen explained that the job of forest guides and gypsy drivers in the core area was easier than their counter parts in the buffer area, as in the core area they knew where a territorial predator may be spotted. Predators have their defined territory in the core area. But in the buffer zone, they are always in movement, so the guides also need to move throughout the zone in an attempt to spot them.

Literally, we did not find even a single spotted deer, which was very unusual compared to our experiences in Indian rain, and dry or moist deciduous forests, thus far. The most common animal in this type of forest is the spotted deer.

However, much to our surprise, we spotted a big male antelope looking at our gypsy with fear and curiosity. Driver Ashish brought the vehicle to a halt, so we could take pictures. Initially we suspected that it was the Indian Muntjac, but later we realized that it was one of the ungulates (herbivores with hooves)– a four horned antelope or Chausingha – a rare sighting in the forest.

Adjacent to where the Chausingha was grazing, was a sacred grove decorated with a lot of colourful scarves (*dupatta*, a part of the traditional attire of Indian women). Guide Praveen told us the story associated with the grove. According to folklore, a village woman was once chased by a tiger. As she ran for her life, she threw her *dupatta* and the tiger pounced on the *dupatta* instead of her, and ripped it apart. The woman's life was spared. After this incident, the local villagers started worshipping the place and offered coloured scarves, symbolizing and seeking protection from tiger attacks.

Generally, tigers of TATR are not known to be human eaters. However, just two days prior to our exploration, a tiger reportedly killed a village woman. Driver Ashish mentioned that there were more such cases of tiger attacks on humans, but not all were reported officially. TATR is a good maternity centre for Bengal Tiger and the number of tigers is on the rise. As per the most recent statistics (2022), there are 115 tigers in a 624-km^2 forest area. Not enough space for such territorial animals. Based on news published in a national daily – *"For more than four years now, one person dies in tiger attacks around Tadoba every month—a frequency of conflict higher than anywhere, recorded, except the Bangladeshi Sundarbans, in recent times"*. In TATR, most of these incidents took place in the buffer zone.

Our first safari ended at 6:30 pm. Key species spotted included male nil gai, northern plain langur, female gaur, herds of sambar, male wild boar and twenty-three different species of birds.

From the following day, all safaris were in the core zone. We started out at 6:00 am. The early winter morning was dark and freezing, with a temperature around 7-8°C. In the open top gypsy, in the core area of TATR forest, the chilling wind pierced our bodies. Guide Eknath and driver Nikhil were hopeful and enthusiastic for tiger sightings. The previous evening, a tigress with her cubs had been spotted near Panderpouni water hole. By now we were familiar with the kind of enthusiasm from the forest guides which eventually yielded nothing. We were, thus, not as cheerful as our fellow forest mates. Besides, we were struggling to keep our fingers on the camera shutters in the biting cold. Gradually the light was improving. Accordingly, we adjusted exposure and ISO setting of the cameras. At around 6:45 am, a strong call of a spotted deer was heard from the northeast direction.

The call did not excite us, as we had learnt that the warning call of a spotted deer was hardly trustworthy.

"Wild boars are running away!", both Eknath and Vedavyasa whispered at the same time.

"Similar situation we witnessed in Kanha, near Munna's hideout." I whispered back to Vedavyasa. I was not optimistic.

An entire herd of spotted deer and two wild boars ran in the opposite direction. Eknath asked Nikhil to turn the vehicle around and to move towards waterbody number one, where a forest department watch tower was installed. Skilled gypsy driver Nikhil parked the vehicle diagonally opposite to the watch tower and in a few seconds, T12, *aka* Maya, the queen of TATR, appeared through the bushes. She was moving slowly towards a herd of spotted deer; waiting for a kill. The spotted deer furiously let out a warning call.

The life of the tiger is entwined with the forest. The colour, built, size, and habitat are attuned to that forest. A tiger moves around the forest like a predator. A predator must be superior to its prey, or else it will be difficult for him to survive. Whether it is a deer, an antelope or a gaur, the tiger must employ both devious and robust tactics to dishearten the prey. Nature has bestowed upon tiger all the requisites to be a good hunter. He is akin to a destructive hunting machine- the supreme hunter of the forest. There is no animal in the forest that hunts the tiger for meal; and almost every animal can be a tiger's prey. So, the forests are filled with terror for the tiger, and the celebrated tigress of TATR, Maya, moving about in her territory at Panderpouni, depicted all these features. She was hungry, and stalking the herd of spotted deer. We watched her movement for an hour before she disappeared into the thick forest.

Maya grew up as part of a recognized and noticeable family by the Telia Lake, with three siblings - two boisterous sisters and a shy brother. Maya was the most rowdy and gregarious of her family.

When we spotted Maya for the first time, through apertures of trees, we held our breath for a while. We watched awestruck, in complete disbelief, as lady luck finally favoured us. We were oblivious to what was happening around us for the next half hour, as our eyes stayed glued on the viewfinders of the cameras - left hand occupying and adjusting lenses and the index finger of the right hand restlessly pressing the shutters. We noticed nothing but the beautiful creature; we heard nothing but the sound of shutters. Beyond Maya, space-time continuum was at a standstill. Her "Maya", magic spell, hypnotized us, the mere mortal spectators.

After Maya disappeared into the dense forest, we clicked a water hen in water hole number one. Shortly thereafter, Eknath and Nikhil turned their gypsy towards Tadoba Lake via Jamni, in the hope of encountering another vivid tigress of Tadoba, Choti Tara and her cubs. But it was not to be, despite combing the forest for two and a half hours.

While passing through the Tadoba Lake, Nikhil stopped his gypsy again and Eknath exclaimed *"Tiger"!*

The very word tiger inspires awe and evokes an image of courage and cruelty. A huge male tiger T54, *aka* Matkasur, was spotted near Tadoba Lake at 9:30 am, a living image of vigour and ferocity. He was moving along the lakeshore, pausing intermittently, and looking at the water. A huge marsh crocodile was basking on the bank. Matkasur tried to attack it, and we heard a large splash as the crocodile jumped into the water to save itself. The mighty Matkasur continued walking along the brink of the lake and *en route*, halted and smelt tree trunks. They do so, to identify the smell of their or any previous tiger's urine to mark and identify their territory. We followed him in the gypsy, and after a walk of fifteen-twenty minutes, he crossed the road right in front of our gypsy and vanished into the forest on the other side.

The safari ended at 10:30 am. Other key avian species identified that day were the bronze winged jacana, pied bush chat and a few birds of prey like the oriental honey buzzard, white eyed buzzard, and changeable hawk eagle. As we exited the forest, we spotted another elusive, nocturnal animal - a tree shrew, and before we reached our hotel at Chimur, a venomous Russel's viper snake sprawling near a paddy field.

We began our third safari the same afternoon, between 2:15 pm and 6:30 pm. Pugmarks of a female tiger and a cub were noticed at around 4:00 pm. But the animals were nowhere to be found.

The fourth Safari started at 6:15 am the following day, concluding at 10:30 am. The forest was very quiet that day, with no indication of any big cat movement. This reminded me of the experiences in the forest of Pench and Kanha the previous summer.

At around 8:30 am, pugmarks of a leopard and a jungle cat were found on the way towards Navengaon area. Around 10:00 am, near Panderpouni, we heard mild warning calls of sambar and spotted deer. We interpreted the calls to be Maya and her cubs' movements from one side of their territory to the other.

During our return, Nikhil, the driver of the gypsy, briefed us on the tiger community of TATR. He explained the conflict between Maya and Matkasur. Matkasur wanted Maya to surrender, but the cubs posed a hindrance. Matkasur once attacked her cubs. Maya and her sons, fighting together, defeated him. Maya's cubs were borne by the male tiger Gabbar (also known as leopard face) *aka* Sher Khan *aka* Ma7 (TAD), who was once the undisputed king of TATR. After the rise of Matkasur, the conflict between Gabbar and Matkasur was inevitable. A recent fight, probably over Maya, had been reported at waterbody number ninety-seven. Another tigress, Choti Tara, with young cubs to protect and feed, is presently incognito in the forest. Cubs of Choti Tara were borne by Matkasur. Maya had three cubs with Gabbar. Owing to frequent attacks by Matkasur, a male and a female cub were separated from her. Now the parted male cub could not be reunited with Maya, as his brother had grown up and would not allow him to come close to their mother. However, he would have no problem when his isolated sister returned, as he would soon require a mating partner.

This suggests that Maya, *aka* T12's sub adult cub, had the potential to challenge its peers, the male tigers of TATR, over right to territory.

From the beginning of this exploration series, I had noticed that Vedavyasa had been restless. One evening, at the resort, as whiskey flew through our veins, allowing our subconscious selves to reveal itself, he disclosed his extra-marital affair with his former college sweetheart. The guilt of a husband and a father was clearly evident.

The lady was known to both of us for her fine literary skill. What I did not know was that she was divorced twice before she started dating Vedavyasa.

Much like how the fictitious character Prithu in Guha's novel was confused with his polygamy, so was my friend Vedavyasa, struggling to justify the same.

This confusion and dilemma can be easily explained by an analogy with the Bengal Tiger.

Prithu tried to rationalize his polygamy by saying there are men who are like tigers of a forest. Such men copulate with women and give them children, but never sacrifice their freedom to those women. There are men who have shown how to live life without women. He knows such men.

In the forest, both the tiger and tigress live and survive alone. They come close to each other to mate but never give up their independence for each other. They are polyamorous. And that unequivocally makes them the icons of essential liberty.

Although unaware, the restless polygamous Vedavyasa was just trying to establish that essential liberty by dating a polyandrous woman.

This, like nothing else, perhaps, explains Vedavyasa's obsession with Bengal Tigers. Being a single man, I had the liberty to be intimate with many women. A Bengal Tiger analogy further reinforces my moral conscience. Whereas Vedavyasa, despite having a strong urge for polygamy, was caught between societal norms and morality. Therefore, he needed a Bengal Tiger analogy to justify his polygamy, thus the obsession for the animal.

The fifth Safari started at 2:30 pm and that was our last safari through Kolara gate. Our subsequent plan was to move towards Moharli gate, around forty kilometres from our current base. Along with guide Dilip and driver Vinod, we started towards the northwest direction. Afternoon in the forest of TATR was quite bright and warm with temperature between 30-35° C. After a drive of thirty minutes, we spotted pugmarks of a female with cubs. We followed the pugmarks which lingered into southeast direction. Fresh pugmark of sloth bear was spotted along the way. After driving a few kilometres, we moved back to the northwest direction. Pugmark of male tiger was observed, along with mild call of sambar. Our previous guide Eknath was in another gypsy ahead of us, and he signalled to move towards waterbody number seventy-nine, close to Nawachila.

We, along with six other gypsies, stopped in front of waterbody seventy-nine at Nawachila. We waited for fifteen minutes, but there was no indication of any movement. The call had stopped a while ago. One after another, gypsies left the place. Tourists who regarded forest as a zoological park, lost patience in no time.

However, Dilip and Vinod decided not to move at all. If there was any possibility of sighting a tiger at all, under the circumstances, it was in this spot. The logic was simple. Fresh pugmarks followed the route and faded near the bushes, on the side of the forest path. The tiger moves as stealthily as a shadow. It is difficult to believe that this animal, weighing 150-250 kg, can move in complete silence. The tiger's paws are padded. So, their heels are cushioned as they walk, and dry leaves or twigs do not crackle under his foot. But since their paws are padded, they prefer not to walk in thorny undergrowth. The tigers roam the paths in the forests and the roads. Therefore, there was a strong chance that a male tiger whose pugmarks we had followed, had a temporary hideout in the undergrowth alongside the forest path. He would come out at some point in time. But when was anyone's guess. Perhaps after dusk, once the tourists left the forest at the closing hour of safari, as set by the forest department.

After a wait of forty-five minutes, at around 3:45 pm, a familiar cackling noise pierced my ears and I muttered, *"Langur's call!"*.

Dilip nodded in agreement. The langur's call was heard twice. Vinod swerved the gypsy northwest, towards the direction of the call.

I screamed, *"Stop, stop!"*

We spotted around 5-6 langurs seated atop a tree – restless and giving out warning calls - as frequently as five times, and gazing below towards the forest. Dilip advised that we return to the original place and wait there. Vedavyasa assured, *"Definitely there is a tiger, and there is no doubt about it. It's only a matter of time before it comes out in the open!"*

Vinod retracked and parked the vehicle in front of waterbody number seventy-nine. The following fifteen minutes were spent waiting, in apprehension, realigning position of cameras, checking and readjusting camera settings and anticipating the direction from where the tiger would emerge and the corresponding light setting requirements of that direction.

"Alarm call again!" yelled Vedavyasa and Dilip in unison. A spotted deer was bellowing ceaselessly, a life-or-death call, from no more than five hundred meters from our gypsy.

Pseudo Ecotourism

It was confirmed. The forest declared to every living and non-living being in the wilderness of TATR, as the terror of TATR, the most dreaded predator of any Indian forest, manifested in proximity.

Other gypsies were returning one after the other. Everybody in the forest had heard that call.

At around 4:00 pm, a subadult male tiger appeared near waterbody number seventy-nine, at Nawachila. He was the male descendent of T12, *aka*, Maya. Our gypsy was the closest, within two hundred meters, from the fascinating creature.

We froze, with our eyes on the view finder, bodies bent over the side railing of the gypsy, left hands on lenses, placed carefully on bin bags, and index fingers of right hand not knowing how to stop pressing the shutter.

Through the viewfinders in the silent foothills, emerged a long proportionate brownish-orange or tawny body, with black stripes, and a round majestic head – slowly coming closer and closer. With every sturdy step, he exuded the unmistakable message as to why every animal in the forest should be terrified of him. Through the viewfinder his head appeared to grow bigger, as he slowly approached us, conquering distances, from two hundred meters to hundred meters to fifty meters. His bright yellow eyes were fixed on us, sending chills down our spine, putting a strain on our nervous systems. Was this the moment to throw the camera away and run for dear life?

No way! This was the rarest moment of my life, perhaps never to experience again!

Our eyes stayed glued to the viewfinder, and our right index fingers on the shutter. We had been yearning for this moment for a long time, since our trip to Nagarhole and Bandipur.

He came within five feet of our gypsy, growled lightly, and started moving towards the southeast, sniffing everything around him. He smelled the urine spread by himself or other tigers in the vicinity, to identify the safe territory. After all he was a cub, an adolescent cub, learning how to live life in the forest without his mother's protection. To spread urine further so as to mark the territory, he continued walking along the forest path in the same direction. All the gypsies (at least 50 of them, if not more) raced after him. In an attempt to give their respective tourists, the best possible view of the "road show", the gypsies collided with each other.

As an aside, engulfed in the excitement of the moment of sighting him, none of us really paid attention to his growl in front of our gypsy. We discovered the growl a couple of years later, when we replayed the soundtrack recorded during exploration.

The road show continued for about ten minutes, before he disappeared into the deep forest. The last five minutes, we shut our cameras, and look in the whole exhibit with our naked eyes, rather than the viewfinders of our cameras.

Natural tools enjoy natural phenomena best.

That was Bhola. For most of the forest guides and gypsy drivers, this was the first moment they had spotted him alone - travelling beyond his territory and moving from one part of the forest to the other.

Few weeks after we returned from Tadoba, Vedavyasa received news from a trusted source that Bhola had a fight with T54, *aka*, Matkasur, near Panderpouni, resulting in latter's defeat and eventual expulsion.

Perhaps, very soon, TATR would witness the coronation ceremony of their new crown prince.

Next morning, we left for Moharli gate and arrived at the Maharashtra Tourism Development Corporation (MTDC) resort post noon. We did not have any safari planned for the day, hence, in the evening, we headed for the entry gate of the core area of the forest to replenish our rations. The plan was to walk the two kms between the MTDC resort and the Moharli gate at about 7:00 pm. However, we had a last-minute change of plan and booked a cab to Chandrapur town instead, which was at a distance of thirty-five kilometres from the resort. The road between MTDC resort and Chandrapur passes through the forest area of Tadoba. We encountered a palm civet on the roadside, both ways of our trip. Driver Palash informed us about the countless sightings he had had of leopards while driving through this road, and the incidents of leopards attacking local villagers. The tale of a human-eating leopard that had killing 5-6 villagers, before it was eventually caught by the forest department and sent to rescue centre, was particularly haunting.

And then he mentioned something, which left us shivering. That evening, as he made his way to pick us up, he caught a glimpse of a leopard near the MTDC resort. He added that this wasn't an unusual occurrence. Our original plan of walking the two kilometres between MTDC and the entry gate of the forest at 7:00 pm, had clearly been unwise and we were saved by the bell.

The sixth safari and the first one from Moharli gate of TATR began at 6:30 am. We headed southwards, reaching Aswalhira and then Telia Lake, known as T24, *aka*, Sonam's area. Sonam resided with her adolescent cubs. After an hour and a half hour of driving through the forest, we started moving towards the north and, at around 8:45 am, arrived at Jamni Lake. Spotted deer gave out strong calls, but the safari ended at 10:00 am without a glimpse of any big cat.

The afternoon safari started at 2:00 pm, again towards the south. After crossing Telia Lake, we reached near Jamunbudi. 5-6 gypsies were already waiting there. Apparently, there had been a warning call from the other side of the lake. We waited for about thirty minutes. A ruddy mongoose running here and there searching for food, gave us ample photo opportunities. As we moved eastwards, we spotted fresh pug marks of a female tiger. We drove further for about a kilometre or two, and halted after seeing a couple of gypsies waiting on the forest path in the Ayanbodi area. Apparently, T12 (Maya), was sleeping in the bushes and people were waiting in the hope of catching a glimpse of her. The anticipation was that she would wake from her slumber in a while and walk out of the bush in style and give us a road show.

This game of anticipation reminded me of the trip to Bandipur - the surging sense of respect that I felt for my fellow wildlife enthusiasts during my first ever safari in that tiger reserve.

On the contrary, in the Ayanbodi area of TATR, I only felt contempt at the wildlife enthusiasts gathered there. Their anticipation game appeared to be a desperate attempt to achieve unrealistic aspiration for fame and glory, which is otherwise elusive to the affluent urban folks in their mundane corporate life.

Gypsies began queuing up, and in no time, there were at least 30 gypsies, that had arrived from all six gates, hopeful of seeing the celebrity tigress of TATR. The myriad visitors included the "zoological park type"; "selfie type"; "DSLR type"; "self-proclaimed forest and wildlife experts"; and the forest guides. gypsy drivers. Speculations followed, on the route that Maya would giving us the "road show". Each time she moved her head or shook her hind legs, or swayed her tail to keep flies away- the excitement heightened.

After an hour and a half of suspense, Maya woke up and quickly dissipated deep inside the forest. What an anti-climax!

In the forest silence is profound. Lend a keen ear and one can listen to the quietude. One would be ignorant to think he can witness the mysteries of the forest unfolding in just a couple of hours of a jeep safari. The involvement of Edward James Corbett or Kenneth Anderson with India's wild was long and persistent, lasting decades.

In our eighth safari in TATR, a strong alarm call was ascertained from Jamni waterbody. When we arrived at Jamni, a few gypsies had already assembled. Reportedly, Choti Tara had crossed the forest path just two minutes prior. The spotted deer were still giving calls. We decided to wait there and were all ears to Sanjay's story of "False Mating".

In September 2016, Maya was seen mating with Gabbar, Sanjay voiced. Maya was bold enough to engage in such strategic "False Mating".

"False Mating" is a mother's desperate measure to confuse all the male tigers in the forest, to save her cubs. A male tiger, typically, does not kill his own cubs, but he manoeuvres to eliminate other contender's genes. When a female tiger copulates with multiple male tigers, all her pairs in the forest believe her cubs are their offspring and allow them to thrive.

Some local naturalists opine that Maya's behaviour is evidence of a crafty new strategy to safeguard her cubs' survival. "False mating" exists among many mammals—including bears, lions, and bottlenose dolphins. Male tigers kill the cubs of their rivals whenever they can, so as to precipitate a new oestrus cycle and impregnate the tigress with their own offspring. Tiger moms typically seek to protect their cubs from such a fate for 18 to 24 months, before pushing them out to establish their own territories. (Tiger fathers have no role in raising the young, so no help there.) But the crowded conditions in Tadoba and other Indian national parks are making that increasingly difficult. The ranges of several roving rivals frequently overlap with the dominant males, bringing danger precariously close to vulnerable cubs.

According to Bilal Habib, a carnivore researcher at the Wildlife Institute of India, *"In high-density areas, where there are more males, the best strategy for a female is to try to leave the cubs early, go with the males, and then go back and look for her litter again,"* Habib explains. *"A brawl with a male might turn out to be lethal for her and the cubs."*

We waited at the Jamni waterbody for an additional two hours, and there was no indication of any big cat movement. Eventually we left the forest, ending the safari at 10:30 am.

The ninth safari started at 2:30 pm and we kick-started towards Jamni lake. We spotted a male sloth bear to begin with. On sighting the gypsy, he concealed himself in the dense woods. We tracked him along the forest path of Aswalhira, which was covered by heavy bamboo trees. We spotted him again. This time the bear was within hundred meters from our gypsy. He crossed the path and hid again inside thick vegetation.

After the not so "sloth", rather "busy" moments with the bear, we travelled up to Jamni Lake, then Tadoba lake, Panderpouni and finally Telia. News emerged that T24, *aka*, Sonam, an adult female tiger was spotted with her subadult cubs. Two gypsies were already waiting, and the guide from one of the gypsies asserted, *"Sonam is there, sitting in the grass land".*

The grassland of Telia zone is very thick and an ideal hide out for tigers. With little or no effort, the dark stripes on pale fur, breaking up an outline of long slender body, lying in the grassland and well camouflaged – was spotted – the white spots behind the black ears – a characteristic mark of tigers – were also noticed. The presence of the beast resting in the grass land was conspicuous. What was not obvious was if the tiger was an adult, alone or with cubs.

The tiger stood up and started moving, clearly visible even with naked eyes. Sanjay confirmed the striking four-legged enigma to be Sonam. Sonam is part of the famous litter of four very illustrious female cubs, brought up by Madhuri in the Telia Lake area, overseen by their caring father Scarface. She has a visible 'S' shape mark on her right neck, but through the thick grass, we were unable to discern that.

Sonam disappeared into the grass and we moved towards the fire line, in the hope that she would come out. We waited for an hour, until 6:00 pm, but she did not appear.

We concluded our safari at 10:30 am of following day and retreated to the MTDC resort to culminate the TATR exploration.

As we returned to the comforts of our homes, we reminisced the phenomena of the forest over the past week, and the wisdom it imbibed us with. Particularly, the story of Roshan, the owner of a souvenir shop near the Kolara gate of TATR. He worked as a tour guide, and assisted the forest guards for tree cutting contracts. He took daily wage workers from local villages into the forest. On one such occasion he was attacked by Kankrajhuri, a famous male tiger, in the buffer zone of TATR. To save himself he climbed up a tree and, in the process, suffered an injury. Thankfully, he was rescued by the forest guards. The incident left Roshan traumatized, and he ceased operating in the forest and thus, the souvenir shop.

Roshan enlightened us about Kankrajhuri. He generally roamed in the buffer zone, where he was seldom defied by humans. Owing to scarcity of prey and minimal exposure to humankind, the tigers in the buffer zone were more inclined to attack humans.

The number of tigers is increasing in TATR, the so-called "maternity centre" of Bengal Tiger. The growing tiger population has resulted in congestion, throwing this tiger reserve at the risk of aggravating inter and intra species conflict.

Is it a consequence of human's obsession for the demigod he once created of the tiger?

Not sighting tigers in the previously visited tiger reserves of Western Ghats and Central India, created anxiety in our minds about not achieving the so-called 'fame'. And that had compelled us to choose a supposedly easier destination for tiger sighting.

At this 'easier' destination of Tadoba, in the past few days I witnessed the transition of the human-created demigod into near-human life form. Bengal Tigers, here, have human names and human like complicated relationships. Here tiger sighting in the wild requires the same effort as that in a zoological park.

Over the last couple of decades, tiger tourism has become an easy tourism and an easy way to achieve fame.

Obsession with fame and fear of not achieving it, has converted ecotourism into pseudo ecotourism. Enthusiasm for nature and wildlife has become synonymous to chasing this glamourous species.

This is how ecotourism becomes tiger tourism and wildlife photography becomes tiger photography. The bio-spherical egalitarianism[1] is overlooked, leading to ecological collapse.

This gives birth to neo ecotourism as a product of greening capitalism, in turn creating the concept of tiger tourism.

---

[1] *Bio spherical egalitarianism is concerned with the rights of other species independent of their interactions with humans. Basically, it is a theory which states every species in this planet have equal importance by virtue of their own existence.*

CHAPTER FOUR: Fame Breeds Arrogance

We were delighted after our first ever tiger sighting in the wild. We left Tadoba feeling high and mighty, and with the pleasure of being part of that elite class of wildlife enthusiasts who had seen tigers in the wild and had successfully captured their images.

Author Amir Yawari, in his article titled, *Why Everyone Wants to Be Famous (and why it's a problem)*, explains, *"We all have a deep psychological need, comparable to the need for food and water or for shelter, that is to be approved by people. This is why fame is so attractive, and it is what fuels everyone's desire for fame in the first place."*

After our Tadoba exploration, we were assured that the ecotourists, who consider tiger sighting in wild as symbol of elitism, would start recognizing us as elite wildlife enthusiasts.

But deep within I knew something was not quite right.

Since the visit to Tadoba, I had developed stronger affection for this animal, but I struggled to feel the same regard and admiration, that I had felt for this apex predator when I read Jim Corbett's *"Man-Eaters of Kumaon"*.

Their human names, human like relationships and their proximity to us in forest, made them less formidable and more adorable.

Nevertheless, sighting of Bengal Tigers in Tadoba gave us an opportunity to feel special about ourselves. It created opportunity to be noticed in our social media circles. And that which brings gratification warrants repetition. But not in Tadoba, elsewhere, at a more "elite" and "glamourous" location.

Based on a newspaper report on 17th March 2017, the previous morning in the Ramnagar area of the Corbett tiger landscape a tiger had injured a boy and killed two people. The forest department personnel arrived at the site of the incident, and after some efforts, were successful in immobilising and caging the male tiger, aged about five years. According to information received, Muradabad (Uttar Pradesh) native, Ramdas and his family, worked as labourers in the Dabka River in the Terai area of Kumaon in Uttarakhand. On the morning of the incident, at about 8 o'clock, while on a break from the quarrying activity on the riverbed, Ramdas and his wife, Bhagwati Devi, went to the woods of Dabka in Belpadao range of Terai west forest division to collect firewood. His son Sachin and a few other people accompanied them. It was reported that as they exited the woods after collecting firewood, near the Dabka River, a tiger attacked the group. The big cat lifted

Bhagwati Devi and carried her into the woods as the shocked group accompanying her shouted and raised an alarm. Instead of scaring the tiger away, the noise had the opposite effect as the tiger returned and attacked the group, injuring Sachin.

The Bengal Tigers of Corbett National Park and Tiger Reserve have a reputation for being human hunters. Afterall the stories of *"Man-Eaters of Kumaon"* are from this landscape.

Therefore, what else could cause our fame to rise further, than exploring Corbett National Park?

Jim Corbett National Park, the oldest national park in India, was established in 1936 as Hailey National Park to protect the endangered Bengal Tigers. The park was the first to come under the Project Tiger initiative. After considering the immense significance of Corbett Park in tiger conservation in India, Vedavyasa and I decided our exploration for Bengal Tiger would remain incomplete if we do not pay a visit to the oldest national park of the country.

Hence, one spring evening, we boarded Ranikhet Express from the old Delhi railway station. The train, which started at 10:30 pm, reached Ramnagar the following morning at 5:30 am. Our guide cum driver, Nabi, who would be part of our exploration for the upcoming week, was waiting for us at the station with his safari gypsy. When we met this sexagenarian gentleman for the first time at Ramnagar station, we had no idea what was awaiting us in the forest of sub-Himalayan state Uttarakhand, in his company.

The pre-exploration phase was far more stressful than for any of the other explorations.

The turmoil in Vedavyasa's relationship with his college sweetheart, Ambalika, created a lot of uncertainties on the possibility of our visit to Corbett Park.

With no resolution to the apparent dissatisfaction with his marital life, Vedavyasa decided to leave his monandrous wife Vatika, and move on with polyandrous girlfriend Ambalika. They decided to make Corbett Park the place for the official declaration of their togetherness. Therefore, as per the initial plan, Ambalika was also part of the trip.

However, a few weeks prior to our trip, when Vedavyasa shared our train tickets and forest entry permits with me, I was surprised to see Ambalika's name missing.

Aware, as I was, of Vedavyasa's recent tendency for mood swings, I said nothing about this sudden change and quietly boarded the train.

We reached Dhangari gate of the park at 7:30 am, and after finishing all entry formalities, including verification of permits, we arrived at the Forest Rest House (FRH) of Gairal zone, where accommodation in the dormitory for two nights had been arranged.

Corbett National Park is divided into five ecotourism zones for proper management of tourism activities in the tiger reserve area. These zones are Dhikala, Bijarani, Jhirna, Dhela and Durga Devi. Dhikala zone

Pseudo Ecotourism

holds the celebrity status among all tourist zones of the Corbett National Park. Dhikala is well endowed with spectacular wildlife, a pure bliss for wildlife lovers. Our ecotourism permits were obtained for Dhikala and Bijrani zones.

On reaching the FRH, we were welcomed by frequent warning calls of barking deer coming from deep within the forest, confirming movement of big cat or at least carnivores nearby.

We dropped our rucksacks at the reception and grabbed a quick breakfast, before heading for the safari. Vedavyasa was unusually quiet during breakfast. In spite of the frequent alarm calls of barking deer, the otherwise hyperactive Vedavyasa, remained indifferent.

However, as we navigated through the enchanting woods of Kumaon, he slowly returned to his usual self. We entered the main forest through Gairal zone and continued driving up to FRH of Dhikala zone. Morning safari ended at 10:30 am. We took a break of four hours to have lunch and to rest. The afternoon safari began at 2:30 pm, but in the opposite direction, i.e., from Dhikala to Gairal, and continued until 6:30 pm.

The most exciting part of the afternoon safari was being chased by elephants, and our first exposure to Nabi's philosophy of surviving in the jungle. *"This is forest, and anything could happen at any time!"* Until the last safari in this park, he would put us in such "threat to survival" situations, and repeat this statement each time.

At around 3:30 pm, near Rongigarh area of the forest, we spotted two adult female elephants with a calf. They were coming from the Ramnagar riverside. As our gypsy got closer to them, the matriarch looked at us and raised her trunk – that was the first level of warning by an elephant. People trained in jungle survival understand this behaviour of the elephant.

We cautioned Nabi, but he muttered his survival philosophy and continued moving towards her. She shook her head and flapped her ears – second level of warning. The next level would be nothing but chasing, and that is exactly what happened when we ceased to stop. The matriarch charged towards us, and we had no option but to retreat. Parade of elephants with a cub, is always dangerous as they are extremely concerned about their calves' safety and do not like any other animals or human to come close.

Once we started retreating, the herd started moving in the opposite direction into bushes. We came to a halt, and observed their movement from a distance. We watched as an adult tusker (male elephant) appeared from the riverside and followed the herd.

We hadn't yet regained our composure after being chased by the matriarch, yet Nabi started following them again. After a short while, the second female in the group noticed us. It was now her turn to warn us. She raised her trunk and flapped her ears. This behaviour is typical of elephants. All the female members are equally concerned about the safety of youngest member of the family. This time we decided to not allow it to escalate. Unanimously we agreed to leave the place leaving the herd undisturbed.

The safari on the second day started at 6:00 am from Gairal FRH, and we reached near Dhikala grassland at around 7:30 am. We dedicated the first few hours observing behavioural patterns of Asiatic elephants.

Imagine the great grandmother of a traditional Indian family. She always picks the menu to be served at a family gathering. The sisters, aunts, and mother spend time in the kitchen in preparing the menu. The teenage brother leaves the gathering and joins a group of other men to drink, which was obviously not part of the menu. Much like this young gentleman, in the elephant family, the adult male elephants leave their herd and form a separate bachelor herd. We encountered a similar bachelor herd that morning at Dhikala grassland.

Like many animals, elephants form a hierarchy within their social structure, thereby reducing conflict over resources (such as food, water, and space). Among elephants, a matriarch (the oldest and wisest female) leads her bond group of related females to find food and water and to avoid predators. When the herd becomes too large for the available food or water supply, some of the females often split from the herd and form their own groups, each headed by an older relative. Elephants thus live in fission-fusion societies.

Scientists continue to investigate the complexities of the social structure among elephants.

Dominance in males is a little different from that in females, or cows. Males, or bulls, form bachelor herds when they reach sexual maturity. For example, while the dominant cow is the herd leader, the dominant bull is usually the individual that mates with the most females and beats out other males in contests of strength. Interestingly, dominant bulls that are in musth tend to remain in musth (and maintain a higher production of testosterone) longer than younger, less dominant bulls.

In the Dhikala grassland, we observed for a significant duration, a conflict between three tuskers over dominance. The biggest among them did not allow the smallest one to be part of the herd. Initially we thought the smallest one was not related to the other two, and so they were preventing him from joining the group. The smallest one was trying to climb over a ridge, near a dry river body at the grassland. The biggest one deterred his efforts by shaking his head vigorously to express his unpleasantness. Soon, they challenged each other and after letting out a huge trumpet, they locked their trunks and started pushing each other. The smallest one gave up after some time but did not leave the group. All three of them started moving together and disappeared into the distant grassland.

Shortly thereafter, we heard the trumpet, and all three of them reappeared. This time, the medium sized tusker started pushing the smallest one. The two of them engaged and started pushing each other. The biggest one joined them after a while, and both together started pushing the smallest one. It continued for some time, eventually the smallest one submitted. They started moving together and disappeared in the bushes. We suspected it was a conflict between them to establish dominance over their newly constituted bachelor herd.

Although we were busy with elephants for two days, we were yet to have any encounter with any descendants of any character from Corbett's *Man-eaters of Kumaon*.

The early summer sun in the forest of Uttarakhand shone brighter as the day progressed. We left the grassland and after proceeding a few kilometres, we saw a couple of gypsies waiting near a waterbody. We heard them whisper - *'tiger'*. In a regular forest this word has a different significance for the tourists, photographers, forest guides, and gypsy drivers, compared to in Corbett Park, where it is nerve-racking, to say the least. When you roam in the park where the grabbles, water droplets, leaves and winds bear the legacy of Jim Corbett, on hearing the word "tiger", your senses are heightened, your ears pick up the slightest sound, and your eyes tend not to miss the slightest movement. You can feel your heart pounding in your chest. Bengal tigers, although plentiful, are not easily spotted due to the abundance of foliage - camouflage - in this reserve.

Thick jungle, the Ramganga River and plentiful prey make this reserve an ideal habitat for tigers who are opportunistic feeders and prey upon a range of animals. The tigers in the park have been known to kill much larger animals such as buffalo and even elephant for food. The tiger preys upon larger animals only in rare cases of food shortage. There have been incidents of tigers attacking domestic animals in times of shortage of prey.

After a few tense minutes, we spotted a female tiger in the dense bushes, her tawny coat nicely camouflaged in the surrounding sub-Himalayan foliage. She slowly moved into the deep forest. That was our first tiger sighting at Corbett Park after our previous encounter with the gorgeous animal in the forest of Tadoba in Maharashtra. At 10:00 am, we concluded our morning safari and arrived at Dhikala FRH for breakfast and rest for the next four hours.

We started our afternoon safari at 2:30 pm, again from Dhikala to Gairal. As we drove through Thandi Sarak, we spotted a female elephant with a calf. As we debated whether or not to follow them, on our left, we heard branches snapping. We suspected another elephant hiding in dense foliage.

It was not a good idea to be sandwiched between elephants both in front of and behind the gypsy. In the case of elephant chasing us, we would have no escape route. Therefore, we reversed our gypsy and waited at a distance from where we kept an eye on the source of the sound. Soon after, two elephants appeared uphill. They were climbing down, breaking branches. We let them go and turned towards Kalichar. Nabi told us that Thandisarak is known for elephant movement. The abundant tree coverage, keeps the place cool, and elephants prefer this part of the forest for movement. He explained that consequently fewer tourist gypsies used this forest path. I wondered why, then, he had brought us there.

I enquired and he replied, *"This is a forest, and anything could happen at any time!"*

Nabi had a knack to test our nerves by putting us repeatedly in "threat to survival" situations.

This perception of "threat to survival" is very grave in materialistic human civilization from where urban affluent people come with an aspiration to become famous. Therefore, they never do anything without a plan to deal with such perceived threat. When they fail to strike a deal with such threat, they either run away or destroy the source of threat.

But the same humans who make their living out of the forest are indifferent to this threat. They believe, *"This is a forest, and anything could happen at any time!"* They accept this so-called threat as accepted norm of living in the forest with other non-human life forms. Ironically, they have no aspiration of becoming famous. At the same time, they are less obliged to compromise their essential liberty; and are, thus, less envious of non-human life forms.

This was the fundamental difference between people like Nabi who are dependent on the forest for their livelihood, and wildlife enthusiasts like us, who need an escapade through the illusion of living a non-human life, in an attempt to become famous.

After driving four-five kilometres, we spotted a parade of elephants walking slowly, in a single file, towards the waterbody at Kalichar. They were at least twenty in number, including – an adult male, adult females and calves. The male was at the front, calves in the centre, followed by female or cow elephants, and the matriarch at the end. This is a typical formation of a parade of elephants that is in movement. *Disney* wasn't deceptive in the movie, *The Jungle Book*. Elephants do walk in a single file when they are on the move, for instance while in search of food and water. The calves often hold on to their mother's tails with their trunks to keep up, while other female elephants surround them to protect from danger.

Female family units range from three to twenty-five elephants. At times a herd of female elephants join groups of bull elephants to form larger clans. Herd aggregations of 500 to 1000 elephants have been recorded in Corbett Park around watering holes and other sources of food and water. Herd aggregation has also been documented in areas where poaching is rampant.

The parade was headed to the river to drink and bathe. Within a few minutes, another parade appeared from the riverside, returning after bathing and drinking. The leading male of the retreating parade stopped; the whole parade followed him. He raised his trunk towards the approaching parade and shook his head. In a moment, the parade approaching from opposite direction changed their course, taking a different route to the river. Neither parade wanted to bump into each other causing unnecessary commotion and conflict. It was an amazing display of discipline and mutual respect in the wild.

There was also a possibility that the two herds were interrelated. Although they tend to be close, an elephant family can split. This decision is influenced by ecological factors, such as the availability of food and water in the area, and social factors, such as how well the elephants get along, the size of the group or the death of a matriarch. As such, different herds living over a vast terrain may be interrelated. These 'bond groups' keep in touch with each other through rumbling calls and usually stay within a mile of each other. Conservationists believe that in the vast grassland of Dhikala, there must be at least a few interrelated herds.

We followed the parade that was headed to the waterbody and observed their bathing activities from a distance. We witnessed how female members of the group pushed the calves into water, submerging them, to ensure their whole body was washed and cooled, and eventually pulling them out of water as the herd prepared to leave. Babysitting is an important aspect of elephant behaviour. Female elephants (cows) help look after each other's calves. Babysitting other female's calves is important for elephant development; young females learn how to look after the young, and the calves are shown how it is done. The survival rate of a calf greatly increases when more females are present and willing to take care of it.

Bathing together is another typical behavioural pattern of elephant, which shows strong family ties. They love to bathe in the river; using their trunks like a hose to spray water across the body. To help protect the skin from parasites and insect bites, elephants wallow in mud or spray dust on their wet skin. Once the mud and dust dry, elephants scratch their body against rocks or trees to remove the parasites.

As we were leaving the place, we saw another parade walking towards the river.

As we left the forest for the day, a huge lone tusker was bathing alone. He saw us too, raised his trunk and soon after left the water, climbed uphill and started walking towards the grassland nearby. Clearly, we interfered with his privacy. We waited there for some time and watched his movement. He was a full-grown adult and his male reproductive organ suggested that he was in musth and ready for mating. In all likelihood, he was going to join a female herd. We had seen a group of cow elephants and another tusker too, in the distant forest. As we were exiting the forest, at around 6:00 pm, there was sudden intermittent warning call of barking deer and peafowl.

The elephants were also a little restless, trumpeting. The presence of tiger was suspected. Unfortunately, it was time to leave the forest.

Living solitary life or surviving alone in the forest is not an exclusive behaviour of the Bengal Tiger. It's a way of life for the Bengal Tigers. However, family life-oriented animals like elephants, also enjoy being solitary at times.

Living in solitude and being able to survive alone is then, clearly, an animal instinct. An important component of essential liberty that non-humans embrace while the human sacrifices.

The following day we prepared to leave Gairal FRH. We packed our rucksacks and loaded it in the gypsy. Accommodation for the night was booked at Dhikala FRH. Around 6:00 am we set out on our safari. The usual route to enter the forest from FRH, was to turn right at the solar powered electric fence. However, Nabi wanted to try an alternate route and turned left instead. That was another speciality of Nabi; he never followed the conventional route of ecotourism marked for tourists, thus increasing the risk. I must admit, that this also increased the thrill associated with the adventure.

Two to three hundred meters into the route, we saw something sitting on the road with its back to us. It appeared unaware of our presence. Initially, it looked like a rabbit with its two ears visible on its head. The colour and size were not very conspicuous, as it was just dawn. Whatever it was, we decided to stop. It took a few moments before it hit us. There sat a tiger on the forest road, stalking a herd of spotted deer.

Hyperreactive Vedavyasa could not control his excitement and screamed *"Tiger! Tiger!"*

As he exclaimed, it noticed us. It instantly stood up and ran into the deep forest adjacent to the road. However, before it disappeared in forest, we realised it was a full-grown adult female tiger. We had taken her by surprise. Alarmed, she quickly ran into thicket. We decided to stay there for some time. After about five-six minutes, there were strong warning calls from barking deer. The jungle fowls joined the call soon after. This confirmed the tigress was still nearby and on move. Eventually the tigress appeared from our left, where she had entered a while ago.

The female tiger came out in the clear, turned towards us and fixed her gaze on us, watching us as intensely as we watched her. A gazing contest of sorts.

I was reminded of Corbett's words. *"The same sense that had conveyed the feeling of impending danger to me had evidently operated in the same way on the tiger...."* The Kanda Man-eater, Man-eaters of Kumaon.

With her gaze still fixed on us, she lowered her upper body slightly, leaning in towards us. For a moment we thought she was preparing to leap, and chase. Afterall, she was merely hundred meters from us. Perhaps she changed her mind, as she crossed the road and went to the other side of the forest. Vigorous warning calls from both sides of the forest continued. There were quite a few spotted deer roaming around. The tiger was perhaps hungry and preparing for a kill. If we stayed long enough, we could perhaps witness and capture that breath-taking moment in our cameras. At the same time though, we did not want to disturb her morning work, or interfere in the natural phenomenon of her survival. Nabi was appreciative of these thoughts, and we left the place leaving the prey and predator in the lap of nature, to their natural fate.

Nabi's consent in leaving the place and allowing the tigress to plan her hunt was revelatory. Post the trip to Tadoba, I was beginning to feel that we were losing respect for animals, considering them merely as adorable wild pets of the forest. The forest dwellers of Corbett Park however, still appeared to have respect for the privacy of the animals, and a certain regard and admiration for them.

We proceeded to Jharana Jhari, and a kilometre into the journey, we found our road blocked. An uprooted Rohini tree blocked our path. A couple of other gypsies were also held up.

Apparently, an elephant uprooted the tree. Evidence of elephant debuckling and fresh elephant poop was all-over the place. Nabi got down form the car, so did we. Tourists are not allowed to get down from the gypsy in the forest, except in designated areas. But this was an emergency. Nabi asked other drivers to help clear the branches. A few tourists came forward to help. Now, we were on our feet in the forest.

Three gypsies, parked at one end of the path and the huge uprooted Rohini tree with thick branches lying on the path. We stood between the gypsies and the tree. The other end of the path, leading to the Dhangarhi gate, was open. Now, if the elephant in question, who apparently uprooted the tree, should appear from that end, we would have no escape route. A guide, Kaleem, had similar concerns, and instantly came up with a solution. *"We will just climb this steep hill alongside the path, from where the tree fell".*

What an excellent survival idea! I visualized a wild elephant following us, as we struggled to climb an uphill slope covered in thorny bushes, with camera and lenses in hand.

Nabi had created yet another adventure for us, albeit inadvertently.

We cleared the loose leaves and branches, and attempted to chop the thick one. But without the right tools, it was not an easy task. I fished out a chain saw and Swiss knife from my survival kit. However, cutting the thick girth of a Rohini tree trunk with such tools was clearly a childish idea.

Most of us were in agreement that it was not possible to cut the whole tree to clear the path with available tools. We decided it would be wise to wait for the forest department lumberjack. The forest officials had been informed. Nabi, however, disagreed as he had minimal faith in the department. He motivated and encouraged everybody to continue the tree-cutting task before the department people arrived.

Amongst us, that day, was the famous fashion and fine art photographer, Mr. Akash (or Akashendu) Das. Nature and wildlife photography was his hobby and he freelanced for *National Geographic*. Incidentally, Nabi and Mr. Das had been in a similar situation on a state highway. Although not in a forest, but nonetheless the situation had been alarming. They were on road and a tornado was fast approaching. Nabi claimed that Mr. Das and he, together, cut a tree much thicker than the tree in question at Corbett Park with Mr. Das's Swiss knife. Mr. Das was indeed a proud owner of a Swiss knife, which he pulled out in support of Nabi's tall claims. But the knife was barely impressive. In fact, it was hardly better than the one I was carrying in my survival kit. Mr. Das, himself sounded much less confident than Nabi regarding the girth of the tree on the state highway, which they had apparently cut through. However, seeing Nabi's enthusiasm and confidence, no one objected. After all, he was the most experienced forest guide present there. Hence, we continued with the task of cutting the tree, resulting in the chain saw snapping, but not before we successfully removed one thick branch.

After the chain saw broke, we ceased our activity and waited for the lumberjack and the officials of the forest department. Mr. Das, however, continued his effort with his Swiss knife, repeatedly muttering that the Swiss knife he used in the previous occasion was better than the current one. His objective, it appeared, was not to cut the tree, but to prove that he had indeed cut through a tree with a Swiss knife, much as how Nabi had described it.

Vedavyasa and I thoroughly enjoyed this drama that lasted two full hours. This was an unprecedented opportunity to be part of the forest, besides the "high" we experienced at the surprise sighting of the tiger. Tourists typically lose patience and express dissatisfaction when their "precious safari time" bought by spending a few bucks, is wasted due to "inconveniences" created by "unreasonable" behaviour of "rowdy" animals. We, however, were in no hurry to get back into our safari gypsy. Standing on the forest path of a tiger reserve on our own two feet and being part of the tree removal activity was more fun and exciting than a regular safari.

The drama ended when the forest department people arrived, cut the tree and removed it in a tractor. We had run out of time for our morning safari and we headed towards Dhikala FRH, where accommodation for the night was arranged in a log hut dormitory.

The afternoon safari started at 3:30 pm towards Kamal Patti and we turned towards Chuha Pani. Elephant population is very high in this part of the park. It is, unfortunately, also infamous for elephant attack. At around 4:00 pm on Sambar Road, we spotted a herd of elephants, females and calves, crossing a waterbody.

Our day ended with a thrilling elephant chase at Thandi Sarak. A herd of four elephants was crossing the road. A gypsy ahead of us suddenly speeded up and overtook the herd. The matriarch of the herd was mighty annoyed. Consequently, she chased our gypsy, as we were following the other. We quickly reversed the vehicle and sped away.

As per a study conducted in May 2019, titled *Fact check: Are Tigers eating elephants in Corbett National Park?* by Ms. Deepika S, published as an article in *oneindia.com*, Corbett has a unique ecosystem with 252 tigers and approximately 1,200 wild elephants, whereas other national parks like Ranthambore, Kanha and Bandhavgarh mainly have tigers.

As stated in the article, an official study conducted between 2014 to 31st May 2019, revealed that around 21 elephants, nine tigers, and six leopards died due to infighting during this period of study. What is particularly significant is that of the 21 elephants that died, 13 were killed by tigers, predominantly the young elephants. The article attributes this to the fact that hunting an elephant requires lesser energy as compared to hunting a sambar or a spotted deer. Besides an elephant provides a larger quantity of food. Even in cases where elephants were killed in infighting, tigers were found eating their body parts.

This study, indeed, signals a worrying trend. It is well known that tigers and elephants share a mutual respect, and tigers usually don't eat elephants. This peculiar aspect of tiger-elephant conflict needs further studies.

The following day around 10:30 am we finished our safari in Dhikala zone and returned to our log hut for breakfast. We packed our bags and left Dhikala zone. We would be spending the subsequent three nights at Bijrani zone.

Our safari in the Bijrani zone commenced at 3:00 pm. Nabi received intelligence that a tigress had been spotted in a particular section of the forest. We rushed towards the forest, and waited at the point where she been spotted in the morning. We waited for an hour. A short while later, a gypsy on its way back informed us that an old tigress was spotted lying on the ground near Chital *more* (*more* is Hindi for 'crossing').

When we reached there, we noticed there were at least five gypsies, and more were coming in. It was a narrow path with dense undergrowth on either side. Only two gypsies could move side by side. As a result, in no time, there was complete chaos with a long line of approximately 30 gypsies with some 200 tourists across all gypsies – all of who were in competition to reach a convenient spot from where to eye the animal. The impatient tourists were desperate to see the tigress, a lifetime opportunity, and take pictures of her, making the situation at sixes and sevens.

All of a sudden Vedavyasa jumped up from his seat and leaped onto the adjacent gypsy. From there he jumped on to another one and then to another one.

By the time Nabi realized what he was up to; Vedavyasa was on the gypsy closest to the place where the tigress was lying.

All these acrobatics, to take an image of the tigress. He was desperate to take an image of the Bengal Tiger of Corbett Park. He was also desperate to show his ability to do so to the mostly non photographer ecotourists despite the chaos, or perhaps because of it.

Nabi started scolding him and he returned to our gypsy by doing similar stunts.

This act of Vedavyasa, however, had a ripple effect. The other tourists let go their desperation and decided to act.

As it is, they were prepared to do anything to have a glimpse of that tigress. They now started pushing and shoving each other and jumping from one gypsy to another. Some of them got off from the gypsy and walked and ran on the forest ground to reach close to the tigress - even if that meant risking their lives.

It had completely escaped their notice that they were in a wild forest, dealing with wild animals, and not in a zoological garden where animals were held captive. The superiority and ego of being a human was on shameless display. So also, their stupidity. The thought that non-human life forms cannot cause the human any harm was apparent. And if this had resulted in a counterattack by the animal, whose peace was being destroyed and patience tested, then of course, as per the laws of human civilization, it would be the fault of the animal herself. Consequently, punishment would be meted out to her by the so-called superior species of this planet.

Incidentally, like most of our explorations thus far, that day, Vedavyasa and I were the only wildlife photographers while the rest of the visitors were just ecotourists.

General tourists follow the path shown by wildlife enthusiasts.

Nabi was the only gypsy driver who went furious and started cursing all visitors gathered there. In response, one young woman reasoned with him quite logically, *"If tiger does not come to us, then we have to go to the tiger, right?"*

Sounded much like the human principle followed by religious devotees in Amarnath, Kedarnath, Vaishnodevi, Ajmeer Shareef, Palestine and many other pilgrimage sites. God does not come to them, so they go to God.

But does this behaviour reinstate the demigod status of Bengal Tiger?

Regardless, the tigress remained calm. In fact, she was completely indifferent, enjoying her siesta in dappled sunlight. Apparently, she was old and injured, and had been unable to hunt for the past few days, which had further weakened her and reduced her pace. However, one couldn't ignore the potential that such circumstances might turn her into a human-eater.

Corbett mentioned in his note in *Man-eaters of Kumaon*, *"A man-eating tiger is a tiger that has been compelled, through stress of circumstances beyond its control, to adopt a diet alien to it. The stress of circumstances is, in nine out of ten cases, wounds, and in the tenth case old age."*

Tiger attacks are an extreme form of human–wildlife conflict that occur for various reasons and have claimed more human lives than attacks by any of the other big cats. The most comprehensive study of deaths due to tiger attacks estimates that at least 373,000 people died due to tiger attacks between 1800 and 2009, most of these attacks occurring in south and southeast Asia. Over the last five centuries, an estimated one million people have been eaten by tigers. In southeast Asia, attacks gradually declined after peaking in the nineteenth century, but attacks in south Asia have remained high, particularly in the Sundarbans.

Near Corbett Park and surrounding areas of the park in the state of Uttarakhand, every year news of tiger attacks is reported.

Statistics released in 2017 by India's Ministry of Environment reveals that 1,144 people were killed by wild animals between April 2014 and May 2017. That figure breaks down to 426 human deaths in 2014-15, and 446 the following year. The ministry released only a partial count for 2016-17, with 259 people killed by elephants up to February of that year, and 27 killed by tigers through May. India's population of 1.42 billion is still growing, and as it does, it is increasingly encroaching into the country's traditional wild spaces and animal sanctuaries, where people compete with wildlife for food and other resources. The growth of human settlements is often seen as economic development. But for some who are living on the edge of wildlife borders, this development can come at a high cost.

We have taken away space from wildlife, and now we visit national parks, which do not provide adequate space for them, all in the name of our love for nature and wildlife. At the very least, we must be empathetic towards nature and wildlife when we trespass into their space.

That afternoon, unfortunately, the tourists in Bijrani zone, appeared completely ignorant about any behavioural requirements in the wild forest and with no respect for wild animals and nature. Soon they turned violent, as if a million dollars were at stake and the only way to recover it was by seeing the tiger. Amidst this chaos, a tourist jumped on our gypsy and damaged the bonnet. Nabi was furious and decided to leave the forest immediately, but not before verbally thrashing the mature adult man in front of a full house constituting tourists and forest guides.

That afternoon, hundreds of tourists, drivers and forest guides made it clear that we human beings are only concerned about our own amusement and have minimal respect and empathy for nature and wildlife.

Nabi was visibly disappointed, and Vedavyasa deeply ashamed. He sat in the gypsy with eyes downcast and spoke nothing until we left the place. When we were well out of the area, he started defending himself without any provocation. He picked up flaws in my behaviour from many previous occasions.

I did not want to get into any argument with him and allowed him some time to regain his composure.

Later in the evening, when he was more relaxed and prepared for a normal conversation, I realized that things were not well between Ambalika and him.

After getting involved with Ambalika, he realized his freedom of being himself was further compromised.

It was for this reason that he had wanted to leave his wife, Vatika. Clearly going to Ambalika didn't solve the problem, instead it only made the situation worse.

Like Prithu of Guha's novel, Vedavyasa too desired a solitary and free life, but did not know how to live without a woman. It was this self-contradiction that caused such desperation in the forest that afternoon.

It is only the Bengal Tiger who is privy to that. Tigers and tigresses know how to live with each other without giving up their freedom.

It is the prerogative of the non-human. Even human Mowgli did not have this privilege.

"Man-pack and wolf-pack have cast me out", said Mowgli, "Now I will hunt alone in the jungle" ...But he was not always alone, because years afterward, he became a man and married. But that is a story for grown-ups. – Rudyard Kipling, The Jungle Book.

Next morning, we found Nabi visibly upset. He explained that it was not just because of the behaviour of the tourists. He was sorry for abusing the gentleman who jumped on our gypsy in front of his family members, other tourists, and guides. He decided it would be better to visit some of the relatively unexplored parts of the forest, rather than going through the general route, taken by all tourist gypsies. That was probably a way to avoid unruly tourists. No doubt, last afternoon's experience had shaken us all. We, thus, took a not-so-regular route, and upon noticing pugmarks of a tiger, followed it, reaching up to Ringora.

In Ringora, rumour was rife that a young female tiger was roaming in the forest and had been sighted by a few tourist vehicles. There was speculation that the young female sought territorial dominance over the oldest tigress of Bijrani zone. Nabi indicated that there was a possibility of sighting the young tigress in Ringora.

Around 7:30 am, we heard a strong call of barking deer. We waited for some time and moved towards Chital Road, the territory of the old tigress. At 8:00 am, near Nalah of chital road, we found the old tigress walking on the road and gradually going inside the forest.

Females are likely to stay within fairly proximity to their mother, despite not necessarily having a relationship with her in the future, while males are likely to go further away. Therefore, there was also a speculation that the young female was the daughter of the older one, whom we saw at Chital Road.

A female tiger reaches sexual maturity at between three and four years old of age and will likely have her first litter then. Males are about a year older than their female counterparts are when they reach sexual maturity; that is, between four and five years old. Females usually wait about 2.5 years between pregnancies. However, if she loses a litter, she can produce another one within five months.

The old tigress of Bijrani would avoid a confrontation with the young one, if she indeed was her offspring. Tigers are generally sensitive about their own gene pool.

One evening at Corbett Park, Vedavyasa told me that one of the main reasons of conflict between Ambalika and him was his daughter. Ambalika had a son from her previous marriage, and she wanted that her son get priority in parental care over Vedavyasa's daughter.

Another evening, in the forest of Kumaon, Vedavyasa asserted, *"I have to protect my gene pool"*.

Bengal Tigers ensure this protection without any self-contradiction. Perhaps it is this ability of Bengal Tigers that further increases human obsession for them.

Although, infanticide by tigers is a common practice as we heard the stories of Matkasur in Tadoba. However, eminent tiger scientist Dr. K. Ullas Karanth, in his book *Among Tigers*, candidly mentioned, *"Infanticide has been a successful evolutionary strategy. It has nothing to do with individual tigers being good guys or bad guys according to a human yardstick of morality."*

That morning, we found the old tigress very weak and slow in movement. Her skin was dark and sagging. Naturally, tigers live longer when they are in captivity, since they are not under threat from poachers, starvation, or fires. They receive protection and medical assistance as and when necessary. Therefore, tigers in captivity have been known to live for about 26 years. Those in the wild must fight and fight hard to survive. For this reason, their life is shorter, at an average of 10 years.

This Corbett National Park exploration conveyed a hard message to all so-called wildlife enthusiasts and photographers - and that is to show respect to forests and its flora and fauna. This includes forest dwellers and forest guides as well, who earn their livelihoods from nature's bounty.

Photographers visiting National Parks are ready to put everything at stake for spectacular images of this magnificent creature – the Bengal Tiger. And in the process become impatient at the thought of losing precious time on their priceless tiger safari.

For such photographers, Jim Corbett has a clear message. *"For ten years I stalked through many hundreds of miles of tiger country, at times being seen off by tigers that resented my approaching their kills, and at other times being shooed out of the jungle by tigresses that objected to my going near their cubs. During this period, I learnt a little about the habits and ways of tigers, and though I saw tigers on, possibly, two hundred occasions I did not succeed in getting one satisfactory picture."- Jim Corbett, Man-eaters of Kumaon.*

Our exploration in this oldest and legendary tiger reserve of India, spanned two main zones – Dhikala and Bijrani. Of the two, Dhikala is closer to the heart for most wildlife photographers of this country, although possibility of tiger sighting is more at Bijrani.

This is precisely why general ecotourists like to visit Bijrani more than any other zones, whereas Dhikala is the favourite destination for wildlife enthusiasts. Dhikala has variety of forest types, backwaters, river, wooded areas, grasslands, marshes, and various ecosystems hosting different forms of life. Once you start chasing the tiger, you miss all else.

Eminent wildlife photography mentor from Bangalore, Kesava, once mentioned, *"Don't fix the expectation of sighting a tiger while going into any park. In my humble opinion, you must leave the expectations behind and take only curiosity along. You will see a lot more."*

As I visited park after park of this subcontinent with lesser and lesser expectations of sighting a tiger; the more enriching my experiences became.

I returned from Corbett Park with another realization – we love our tigers and like to possess them like a trophy so as to elevate ourselves to the class of elite wildlife enthusiasts (read wildlife photographers and ecotourists) for fame. But we do not fear them anymore.

Less fear and respect for the tiger and any other wildlife breeds arrogance. Therefore, we do not hesitate in jumping out from the gypsy inside a tiger reserve, or walk on forest path in a National Park, or shove and push fellow ecotourists to reach closer to the animal we desire to see.

This arrogance borne from so-called fame, makes people turn a blind eye to the reality around them.

After the shameful incident of jumping out from the gypsy in Bijrani zone, sensitive Vedavyasa's enthusiasm to participate in a wildlife photography exploration appeared much lower than usual. The Corbett Park incident and the unending complications of his emotional life had significantly deteriorated his confidence.

One Christmas vacation I stayed with Vedavyasa at his office quarters at Balipara, where he was posted as a site engineer for a 400 KVA transformer installation project of *National Power Grid Corporation*.

On Christmas Eve, we had a unique party with other engineers and contractors within the switch yard of

400 KVA power station. The menu was special and included Assam's special duck meat, Bacardi and Goan country liquor – feni, which I had carried with me.

The party was an eye-opener. It helped me understand Vedavyasa's recent psychological conundrum as I had perceived during our trips to Tadoba and Corbett Park.

In Guha's novel, Prithu expresses his unhappiness with his profession several times. He was a natural poet, a creative person. He admitted that his engineering profession was nothing but a means of making a living. He would have been unable to make a living by being a mere poet. He knowingly but helplessly embraced the path towards temporary protection, to meet the demands of his materialistic lifestyle. However, he knew for sure that his true talent lay in writing poetry.

In the material world, not everyone is fortunate enough to pursue their passion as profession. Of course, the question of being fortunate arises only when someone is clear about what his or her passion is.

Often people fail to recognize their real passion, owing to their urge for earning temporary protection to secure a materialistic lifestyle. They, thus, choose a path which assures them commercial success. People embrace the path and mistake that as their passion. After spending a significant part of their life-journey on that path, when their true self rejects the path, it is with a heavy heart that they realize that they were not following their passion. Often, they also realize that they never even tried to explore what their real passion was.

When the monotony of their professional as well as materialistic life compels their true self to reject the path they embraced so far, they become desperate to find a passion as an escape. They may manage to find a passion but that may never become their real passion. Very often such passion provides short term relief from the mundane as such passion is nothing but mimicking someone else's passion - a pseudo passion.

People who are in the wrong profession are often unglorified in their professional circle, because of their lack of dedication in the profession they pursue. Therefore, they desperately use this pseudo passion to restore their lost glory.

I am unsure about Guha's Prithu, but for real-life Prithu(s), this is a common phenomenon.

The Christmas Eve party within the switch yard of 400 KVA power station of *Balipara National Power Grid Corporation*, revealed that Vedavyasa was an unglorified power transmission engineer.

It was quite apparent by the way he was treated by his colleagues and contractors at the party. He was never humiliated, at least not in front of me. But he was made a laughingstock on multiple occasions because of his lack of willingness in completing his work and his persistent alcoholism.

To his colleagues he was a crazy alcoholic, with a reluctance to finish his work on time.

I stayed with him for two more days and witnessed the treatment he was meted out by his colleagues.

On the morning of Christmas, we went to Nameri National Park, situated fourteen kilometres from the power station. Nameri National Park is a national park in the foothills of eastern Himalayas in Sonitpur District of Assam.

We crossed the 40 feet deep Jia Bhoroli River, and started our walk in the bushes at about 1:00 pm. The Jia Bhoroli River of Assam has been famous since the time of the British for golden mahseer angling. While crossing the river we spotted a few cormorants and lesser whistling ducks. Our guide, Lalit Bohra, asserted often enough that it was risky to see wildlife when you were on your feet on the forest path.

We saw a few tokey geckos busking in the comfort of their tree hide. After a thirty-minute bush walk, we heard animal movement on our right, from the nearby shrubs. Lalit noticed a porcupine slide through the deep forest. After an hour, as we walked along a waterbody, Lalit suddenly asked us to stop. We saw a herd of water buffalo led by a huge bull. Wild buffaloes could be quite dangerous when threatened by human presence. Escaping them could be difficult in the event that they charged. Therefore, instead of standing and being shutter happy, we quickly crossed the place and hid behind a watchtower nearby. The herd also turned around and disappeared within the forest. Perhaps, they were coming for water, but retreated sensing our presence. Once they disappeared, we emerged from our hideout and tried to follow their course only to see them going deep into the forest.

We continued walking, and another thirty minutes later we reached another watchtower, and climbed up to the top. We waited for an hour. We saw a huge male gaur grazing. We also spotted a couple of female sambar deer.

A group of students along with their professors from a local college were visiting. Undergraduate zoology students, I presumed, pleased to see our future wildlife enthusiasts and explorers.

Vedavyasa, however, displayed phobic anxiety, evident from his body language when he saw student visitors in the park.

At around 3:30 pm, we climbed down from the watchtower, and started walking to exit the forest. As we crossed the grassland, we heard frequent warning calls of sambar deer. That confirmed movement of big cat in the nearby forest. Lalit mentioned that he had spotted two Bengal Tigers, presumably, one female and her subadult cub, in that same grassland a couple of days prior. Possibility of a face-off with Bengal Tigers in the grassland, particularly when we were on our feet, gave goose bumps, and my footsteps hastened. We concluded our three hours trek of the five kilometres long forest trail.

It did not matter how comfortable and up close we sighted tigers in previous occasions. The mere thought of encountering a Bengal Tiger on foot, raised a question in our minds - *Are we prepared for that sort of fame?*

We spent the following day reviewing video footages of a bike rider couples' interaction with local villagers of Sundarbans, as part of an initiative - *"Protest against Tiger habitat loss"* – in the Sundarbans area of West Bengal. Vedavyasa and I sponsored the initiative and planned to create a fifteen-minute documentary to upload on YouTube.

That day, I discovered more of my childhood friend's misery.

He revealed how dissatisfied he was with his profession. Wildlife photography and talking about nature were now the only things he had to prove that he was a worthy man.

His addiction for wildlife photography, although, was making him even more worthless in his profession. As a result, he had degraded in the eyes of his wife. And thus, he decided to leave his wife. But the relationship with his girlfriend wasn't working either, as that too required sacrifice of his independence.

It was difficult to look at his sorrowful eyes when he admitted that he did not know the purpose of what he was doing, whether it was his engineering job or wildlife photography.

Vedavyasa was clearly a victim of the mundane materialistic lifestyle which neither allowed him to choose the right profession nor allowed him the liberty of time to think about his real passion.

Whatever he was doing presently, was but a desperate attempt to regain his lost glory.

A year after my visit with him at his quarter in Balipara, Vedavyasa told me that one evening in an intoxicated state he had smashed his laptop out of anger against society. As a consequence, the unedited video footages of the bike-rider couples' workshop at Sundarbans will never make it as a worthy documentary on any YouTube channel.

That was a few grands that we spent to shoot the event, down the drain.

Clearly, Vedavyasa's obsession with the Bengal Tiger and their ability to enjoy essential liberty, was no longer working as an escapade for him. On the contrary, his inability to pursue the journey towards essential liberty had him even more dejected and frustrated.

The people who were still determined to continue this quest were turning into his enemies, as was evident by the subtle phobic anxiety he displayed towards the students at Nameri.

Pseudo Ecotourism

Our Tadoba and Corbett Park trips had me convinced that the respect created by Jim Corbett through his literary work for this formidable predator had now been diluted in the hearts of wildlife enthusiasts and general tourists visiting the subcontinental forests.

The ease of tiger sighting in subcontinental forests had shown the path of achieving fame without too much effort. This fame bred arrogance removed any and all hesitation in breaking ground rules of the forest.

The market economy of capitalism is waiting for just this. A glamourous trophy with a high price tag and an effortless way to achieve it; and a few directionless people dissatisfied and unglorified in their profession, but desperate to achieve fame to colour their faded reputations.

The subcontinental forests are ideal grounds for greening capitalism. There are tigers as well as depressed affluent class turned ecotourists/wildlife photographers.

Therefore, tiger tourism in the subcontinent is also the perfect way of greening capitalism, as more affluent ecotourists participate and generate more revenue for stakeholders of capitalist tourism markets. In the process, more people make a livelihood and greening of capitalism receives social license to operate. Hence, it serves as a successful tool for "Sustainable Development".

The apparent success of tiger tourism and tiger photography leads to arrogance. Winning a prize through hard work brings humility. However, buying a prize with money and pretending that it was achieved through hard work, is what gives birth to such arrogance.

CHAPTER FIVE: Non-human Shatters Human Arrogance

A couple of decades ago, cinematographer Mike Herd captured the swamp tiger on film for the first time. It was an extraordinary breakthrough, the first glimpse into the secret life of the least known tiger in the world - The Swamp Tiger of the Bangladeshi Sundarbans.

When the documentary, with a running time of fifty minutes was released in 2001, the apex predator of the forest was portrayed in another ferocious incarnation - one of the most efficient predators on Earth, this animal is feared as a killer and a human-eater - the legendary swamp tiger. Entangled, mangrove forest in the Bay of Bengal is the kingdom of this creature and he is rarely seen by humans. These tigers are so elusive that all attempts to track them in these impenetrable swamps typically end in failure.

After two consecutive successful attempts in spotting Bengal Tigers in wild, journey-proud Vedavyasa and I wanted to continue our quest for glory in the tiger territory of this subcontinent.

We wanted to tell everybody, loud and clear, that we were capable of taking it to the next level. To "Mike Herd's level". Thus, we started an informal discussion to explore the Bangladesh part of Sundarbans. A wildlife photographer friend of ours, Sankar, was based out of Dhaka, and was quite active in wildlife photography in southeast Asia. The planning for the exploration of the swamp-land began under the able guidance and leadership of Sankar.

Vedavyasa, however, eventually decided to abandon us, as he struggled to accept Sankar's and my ability in continuing our exploration activities for Bengal Tigers in the subcontinental forests.

The apparent success of the previous two tiger tours, left me highly motivated and desperate to explore the swampland – the formidable and mysterious Sundarbans of Bangladesh.

Yet life had other plans for me!

After a couple of days stay with Vedavyasa at his office quarter, I left Balipara to board a Calcutta bound flight from Tezpur Airport. I reached Calcutta at 11:30 am, via a short halt at Guwahati. Soon after, I flew to Dhaka, and my exploration in Swampland began. The plan was to stay in Dhaka with co-explorer Sankar Singha, at his company guesthouse. Sankar had been posted in Bangladesh for the past few years as an Environment, Health, and Safety Manager for a power generation company. Our itinerary spanned two nights and three days in the Sundarbans of Bangladesh. Sundarbans, a network of estuaries, tidal rivers, and creeks intersected by numerous channels, that encloses flat, densely forested, marshy islands. The total area of the Sundarbans, including both land and water, is roughly 10,000 km^2, about three-fifths of which is in Bangladesh. Thus, we decided that the Swampland exploration should begin from the Sundarbans of Bangladesh, as opposed to India (West Bengal).

After an overnight stay at Sankar's company guesthouse, at Dhaka's posh locality of Baridhara, the following morning we headed towards Kamalapur railway station. We were to board the Sundarbans Express to Khulna. From Khulna, a cruiser to Sundarbans had been arranged. It was the time of general election in Bangladesh, and elections in Bangladesh have always been messy and violent. In recent elections, the country had seen a lot of unrest. Therefore, our tour operator advised us to get into cruiser a day before the election day to avoid any traffic restrictions.

The Kamalapur station was jam-packed. We boarded the train. It appeared that everybody was headed home. It was a long weekend - with Friday a public holiday, followed by Saturday, and elections on Sunday. Our compartment, however, was quite empty as it was an air-conditioned reserved compartment. We placed our bags on overhead bunks and took our seats. We were quite stressed out – more psychological than physical – the hustle bustle of the chaotic railway station probably caused the panic.

Once we saw the calm and clean compartment, we felt relaxed, and the holiday spirit calmed our nerves. We settled down, and soon, we were engrossed in a deep conversation on wildlife and biodiversity.

We almost forgot about our surroundings. Besides, there was nothing interesting around us. The sight of the dingy trackside of Bangladesh railways was not worth viewing or remembering. It was fascinating to hear someone like Sankar, a well-travelled and earnest wildlife enthusiast. He spoke of wildlife of Laos, Thailand, and Malaysia. I shared my experiences of South African Savannah, Scottish Highland, and Sumatran Rain Forests.

The train stopped at the next station, Biman Bandar. A few passengers boarded. A chill went down my spine as my eyes rested on the luggage bunk. My camera bag was missing. For a few seconds I could not believe my eyes. Nevertheless, it did not take long to comprehend the reality!

Yes. I lost my backpack containing the latest Nikon D7200 camera (which I had used but once at Daroji Sloth Bear Sanctuary the previous summer), one Sigma 150-600 mm lens, iPad, one terabyte (TB) hard drive (with all my work), and my official laptop. The hardest part was that my passport was also in the same bag.

I lost the bag. To be precise, someone stole my bag. The contents in it could easily be valued at two to three lakhs rupees.

Pseudo Ecotourism

We disembarked from the train. The Sundarbans trip stood cancelled. Disappointment at cancellation aside, I was more anxious and fearful about what lay ahead, and the anticipation of a tough time.

I was stranded in a foreign land, without a passport. Next few days saw us running between the police station and high commission offices, amidst the tension of election.

I had done a lot of biodiversity exploration, including in remote and risky parts of the world. Chased by wild elephants in dense and muddy forest trail of Periyar; felt the presence of fearsome predators around me; dealt with adverse natural calamities while camping in the forest of Western Ghats and Himalayas; almost sucked in a whirlpool in Sumatra; tent ransacked by baboons in South Africa. But never before had I felt so hopeless during any exploration.

In all previous cases, the situation had popped suddenly, with no time for preparation. The risk was high but the pain and stress of dealing with the situation was short-lived. However, this situation was different. I suffered incremental level of stress for an indefinite period.

I told myself, *"An adventurous life comes with pain!"*

With no passport I was stuck in Bangladesh for an indefinite period. But I am grateful to Sankar. He arranged my accommodation at his company guesthouse and deployed his local travel agent to coordinate with Bangladesh visa processing department. He made his office vehicle and driver available for all the coordination tasks with different departments.

This train incident was a subtle warning by life to people blinded by their obsession for fame and glory. Life was urging me to take a pause before jumping into relentless tiger tourism to prove my worth to the world. The world clearly did not care about my expertise in tiger photography. Rather, all it cares about is how much wealth I am capable of investing in this commodity market called ecotourism.

With elections in the country, I did not have much opportunity to go around and explore the city. Therefore, I utilised that time to consolidate my thoughts on my future exploration plans and as a result, the seed for this book was sown. It was there, that I conceptualized the idea of this book *"Pseudo Ecotourism: In the Shadow of the Bengal Tiger"*.

During my stay in Dhaka, Sankar's wonderful colleagues kept me company. We played badminton in the evenings, and went jogging in a park nearby. His local Bangladeshi cook, Pervez, was an artist in preparing Bangladeshi delicacy. Apart from the uncertainty in going back home, ironically, I was enjoying my stay at Dhaka.

After few weeks, I returned to India. I spent the subsequent eleven months, reassembling resources, improving my photography and writing skills, and roaming the rainforests of Western Ghats. I realized that while the train incident in Bangladesh had forced me to pause and re-think the worthiness of tiger tourism with which I had started to achieve fame, its effect did not last long. It was time to plan another trip to the swampland.

A writer and conservationist friend of mine from Bangladesh, Foridi Numan, wrote in one of his articles on *Exploring Nature* published in the e-magazine *The Holocene* – "*Sundarbans – an enormous, extensive, vast, reticent, quiet, tranquil, harrowing, and mysterious forest; the habitat of fearsome carnivores and predators; the largest mangrove delta of the world; commonly known as Swampland, an inexplicable wonder of earth.*"

By "inexplicable wonder of earth", Foridi Numan clearly meant the Bangladesh part of Sundarbans. This time, however, I decided to make my comeback to the swampland in the Sundarbans of West Bengal (India).

The mystery of world's largest mangrove forest and the only mangrove tiger land are inseparable from the fascinating story of the deity "Bon Bibi". The name Bon Bibi literally means lady of the forest. Since the appellation Bibi is used by Muslim women as an all-purpose surname that makes it a unique name for a Bengali goddess. Jnanpith and Sahitya Akademi Awards winner, Indian writer, Padma Shri Amitav Ghosh in his environmentalist novel *The Hungry Tide*, published in 2004, mentioned two accounts of the Bon Bibi story of *"Dukhey's Redemption."*

Bon Bibi is believed to be the daughter of Berahim (Ibrahim), a faqir from Mecca. When his first wife

Phul Bibi could not bear a child, Ibrahim (locally known as Berahim) married Golal Bibi with Phul Bibi's permission, on the condition of fulfilling a wish of hers in future. At the same time, Allah (God) decided to send Bon Bibi and Shah Jangali from heaven to the Earth for a divine mission. He instructed them to take birth as the children of Golal Bibi. When Golal Bibi became pregnant, Ibrahim left her in a forest as wished for by his first wife. He kept his promise of granting her a wish. Bon Bibi and Shah Jangali were born to Golal Bibi in the forest. Allah sent four maids from heaven to take care of them. Golal Bibi abandoned Bon Bibi in the forest and left with Shah Jangali in her arms. Bon Bibi was raised in the forest by a doe. After seven years, Ibrahim realized his mistake and took Golal Bibi and her two children to Mecca.

One day, while praying at the mosque of the prophet of Islam, Bon Bibi and Shah Jangali received two magical hats. With the help of the magical hats, they flew to the country of eighteen tides (*atharo bhatir desh*) in Hindustan (India). Another version has it that they were brought to the country of eighteen tides by Gibril[2]. After reaching the country of eighteen tides, Shah Jangali gave the *azan* (call to prayer). The country of eighteen tides (the Sundarbans) was under the control of the demon king Dokkhin Rai. The sound of azan reached his ears. He sent his friend

---

[2] *In Islam, the Angel Gibril or Jibril is the bringer of good news. He is mentioned in both the Qur'an and the Hadith.*

Sanatan Rai to enquire. When Sanatan informed him about the duo, he decided to throw them out of his territory. As he prepared to go into battle, his mother Narayani prevented him from doing so and she herself went to fight with her army of ghosts and goblins. After a long battle Bon Bibi defeated Narayani. Out of mercy, she returned half of the erstwhile kingdom (the deep forest of Sundarbans) to Narayani and her son. Narayani thus befriended Bon Bibi. While the inhabited part of the Sundarbans is believed to be the realm of Bon Bibi, Narayni's son, Dokkhin Rai, is still believed to be the ruler of the deep forest.

As Ghosh narrated in his novel, *"The jungles of 'the country of eighteen tides' were then the realm of Dokkhin Rai, a powerful demon king, who held sway over every being that lived in the forest - every animal as well as every ghoul, ghost and malevolent spirit. Towards mankind he harboured a hatred that was coupled with insatiable desires; he had a limitless craving for the pleasures of human flesh, and when overcome by desire he would take the form of a tiger in order to hunt human beings."*

The Sundarbans's folklore says, Allah chose Bon Bibi to end Dokkhin Rai's tyranny – a task accomplished easily enough after a short trip to Mecca and Medina. Bibi, however, decides not to kill Rai and instead makes him promise that he will not harm anyone who worships her. In the Sundarbans, where death can come quickly, its inhabitants have worshipped Bon

Bibi for centuries as protection from the jungle's many dangers.

This is the mythological connection of human being, Sundarbans Forest, and the apex predator of Sundarbans – the Bengal Tiger, also known as swamp tiger.

According to most wildlife biologists, the mangrove or swamp tigers of Sundarbans, are unlike others. They are physically smaller by as much as 50%, have smaller home ranges, are less shiny, and are by all accounts, less afraid of humans and more aggressive than Bengal Tigers elsewhere. They are also the only tigers in the world to live in a mangrove forest, and they dominate the landscape with their fantastic swimming ability. Nobody really knows why the Sundarbans' tigers are so aggressive. But there are some common theories among scientists and researchers that the saline environment keeps the tigers in a state of discomfort making them more aggressive. Additionally, their habitat, prey stocks, and fresh water supply are shrinking, forcing them into contact with people; also, it is believed that the human eating behaviour is learned. Female human-eaters pass this behaviour onto their cubs when they feed them human flesh.

Regardless of which of these theories is true, when all is said and done, quite a few people end up in the jaws of tigers each year. Officially, tiger deaths number between 30-50 yearly. This is thought to be an underestimation, in part because many of the people killed are not reported as in all likelihood they were attacked as they were collecting resources in restricted areas, and their families fear that if they report their permits would be taken away. The people most at risk are honey and wood collectors, and fishermen, since these jobs require the workers to go deep into the forest, increasing their likelihood of encountering tigers. It is not uncommon for tigers to attack men on fishing boats.

Just three days before my trip to Sundarbans, my photography mentor for this exploration, Santhosh Krishnamoorthy, a Bangalore based wildlife photography tour operator mentioned that he had credible intelligence from his local contact at Sundarbans, of tiger sighting and a fisherman having been picked up by a tiger near a watchtower.

These stories and news from the forest created an exciting pre-exploration mindset coupled with anxiety as I began my journey.

The Bangladesh train incident was a mere anthropogenic disruption to my tiger tourism. It was nothing but an act of petty crime in a poverty-stricken third world nation. That act was not sufficient to question my materialistic arrogance of human supremacy and obsession for possessing a precious prize (a picture of the Bengal Tiger of subcontinent).

My human arrogance induced tiger tourism needed a challenge from non-human life forms to create a significant and long-lasting impact.

Indian Sundarbans awaited me with that challenge.

One winter morning at 8:00 am, I flew into Calcutta. After the arrival of other photographers and nature enthusiasts from Bangalore, Kochi, and Delhi, at around 10:30 am, we started a three-hour journey towards the Godkhali Feri Ghat (Jetty). After walking hundred meters through a narrow rural market, we found ourselves in front of the huge entry gate of the dock, where it was written, *"Welcome to the only mangrove tiger land in the world – Sundarban Tiger Reserve"*. An emotional moment. After a failed attempt in Bangladesh, I was finally at the verge of stepping into the most mysterious and feared Bengal Tiger habitat of the world. It was also a stark reminder that despite being born and raised in Calcutta, and studying Environment Management from a Calcutta based institute, I hadn't ever visited this mysterious land before. This becomes particularly shameful, because the then Director of Sundarbans Biosphere Reserve, and Principle Chief Conservator of Forest (PCCF) of West Bengal, Mr. Atanu Raha, was a visiting faculty teaching us Wildlife Management. He organised annual field trips to Sundarbans. Somehow, I could never make it on any trip during my two-year post-graduation study.

We cruised through Vidyadhari River and other rivulets and creeks of the mangrove forest of Sundarbans. Besides six photographers, we were accompanied by Santhosh's local naturalist and point of contact, Riddhi Mukherjee, local forest guide

Samar Joardar, and boatman Gaurango Mandal, who was also the owner of our safari boat named *Golapi*. There were two additional members in the crew – cook cum assistant Babusona and assistant Sukumar, who had worked as forest guard with the forest department for twenty-five years and was witness to human eating behaviour of swamp tigers, twice.

The eco-geography of this area is totally dependent on the tidal effect of two flow tides (when sea level rises over several hours, covering the intertidal zone) and two ebb tides (when sea level falls over several hours, revealing the intertidal zone) occurring within 24 hours with a tidal range of three to five meters and up to eight meters in normal spring tide, inundating the whole of Sundarbans in varying depths.

Throughout the day we saw six different types of kingfishers. In Sundarbans, typically eight species of kingfishers are found including local species of common, white throated, pied, ruddy kingfisher, migratory black capped, brown winged, collard, and stork billed king fisher. On the first day we spotted black capped, brown winged and collard kingfishers several times. Among them collard and brown winged kingfishers were quite cooperative in terms of photography. However, the black capped kingfisher was skittish. Over four days, we spotted this species several times, but could never manage to reach close enough to get a satisfactory image. Besides these, we spotted local kingfishers – pied, common and white throated. The other local kingfisher, ruddy, is most common during monsoon season.

In the Sundarbans mangrove forest, dusk happens early. The sun set around 4:30 pm and within thirty minutes thereafter, it was quite dark. While retreating to our overnight stay at Sundarban Riverside Holiday Resort, at Chotto Mollakhali of village Dayapur, just opposite to Sajnekhali Tiger Reserve, our safari guide Samar explained how difficult it was for swamp tigers to survive in this difficult terrain. It is not easy to move and search for prey over mud flats, with sharp and hard pneumatophores popping up here and there. That is why Sundarbans tigers remain hungry most of the time thereby becoming an opportunistic hunter. It feeds on a wide range of preys including crabs, shrimps, fish, crocodiles, monitors, wild boar, spotted deer, rhesus macaque, and of course human. In fact, human population in Sundarbans is tigers' sizeably large prey base.

Our plan for the following day was to get into boat by 5:00 am and start cruising by 5:30 am. The safari would continue until dusk, that is, 5:00 pm. Breakfast and lunch was to be cooked and served in the boat itself. We were to be in the forest for twelve hours and that was the typical schedule for each day that we were there. The entire safari was by boat, as rivers are the roads of Sundarbans. There was occasional dismounting to visit a few watchtowers and for canopy walks from where we could get an insight into how the forest looks from within.

Pseudo Ecotourism

As had been agreed, the six of us gathered at the main gate of our resort, only to find it closed with two heavy locks. There was a ten feet high iron fence, covered in barbwires, all around. The 6-acre land with 30 rooms, common area, dining area and two ponds was protected like a fort.

When we called the security guards to open the locks, they created havoc. They had clear instructions to not allow guests out before dawn, *i.e.*, around 6 o'clock. On enquiring why, they responded that several times tigers had been sighted just in front of the main gate of the resort. That made my hair stand on end.

Meanwhile, Santhosh called Riddhi, and they brought the boat to the resort's dock. Each forest office and resort within the national park have their own dock, as water ways are the only mode of transportation within the forest.

We moved towards Dobanki Forest Range and watchtower. It was quite dark due to the mist that had formed over the river. The highlight of the day was spotting peregrine falcon and chasing, yet again, the black capped kingfisher for a few rounds, and then eventually giving up. However, a close view of a collard kingfisher waiting to catch fish was quite spectacular.

A huge saltwater crocodile was found basking with jaw wide open on the outward part of the mudflat. Crocodiles do not have sweat glands, and they bask by keeping their mouths open to cool themselves down. Low tide started and the day turned bright and sunny. It was a good time for spotting land and aquatic animal biodiversity on the exposed outward part of mudflat. The inward part is always covered with thick mangrove and it is difficult to anticipate what is going on inside.

We also saw a leucistic saltwater crocodile. Leucism is a condition characterized by reduced pigmentation in animals. Leucism can cause the reduction in all types of pigment. This contrasts with albinism, for which leucism is often mistaken.

Between 9 and 9:15 am, we saw fresh pug marks of a tiger on the outward part of the mud flat. The trail of pug marks continued for a few kilometres, between Dobanki and Peerkhali range, along the mud flat that emerged during low tide. That was our first exposure to evidence of tigers' existence in Sundarbans. We also saw a wild boar grazing; apparently, the sighting of wild boar is rare in Sundarbans. Suddenly, the animal started running as if it was running for its life after spotting something dangerous. A few metres ahead, we saw two monitor lizards of different morphs. Although, it was unlikely, the wild boar may have been threatened by the monitor lizards.

At around 11 o'clock we saw another trail of tiger pugmarks on the mud flat near our boat. The pugmarks emerged from the dense mangroves of the mud flat towards the edge of the flat where it merged with water. An indication of a tiger that perhaps went into water. Although, I had seen many tiger pug marks in northern, central and southern forests of

India, I could not recognize the pugmarks in Sundarbans initially. Most of them looked like formless depressions, punched in the sloppy and slushy mud flats.

Then began an intense search with eyes scanning for a swimming tiger, and simultaneously scanning the mud flats around our course, with no luck.

After lunch at 2:30 pm, we did a brief canopy walk at Dobanki range, where an afforestation program had been undertaken for a deer rehabilitation centre. A few important bird species spotted there included crested serpent eagle, lessor adjutant stork, Eurasian curlew, red sank, plover and brahminy kites among others.

On the nearby mud flats at Dobanki range, we saw plenty of mudskippers, screw shells, hermit crabs and fiddler crabs. These are typical aquatic fauna of Sundarbans and mangrove ecosystems. Mudskippers are amphibious fish. There are thirty-two living species of mudskipper. Compared to fully aquatic gobies, these specialized fish present a range of peculiar anatomical and ethological adaptations that allow them to move effectively on land as well as in the water. As their name implies, these fish use their fins to move around in a series of skips.

At 4:30 pm, it was getting dark, and we started retreating. We reached our night stay by 6:30 pm, and by then it was pitch dark. The waterbody was covered in thick mist bringing down the visibility level to a minimum. At night, we heard the sound of crackers from some distant villages. Apparently, it was meant to keep the tiger away, suggesting that it may have been sighted in one of the villages.

The two days of exploration in the mangrove forest of Sundarbans was fascinating. However, not sighting a Bengal Tiger, was disappointing to the six photographers on board.

Each of us had the same dream- to have the glory of sighting the elusive swamp tiger in the mysterious mangroves.

The third day of our exploration, we were awed as usual, at the break of dawn. As the day got brighter, we sighted a few collard and black winged kingfishers. The kingfishers of Sundarbans did not disappoint us. However, the sighting worthy of mention, when the first golden rays fell on Vidyadhari River and cleared the mists, was a pair of Irrawaddy dolphin. They were swimming across the breadth of the river, and occasionally their noses popped out of the water. Irrawaddy dolphins are shy of boats, not known to bow-ride, and generally dive when alarmed. They are relatively slow moving. Therefore, our sighting was also from quite far through telephoto lenses and binoculars. They are more susceptible to human conflict than most other dolphins that live farther out in the ocean, and currently the species is endangered. The pair kept us busy for some time, although taking their images was not easy; as we had merely milliseconds to spot them when they occasionally popped or leapt out of water.

Pseudo Ecotourism

The river and the forest around it were very quiet today. Occasionally we got busy with some birds and tried to follow them. At one point a shikra held our attention for a few minutes, then again, a prolonged quiet moment, then some time spent chasing a cuckoo shrike. Getting a clear shot of the cuckoo shrike was difficult, as it was not perched in a manner convenient to shoot. Therefore, we spent some time to see if it sat on a good branch against a background of green leaves. But luck did not favour us.

Overall, it was a slow day with peaceful cruising among mangroves over the serene Vidyadhari River. At 8 am, breakfast was served. After we were done with breakfast, our crew took a break to finish theirs. Suddenly, Gaurango shouted, *"Bagh! Bagh!"* (*Bagh* in Bengali means Tiger).

He was pointing towards a creek. I saw a horizontal orange-ish patch against the background of white mist and dull mud flat at the merging point of water and the outward edge of mud flat.

Then I heard a huge commotion in our boat and saw everyone rushing towards the front end of the boat as the orange-ish patch was exactly at 12 o'clock position along our course.

Gaurango jumped into his driver's cabin and cruised the boat in full throttle. I watched through my newly bought Tamron 150-600 telephoto lens as the orange patch gradually turned into a sizeable tawny coat with black stripes.

The Bengal Tiger of Sundarbans, at a distance of merely a kilometre from me, descended into the water and started swimming. There was one other boat ahead of us and closer to the tiger. My eyes were moist. It was an emotional moment. I always thought my Sundarbans visit was jinxed. After a lot of patience, trauma, preparation, and investment I was finally experiencing what I had desired. I had waited a long time.

Gaurango cruised the boat in full speed towards the direction of the tiger. Everybody in the boat was giddy with excitement. Both Riddhi and Samar gave Gaurango rapid instructions on movement and direction of the tiger. The tawny coat-black stripe was moving in water like a torpedo released from a submarine. We relentlessly pressed our camera shutters.

In under fifty seconds, the tiger had reached the other side of the canal, emerged from water, shook off water from its body, looked at us and disappeared slowly into the thick mangroves. We were within few hundred meters from him by that time. Riddhi announced, *"We just saw the certified man eater of Sundarbans!"*

For the next four and half hours, we played hide and seek with the most dominant alpha male of Sundarbans, known to have killed only human as his prey over the past three to four years. This is why Riddhi had referred to him as "certified man eater". Riddhi and Samar told us that he was Nantu, the terror of Sajnekhali range. He had been named by local naturalists and forest dwellers. Nantu was be slightly over ten years old. Although experts say that the swamp tigers are smaller than other Bengal Tigers of India; I found Nantu quite huge.

When we saw him at Lebukhali junction, there were only two boats including ours. But the news of tiger sighting spread across Sajnekhali Wildlife Sanctuary and as many as six other boats arrived from different parts of the forest in no time.

We saw him five more times in the next four and half hours over the entire safari zone of Peerkhali number three. He walked through sharp and hard-protruding pneumatophores over slushy mud flats exposed during low tide and back again into the mangroves in the inwards part of the mud flat. Then again, after thirty minutes or so, he came out of the inner mangrove forests, and sat on outward part of the mud flat, facing water. Perhaps he was gauging the water level and current, to decide whether or not to cross the canal. Tigers in Sundarbans generally cross from one side of the forest to the other to assess the prey base in their territory and in search of mating partners. The tide was still low, and perhaps he wanted to cross the river again before water level rose with high tide. Once our boat reached too close to him, he stood up and went into the forest. Clearly, we disturbed him.

After fifteen-twenty minutes, we saw him walking along the edge of the mud flat. All the eight or nine boats were trying to follow him and racing among ourselves to be the first to reach close to him. An intense competition ensued, with boat men, assistants and guides shouting and hurling abuses at each other. This desperation and display of irresponsible behaviour on sighting a tiger, was not new as I had witnessed it several times, starting from Bandipur, then Tadoba, and in Corbett Park as well. The only difference in Sundarbans was, instead of being in gypsies on land, we were in boats on water.

We saw him a couple more times. At around 12:30 pm, he came out of the forest and again sat on the edge where the mud flat meets water. Samar mentioned that he looked desperate to cross the river and the presence of so many boats on his path was preventing him from doing so.

Human arrogance and sense of superiority had them thinking that they belonged outside the food pyramid and that from outside they had the right and power to control this food pyramid for their pleasure and needs.

We displayed our arrogance solely for our pleasure, only to learn a hard lesson the following day, around the same time in a different place.

After a while, the tiger got up and walked slowly over the outward part of the mud flat. With each step his paw went deep inside the mud, but he was cautious. His destination was clearly the creek between the two mud flats. He was looking ahead but not once did he step over the thorny pneumatophores. A single step on the hard and sharp pencil roots, can lead to painful penetration and loss of limbs.

He slipped into water and after a brief swim crossed the ten-fifteen feet wide creek, he stood up at the edge, shook his head to shake off water and went into the forest once again.

With a deep feeling of satisfaction, we took a break for lunch. Samar and Riddhi entertained and enthralled us with stories of Nantu and his human-eating incidents from the recent past. Incidentally, Riddhi is a famous wildlife photographer and more known for taking photographs of Indian Wolf for the first time in the Indian part of Sundarbans in April 2017, and sending conservation circles in India into a tizzy.

Post lunch, we circled Peerkhali number three for two hours, with the hope of another sighting of Nantu. I was reminded of how we circled the carcass of gaur in Bandipur with the hope of seeing the killer tiger. As we exited Sajnekhali Wildlife Sanctuary, we saw fresh pugmarks of another tiger, coming out of the forest and headed towards the river.

Riddhi mentioned that there was a young female tiger and cubs, reported to have been seen many times in Dobanki area. If we were lucky, we might spot them the following day.

We ended the day after taking some close shots of the brown-winged kingfisher and at 4:30 pm, we went to Sajnekhali Wildlife Santuary's river terrapin conservation centre. The conservation centre was home to many large size water monitors.

Seeing the alpha male of Sajnekhali, the elusive swamp tiger, six times in a day, in a span of four and half hours, is not a typical event in Sundarbans. According to Riddhi, such a long span sighting in a day happens once in two years. This information added yet another dimension to our newly acquired glory. Desire for that glory manifests in the commodified tiger tourism industry of this subcontinent.

At the end of the day, Samar gave me a philosophical perspective of sighting Nantu. He said, the sequence of events was destined as the timing of the tiger's movement and our movement was in sync. Had we not wasted time in the failed attempt of getting a closer view of black napped kingfisher; had we not spent time with Irrawaddy dolphin pairs; had we not gone for shikra; and finally had we not made another failed attempt of viewing cuckoo shrike up close; we wouldn't have been there at the junction of Lebukhali at 8:10 am, at the exact time the tiger had crossed the river. We would have gone past the area much before the tiger even arrived. Timing, then, plays a crucial role in humans' interaction with non-human in nature.

Then the day arrived. Neither I, nor my five fellow photographers, mentor Santhosh, naturalist Riddhi, guide Samar and the three crew members of *Golapi* boat would ever forget this day in our lifetime. What we witnessed, we hope, no wildlife enthusiast ever witnesses in any of their exploration in any forest.

The day started as usual at 5:45 am. It was early dawn, and we started progressing slowly through creeks, in the eastern direction.

The day was very quiet and sombre with fewer number of boats on the river. We were occasionally seeing black capped and brown winged kingfishers, plovers, red sank, common kingfishers, etc. We also saw another leucistic crocodile busking on the mud flat. It was already low tide. On realizing our presence close to the edge of mud flat, the crocodile jumped into water creating a huge splash. We had been very close. In fact, our boat collided with the mud flat and that made the crocodile jump into water. Every time we got close to the mud flat, we thought about the imminent danger of wildlife attack. Nevertheless, when the next opportunity of getting a closer view of wildlife presented itself, we repeated the act of going close to the animal, without a second thought.

Perhaps, we were waiting for a special learning and a first-hand perspective of such danger to shatter such arrogance.

We kept moving and saw a pair of rose ringed parakeet, maintaining and re-shaping their nests on a big garjan tree. One of the key species of Sundarbans, a white bellied sea eagle was flying above our course and was challenged a couple of times by an osprey in air.

After breakfast, we took our boat again almost to the edge of a large outward land of an emerged mud flat, to observe a few jumping mudskippers. But when a greater egret arrived, they all hid themselves inside a small water puddle.

Later we got off the boat at Sudhanyakhali Wildlife Sanctuary, in search of the red-tailed green bamboo pit viper, but we did not find any. Instead, we found few monitor lizards, and birds like oriental white-eye, female paradise flycatcher, warblers, and many rhesus macaques.

Around 12:35 pm, when we were exploring the idea of going back to Sudhanyakhali area to search for the jungle cat, our guide Samar, noticed some pug marks on a distant mud flat. He asked Gaurango to take the boat closer to the mud flat, to verify whether the pugmarks were fresh. The intention was to just check the pugmarks and then go looking for the jungle cat.

Once we reached closer, Gaurango identified them as fresh pugmarks and according to him; the tiger had probably crossed the area at around 11 o'clock in the morning. Therefore, we started following the trail of pugmarks, and gradually the trail disappeared into water. We moved on, keeping an eye both on land and water. It was possible that the tiger wanted to reach the other side of the river. When we reached the next mud flat on our course, we again saw fresh pugmarks coming out of water and going towards the next creek. The picture was getting clear. The tiger had moved along the edge and crossed creek after creek, reaching from one mud flat to another. Riddhi informed us that a tiger generally does so when it follows a prey.

There was excitement among us, with the thought of a tiger on hunt. Last evening Nantu had majestically walked through pencil roots, sailed smoothly through water, and had royally surveyed his territory and prey base (human of course in this circumstance!). This got me thinking that he had displayed all the required skills to rule the forest. Almost all. We hadn't witnessed yet, the two most special ones— hunting and courtship. Were we getting close to witness at least one of them?

We continued moving along the mud flat and the pugmarks continued. The pugmarks, like before, descended into the next creek and as we advanced, we found them again ascending through the steep gradient of the mud flat and disappearing into the dense mangroves in the inward mud flat. Here the mud flat was a little different from the previous ones. The outward area was smaller and steeper - almost with a 45° gradient, it merged with water. The mud flat continued but there were no pugmarks. Presumably, the tiger went inside the mangroves.

We reached the junction of Naoboni and Peerkhali number seven. Less than a kilometre from us, was a fishing boat floating close to the edge of the mud flat. Riddhi mentioned that there was a possibility that the tiger had followed the fishermen. I was disappointed. I had been eagerly waiting to see a hunting attempt or kill by a tiger. My heart refused to register that according to rule of nature, an attack on fishermen could also be considered a hunting attempt by a "human-eating" predator.

As we got closer to the boat, we saw three fishermen. One of them was in water, bathing. The psychology of the Sundarbans dwellers had taken us by surprise from the very beginning of our exploration. They are fully aware that there are human eating predators on land and in water, and despite that their livelihood demands unbelievable stunts from them. We were never sure, whether such acts could be considered an act of bravery or stupidity or sheer desperation for survival in the land of "human eating" mangrove tigers, that had made them indifferent to life and death situations.

Perhaps they adhered to Nabi's philosophy. *"This is a forest, and anything can happen at any time!"*

Samar started yelling at them for taking the boat so close to the mud flat and asked them to move away from the edge. But they continued to be indifferent and ignored him. Floating merely six to eight feet away from their boat, we thought that Samar was over reacting. We thought he was being over cautious and exaggerating the gravity of the situation. Perhaps, he wanted to prove to us that his tracking ability and anticipation of movement of swamp tiger in difficult swamp land was quite accurate. The fishermen's attitude towards Samar reinforced the fact that Samar was overreacting.

After repeated warnings from Samar, the fishermen said that they would leave after bathing and eating. It appeared that the two fishermen standing on the boat, facing the forest, had already bathed as they were wrapping clothes around their waist. As we reached closer and caught their attention, they turned towards us and away from the forest. The third fisherman was still in water. The three of them had probably just finished catching crabs and shrimps.

In a couple of minutes, the third fisherman got into the boat. The next minute the thick mangroves behind the boat shook violently and parted. A bundle of "burning bright" flame ejected out like a fired cannonball. A huge lump of tawny coat with black stripes, slid through the steep gradient of the mud flat, with its front legs spread apart, claws of both front paws exposed, jaws open wide with all canines shining in the bright sunlight of mid-day, and bright yellow eyes spitting fire and fixed on its target - the fisherman who had just got into the boat, sitting in between the two standing men.

As the tiger slid, its chin, chest and belly were completely touching ground and its shoulders were slouched. The moment the tiger reached the line where the mud flat and water merged, it let out a thunderous roar as it exerted its full strength by pushing its hind legs and throwing itself on the third fisherman. With the force of that jump both the tiger and the fisherman toppled into water.

The next moment the fisherman lay motion less in water, with his head bent from the neck. Clearly, the tiger jumped on him and caught him by the neck. His neck had snapped, and death had been instant. Tigers break the neck or vertebrae of their prey simply by biting straight through them. Owing to the momentum created by the jump, the tiger couldn't hold onto him in its powerful jaws. Therefore, it swam a little to reach the fisherman's body and picked him again by his neck. Fountains of blood oozed out. The tiger pulled him through water towards the same mud flat from where it had appeared and gradually dragged him along the gradient into the mangroves.

From the moment of its appearance, to disappearing with the dead body, it took less than thirty seconds.

I was at the edge of the side railing of our boat, as the events unfolded. Among the ten members on our boat, I heard a few of them shouting and screaming. I was up front with a clear view of the tiger, and the camera mounted with telephoto lenses was in my hand. But I was completely stunned with the suddenness of the chain of events, although I managed to click a few shots as the dead man was being pulled through water.

When it was over, speechless, we looked at each other in disbelief and fear. Samar's eyes were red and tears rolled down. He had warned them. A little more seriousness from them, and perhaps a little more insistence on our part, could have saved a human life.

Up until then, I had never seen a killing by any predator in the wild. Although, I had watched recoded videos of such incidents in TV channels and in various documentaries. I had seen a fawn picked and dragged by a leopard, and how the mother deer and other deer in the herd looked on helplessly and apathetically as it departed. Unfortunately, it was the same reaction that I observed in the surviving fishermen. As we slowly moved away from the location, we found them quietly rowing away, almost fleeing. No screaming, no crying, no cursing, no display of emotion at all. Much like the herd of deer that looked on at the fawn being dragged away.

In the wild, the hierarchy of the food pyramid binds all animals. In the mangrove forest of Sundarbans, tiger is at the top of the food pyramid, and everything else, including human, are its prey.

The tiger made a sudden appearance, although we had been tracking its pugmarks, we had not really anticipated such a sudden appearance out of nowhere. When it was sliding through the steep slope of the mud flat, all the crewmembers in the boat recognized it as the same tiger that we had seen six times the previous day. The very tiger whose royal movement and athletic strength we had deeply appreciated, and had desired to witness its two other apex predatory behaviours – hunting and mating. One desire had been fulfilled, but what a heavy price we paid.

The alpha male of Sundarbans, the terror of Sajnekhali, the ruler of a territory spanning around

150-200 square kilometres including land and water, between Sajnekhali and Peerkhali. Locals call him Nantu.

Just the previous day, we had admired his beauty and royal movement, which had rightly earned him the title of "Royal Bengal Tiger". Today we saw another incarnation of him with a strong message to all wildlife enthusiasts and ecotourists, *"You believe that I, the Bengal Tiger of the Indian subcontinent is now adorable and less formidable. You are wrong. I remain the demigod of the Sundarbans - to be feared and respected. I, the evil deity and protector of forest."*

The fishermen parked their boat close to the edge of the mud flat, because the water was shallow there. A good place for a bath. Clearly, the tiger had set his target from the very beginning.

When we arrived, and initiated conversation with them, asking them to move away, the tiger might have figured out that we were trying to warn them. It perhaps decided it was prudent to attack right away, before the prey slipped away.

Another possibility was that it may have been us, who distracted the fishermen, and made them look towards us, turning their back to the tiger – giving it the opportunity to attack.

Regardless, we were dumbfounded by the turn of events. We humans, think ourselves as the most superior species on this planet, and find it difficult to reconcile when such believes are shattered. Nature, however, has her own law. One animal had been killed by another. A prey had been killed by the apex predator of the forest.

The surviving fishermen perhaps thought in a similar fashion, hence the apparent apathy - *"This is a forest, and anything can happen at any time!"*

In Corbett Park, Nabi the prophet of Jim Edward Corbett, introduced me to this philosophy of forest dwellers, who do not envy non-human for their access to essential liberty.

More than a year later, the forest dwellers of Sundarbans showed how they live embracing this philosophy, like just any other species in the wild.

Later in the afternoon, when our cook Baboosona, informed his father, a honey collector, of the incident, his dad displayed a similar apathy, announcing that he was planning to venture into the forest the same night.

After a lot of deliberation, we decided to notify the forest department of this incident. When we did, forest officials appreciated it and called for a meeting with us. We met Range Officer, Mr. Bijoy Chakraborty at Sajnekhali forest range office at the end of the day, where we had dropped by the previous day to see the river terrapin conservation project. Mr. Chakraborty took our testimonials, saw whatever images related to the incident we had managed to capture and made copies of those. He also informed us that they were in the process of tracking the male tiger, as there had been multiple reports of human-killing by him in recent times. In fact, the previous week, that very tiger had killed an old villager. Forest department was in the process of laying camera traps over the territory of the killer tiger.

Enroute to range office, we saw spectacular natural phenomenon of osprey swooping in water and trying to catch fish and spotted a golden jackal, an uncommon sighting in Sundarbans. However, our minds were still disturbed. Seeing someone from our own tribe being killed, from such a proximity, was not easy to comprehend and rationalize.

Many of us were unable to sleep that night. Next morning we tried hard to overcome the shocking events of the previous day by putting it in perspective of natural history.

Soon we were discussing the incident from the perspective of photography. Santhosh, our photography mentor, is a professional and seasoned photographer. He had managed to take shots of almost the entire episode, from the tiger leaping on the boat to it pulling the body through water. I was positioned with a full view head on stance with the tiger, and with camera in hand. Initially I was, of course, taken aback with the suddenness of the attack. But the moment I saw the tiger was sliding through the steep mud flat; my photographer instinct woke up and I prepared to focus my camera on the tiger. Almost immediately I was stuck by a paradoxical feeling that "humans are superior". This made me empathetic towards my fellow human brother, and I resisted taking images of him as a prey. For a moment, I was at crossroads between my photographer instinct and morality. I remained undecided on what to do and by that time the dead man was floating on water with a broken neck, with the tiger pulling him towards the mud flat.

On the last day of this exploration, we were low in energy. Although we had recovered from the incident, the aftermath hung in the air. We started our day as usual —boarding the expedition boat on time, assembling our gears, and gathering at the front deck – much like the other four days. We continued discussing the previous day's incident. Perhaps, in the history of ecotourism and wildlife photography, very few people had witnessed such an incident - an incident that was the pinnacle of all our ecotourism activities thus far.

We took a few shots of the saltwater crocodile, shikra, *en route* to our next stop at Sudhanyakhali Wildlife Sanctuary. There we were treated to intimate views of the red-tailed green bamboo pit viper and by the end of the day we saw the peregrine up-close again. By 1:30 pm in the afternoon, we exited the reserve forest and, in an hour, we arrived at Godkhali jetty, and from there we headed for Calcutta in cars that had been arranged and were awaiting our arrival.

Next morning, a Monday, a Bangalore based fellow photographer shared the news clips of an English national daily published from Bangalore. The news clips reported the incident with Nantu. The report quoted a forest department official's statement that a 52-year-old fisherman, Anil Mandal, busy catching crabs and shrimps along with two other fishermen, was mauled to death by a Royal Bengal Tiger. Reportedly, the other two fishermen returned later along with forest department personnel to the site of the incident, and recovered the partially eaten body of Mandal.

Additionally, the report mentioned a passing tourism vessel that had warned them about the movement of *three* tigers in the area. This was only partially true. We were aware of the movement of one tiger, whose pugmarks we had followed.

Another news report in an online English news daily, mentioned that the big cat swam silently and jumped on the boat to catch Anil Mandal. His other companions Kenaram Mandal and Haren Bayen, were so sacred that they fell into the creek, and later managed to board the boat again. No such thing happened. Only eleven people knew precisely what happened that afternoon at the junction of Naobani and Peerkhali number seven. This was just an example of how the news becomes skewed and is distorted in transmission.

Be that as it may, we the unfortunate (or fortunate) eleven, that afternoon, had experienced extreme predatory behaviour by the apex predator. We humans always situate ourselves above the food pyramid defined by nature, and that is the reason for the collapse of ecosystems across the world. The incident at Sundarbans was a mirror. We realized that we are very much part of the food pyramid and very often not at the apex of the pyramid.

Coincidentally, on 11th November 2019, a week before our exploration at Sundarbans, the revised Standard Operating Procedure (SOP) drawn up by *National Tiger Conservation Authority (NTCA)* for dealing with big cats straying into human-dominated landscapes was issued. This SOP had replaced the term 'man-eater' with 'dangerous to human life'. Big cats attacking and feeding on humans would not be called man-eaters anymore. The new guidelines also banned non-departmental individuals, like private sharpshooters, from participating in operations to eliminate/tranquillise or capture tigers in conflict. The development came in the wake of the controversy over death of tigress Avni in Maharashtra in 2018. Environmentalists and veterinarians hailed the removal of the word 'man-eater', which they said was a cruel description. However, the new term was quite broad and hadn't been defined well, they felt, pointing out there could be chances that tigers which haven't killed humans may end up getting the 'dangerous to human life' tag and eventually be captured or killed.

Forest dwellers of Sundarbans, however, know that living with danger to human life is an accepted norm in nature. Therefore, they are indifferent to such danger and do not try to destroy the source of danger.

The Sundarbans trip was a life changing exploration experience for me. I admit, I had started believing that Corbett's depiction of tiger as glorified, formidable apex predator (in *Man-Easters of Kumaon*), and Sy Montgomery's narrative to establish the animal as 'fear mongering almighty' (in *Spell of The Tiger*) may have been relevant when they wrote their novels, but in today's world, such glory and fear have enough reasons to be diluted.

This incident caused a marked shift in my perspective. I now believe that even in today's world there are enough reasons to not allow the glory and fear associated with this predator to be diluted.

The Bengal Tiger's incarnation as food pyramid's apex predator may clearly not be productive in the greening capitalism process of the ecotourism industry. Particularly, if the human is sighted as part of the food pyramid. The ecotourism industry stands to lose their customer base to whom they sell their commodity of tiger tourism.

While the Tiger is a photography subject for the urban dwelling human, for the human co-habiting with the non-human in the same ecosystem, tiger is a fellow inhabitant. This truth is well known to the forest dwellers of Sundarbans.

The Bengal Tiger has become a symbol of elitism to wildlife enthusiasts and ecotourists across the world. They like to acquire Bengal Tiger as a precious prize to showcase their belongingness in the elite class.

These wildlife enthusiasts and ecotourists are real life Prithus' who aspire to live like Mowgli and possess a deep obsession for Bengal Tigers. This aspiration and obsession are nothing but an escape from the monotony of materialistic life.

However, the forest dwellers' connection with Bengal Tigers is markedly different. They do not want to acquire them. Rather they consider them as a threat to survive and perceive that threat as an accepted norm.

The tiger is worshipped as the evil demigod protector of non-human forests. They are aware that living with non-humans requires keeping their demigod happy and away from humans.

This spiritual perception towards non-human and their demigod do not just enable them to live in harmony with non-human but also serves in uniting different communities of humans living in the forest.

As modernity intervenes in the thick mangrove forest, Hindu and Muslim Bengalis separate into their own theological silos. Bengal was partitioned in 1947 along communal lines. Hindu-majority western Bengal became a part of the dominion of India while Muslim-majority eastern Bengal became a part of the Pakistan dominion. Belying this recent history, however, Bengal has a tradition of communal coexistence stretching back centuries. Bengalis, both Muslim as well as Hindu, have lived cheek by jowl in the most densely populated area on Earth. Perhaps nothing symbolises this long history of Hindu-Muslim cohabitation than the Goddess Bon Bibi, worshipped by both communities in the dense Sundarbans Forest on the Bengal coast. Bangladeshi author and nature enthusiast, Foridi Numan wrote about remains of an ancient palace about 20 km west of Raimangal check post, inside the Sunderbans of Bangladesh. Numan writes, *"The ruins of human settlement around the palatial remains were believed to be houses of Dokkhin Rai (folk deity of Sundarbans) and his brother Mukut Rai. As per folklore, Ghazi and Kalu crossed the canal of Dara, around this area, with his tiger disciples, towards Brahmanagar during battle against Mukut Rai, once Ghazi's marriage proposal with Mukut Rai's daughter was turned down."*

Therefore, besides Bon Bibi, Dokkhin Rai had other enemies as well, Gazi and Kalu, if we combine both Indian and Bangladeshi folklore together. In fact, during my winter trip to the West Bengal part of Sundarbans, I saw idols of Bon Bibi, Kalu, Gazi and Dokkhin Rai being worshiped together at one of the Bon Bibi temples at Sajnekhali Wildlife Sanctuary.

Pseudo Ecotourism

The folklore around swamp tigers from these two subcontinental countries still prevail as symbol of communal harmony between Hindus and Muslims.

However, the hegemony created by tiger tourism has a very different agenda.

This hegemony is rooted in capitalism in the name of sustainability (ecotourism in this context). Capitalism is comfortable with this hegemony as there are affluent urban photographers and ecotourists ready to pay a premium to see the apex predator in its natural habitat. An environment where greening capitalism is not conducive, ecology is relegated to the back seat. Ecotourism, then, is also pushed to the backburner and becomes just tourism.

The Bangladesh counterpart of the swampland, which comprises $3/5^{th}$ of the Sundarban Mangrove Forest has a very different model of ecotourism, where ecology has clearly been moved to the back seat.

A month after my trip to the Indian Sundarbans, on a winter-morning at 7:30 am, I reached Khulna, along with my *Viator* tour guide, Shahadat Hossain Bhuiyan, after an overnight train journey by Chitra Express. Commencing from Dhaka, it took ten long hours to cover a mere 550 km to reach Khulna. It was gloomy and drizzling when we reached Jailkhana Jetty of Khulna at the bank of river Atharobhati. Atharo is the Bengali word for eighteen. I was reminded of the eighteen tides in the story of Bon Bibi.

Thousands of tourists had gathered at Khulna to enjoy a vacation during their winter holidays at Sundarbans. It was apparent that this trip was not going to be like my other nature explorations. I was preparing myself mentally for a "picnic" in Bangladeshi Sundarbans.

Bangladeshi Sundarbans receive an average 250,000 visitors annually. Most of them are ecotourists who would like to ascend socially into elite class by possessing a minimum of one tiger sighting story over the course of their life.

However, I noticed in this trip that the gravity of this aspiration was different from what I witnessed in my Indian tiger reserves explorations.

We boarded *Bonobilas*, our 120 feet long and 20 feet wide, three-storied safari ship, equipped with two engines and one motorised country boat tied at the back. The boat, I assumed, was for accessing narrow canals and creeks of Sundarbans during our safari. Bonobilas had a total of sixteen crew members on board, including two shipmasters, two engine mates, two boatmen, five kitchen staff and five attendants. The ship would cruise through Atharobhati River that meets Rupsa and Possur rivers. Possur is the principal river flowing through Sundarbans of Bangladesh.

There were around 68 passengers on board. Shahadat told me that we were cruising through the confluence of Possur and Rupsa Rivers, a special economic zone in Bangladesh. I noticed a lot of industries on either side of the river, with patches of forests and human

Pseudo Ecotourism

settlements in between. There were cement industries, refineries, shipyards, food grain storages etc. No sign of any birds and animals around us, except couple of river dolphins, popping in and out of water a few times. We were cruising in the southern direction, to the southernmost part of Bangladesh. As a few passengers had not arrived on time, we waited at Jailkhana jetty for an extra hour and that had led to beginning of low tide, which eventually delayed our start by an additional two hours. Therefore, we started at 11:30 am, when tide was again in favour, and by 4:30 pm arrived at Gungmari Forest range, the formal entry point of Bangladeshi Sundarbans. Effectively it took almost twenty-four hours to reach Sundarbans from Dhaka. This was a significant contrast from Indian Sundarbans. One can arrive at the formal entry point of the forest, the Godkhali jetty, from the closest airport, Calcutta, in less than three hours.

Shahadat told me that the first time he came to Sundarbans in 1994, he was a student of Geography. Back then they entered Sundarbans from Mongla port instead of Khulna. Presently, the Mongla port is a big industrial area, which has pushed the forest further down. The forest patches in between industries are the remains of the erstwhile Sundarbans. Indeed, the increasing number of heavily polluting factories producing petrochemicals, cement, and leather on the edge of the Sundarbans, as well as new thermal power plants, threaten the mangrove ecosystem. We saw Mongla port as a bustling centre of activity. Several oceangoing vessels were anchored in the harbour and there was a steady bustle of barges hauling cargo. Based on a recent article published in *thirdpole.net*, the Bangladesh government has in the recent past tried to frame rules that seek to mitigate the potential harm to the planet's largest mangrove forest, which straddles Bangladesh and India. It has stipulated that no industrial activity can take place within ten kilometres of the Sundarbans Forest reserve, which is designated as an Ecologically Critical Area (ECA). However, more than 150 industrial units had already been approved in Satkhira, Khulna, and Bagerhat (where Mongla is located) districts before these rules came into force. The sad part is such newly introduced rules cannot be implemented retrospectively. Therefore, the damage caused to this part of Sundarbans is irreversible.

We also passed by the construction site of the controversial Rampal power plant, a proposed 1320-megawatt coal-fired power station at Rampal Upazila of Bagerhat District in Khulna. It is a project of *India Bangladesh Friendship Power Company limited*, owned by *National Thermal Power Corporation (India)* and *Bangladesh Power Development Board (Bangladesh)*. Evidently, this project violates the environmental impact assessment guidelines for coal-based thermal power plants.

Upon reaching Gungmari, our local trip manager Rubel organized necessary permits from the forest range office, but by then dusk had fallen. Therefore, we decided to start early next morning, at 5:00 am, and venture into Katka Wildlife Sanctuary.

In Bangladeshi Sundarbans, tourists are allowed to walk through the forest in selected tourism zones. Katka Wildlife Sanctuary is one such zone. Although initially it sounded quite adventurous, but in reality, it was like hiking in an ecological park, with minimal possibility of any predators on the move. The objective of wildlife tourism in Sundarbans was a fun filled family trip. There was little for wildlife enthusiasts. Throughout the trip I witnessed a complete lack of respect for nature and forest, quite unlike my past experiences. It was acceptable for tourists and crew members to play loud music, speak loudly while trekking inside the forest, throw food and even sanitary wastes into the river.

We spent the night on the ship and enjoyed sumptuous Bangladeshi food. Bangladeshi cuisine has time and again attracted me to the country.

Following morning at 6 o'clock we went to Jamtala beach, followed by Katka Wildlife Sanctuary, part of Sarankhola range of Sundarban East Tiger Reserves. It was a four-hour hike of eight kilometres through grassland, beach, and a forest path full of sundari, garan, and geoan trees. A troop of noisy tourists, numbering a few hundreds, were on foot to explore the forest. Spotted deer and their movement on mud flats of the mangrove ecosystems was evident.

To arrive at Katka Wildlife Sanctuary and Jamtala beach, we had to travel via a motorized country boat, locally known as trawler. This provided the opportunity to see the spotted deer up close.

We cruised through the central river of Bangladeshi Sundarbans, Possur River, and not through canals or creeks close to mangrove forest. This was a major difference compared to the experience of mangrove ecosystems in the Indian Sundarbans. In India, I got to see the ecosystems intimately. Hence, the possibility of spotting mangrove fauna was much higher.

The sky had been overcast for the past two days. By noon the second day, though, the sun appeared through the clouds and the day became brighter. A folk of brahminy kites and few common gulls were circling and hovering around our ship and intermittently swooping into the river to catch fish.

From Possur river, we proceeded to Shela River by afternoon, and for a brief time, we were close to emerged mud flats of the mangrove ecosystem. The vegetation was predominantly garan trees. Few spotted deer grazed on the carpet of protruding breathing roots on the mud flats.

Post noon, we cruised through the southernmost part of Sundarbans, up until Nilkamal Wildlife Sanctuary, commonly known as Hiran point (Hiran is Bengali word for Deer). A trail full of garan, geoan and keora trees with breathing (pencil) roots popped out from the mud flats. There was also a freshwater pond, constructed by the forest department.

Pseudo Ecotourism

So far, we had cruised only towards the south. As dusk set in we started cruising back towards north. We had begun our return journey from Bangladeshi Sundarbans.

The following day, we visited Harbaria Wildlife Sanctuary and Karamjal Deer and Crocodile breeding centre. This side of the forest is infested with rhesus macaque population. On this one-hour long trail we saw a saltwater crocodile busking at the edge of the river and a magpie robin, the national bird of Bangladesh. The part of Harbaria accessible for tourism is connected with dense mangrove forest which is less penetrated by sunlight. This part of the forest is known for tiger sighting. Although Bengal Tiger is even more elusive in the Bangladesh part of Sundarbans than its Indian counterpart, Harbaria is known for the occasional, albeit rare, appearance of this majestic predator.

In general, my encounter with faunal biodiversity in Bangladeshi Sundarbans was significantly less compared to my recent exploration in the Indian part of the forest. Primarily for four reasons–

First, I chose a picnic tourism party, which did not have the requisite expertise to conduct wildlife exploration.

Second, the rivers (Possur, Shela etc) flowing through mangrove ecosystem are much wider than rivers (Vidyadhari etc) in Indian Sundarbans. Such enormous width kept our big safari ships away from the edge of the forest on both sides. Therefore, we could not see through the forest from close quarters.

Third, our safari ship was huge and that prevented us from entering creeks and canals. Whereas, in Indian Sundarbans we could easily enter or sail through creeks and canals, thus increasing our possibility of spotting wildlife.

Fourth, the entire wildlife tourism in Bangladeshi Sundarbans is designed for general tourists where the element of entertainment was given priority and not the academic and conservation aspects of ecology. My tour operator Shahadat told me that most of the tourists expect something that would amuse them and their family members during their vacation. That explained the loud music, sumptuous food, easy trail, and less control over tourists' behaviour. Risks of having predators around might play a spoilsport.

In Indian forests, wildlife tourism is designed for both general tourists and wildlife enthusiasts. The general tourists in India are as eager as wildlife enthusiasts to see a tiger in the wild. In Bangladesh, as we boarded the small-motorized country boat to access islands like Katka or Harbaria, there was always a section of tourists, who prayed to Allah to not see a tiger. An elderly woman even asked her companions, *"Please tell Allah not to send a tiger when we are on our foot in the forest."*

On the contrary, in India I saw general tourists praying to see a tiger in the forest.

Probably the aspiration of being elevated to elite class of tourists is not popular enough in a country, where the need for industrial growth to meet materialistic lifestyle is stronger than the need to escape from the monotony of a materialistic lifestyle.

Evidently the race for fame is less intensive hence, the arrogance bred by fame is also less prominent.

The absence of the collective need to living the "life of Mowgli", encouraged expansion of industrial growth and consequently contraction of Sundarbans.

In Bangladesh part of Sundarbans, the infrastructure is suitable for wildlife tourism for general tourists, and that did not serve the purpose of wildlife enthusiasts from other parts of the world. In our team consisting of 68 members, there was a Dutch guy from Netherlands and a Russian lady who lived in Germany and was accompanied by her Nigerian boyfriend. Both the Dutch guy and the Russian lady expressed their disappointments in a similar vein, at being unable to explore the beautiful biodiversity of Bangladeshi Sundarbans, in the way they had expected to.

The Russian woman asked me clearly, *"I want to see a tiger, how can I make it happen?"*. She had never seen a tiger in the wild, and certainly had an elitist aspiration among ecotourists.

Before boarding the Chitra Express from Biman Bandar station to begin my journey towards Bangladeshi Sundarbans, I had taken some time to meet with Sankar, and the renowned Bangladeshi wildlife photographer Sadat Amin Khan, for whom I had to pick up a Nikkor 500 mm prime lens from Calcutta. Sadat informed me about how they explore Sundarbans, based on their own knowledge, experience and personal contacts with local forest dwellers. Local forest dwellers help them get access to those canals and creeks, where general tourists do not go. On one such exploration, Sankar and Sadat felt the presence of a tiger around them as they hiked through Katka. Sadat saw a yellowish shadow moving quickly through adjacent garan forests. They later discovered that it was another elusive animal of Sundarbans – a fishing cat.

Another conservationist of Bangladesh, who works for *UNDP*, Imdadul Islam Bittu, shared similar stories. When he heard that I had visited Harbaria, he told me that in 2011, when he was exploring that part of the forest with a local forest guide, he decided to take a detour from the regular trail. After trekking a few kilometres, they came face to face with a tiger, sitting on their path. Later, the then Chief Conservator of the Forest, confirmed that it was human-eater and had killed a fisherman few days prior.

Clearly, there are wildlife enthusiasts in Bangladesh, who consider tiger sighting as a sign of elitism. The wildlife tourism infrastructure of the country however does not help in acquiring the coveted elite status.

The lack of aspiration of the general tourist to ascend socially to the elite club, helps in maintaining the fear of tiger. But that does not increase love for the animal. As a result, the industrial expansion in Sundarbans never ceases and the opportunity for wildlife tourism never improves.

On the other hand, the section of wildlife enthusiasts in Bangladesh with a strong urge to become elite, opt for different ways to meet their aspiration.

Foridi Numan began his visits to Bangadeshi Sundarbans in 2004, and on an average, he made eight to ten visits each year. In various articles, he has confessed the risk he took to explore the narrow canals of Sundarbans on a country boat, which took him dangerously close to the edge of the mud flats. He privately organized all his trips by using personal contacts with local forest dwellers.

His narration brought back visuals from the time I visited the Indian Sundarbans. Visuals of fishermen on country boats parked near the mudflat. What happened after that is now known to you, my reader.

After attempting for eighteen years, Foridi Numan with a few friends, in one such risky attempt succeeded in spotting a Bengal Tiger of Bangladeshi Sundarbans. The tiger was sitting on the lower branch of a Keora tree (one of the tallest trees in the Sundarbans mangrove forests).

They clicked images of the tiger for an entire hour. Foridi Numan in his article about this exploration mentions, *"The prince of Bangladeshi Sundarbans appeared to us as adorable as a domestic cat."*

The sign of considering the Bengal Tiger as more adorable and less formidable began to show up among wildlife enthusiasts of Bangladesh.

More accessibility to Bengal Tigers in any forest would affect their demigod and formidable status. From a fearsome apex predator, they were transformed to an adorable creature to wildlife enthusiasts and ecotourists.

Fear for the animal certainly does not help in realizing its role in protecting non-human life forms. This fear would make the animal an undesirable one to human; and as a result, there would be no effort in preventing the degradation of its habitat.

There is a need for striking a balance between fear and love. The forest dwellers' involvement is crucial here as without any aspiration of possessing this animal as a prize, they know that human and non-human life forms are united in nature.

These stories from either side of Sundarbans, emphasize the importance of involving local forest dwellers in ecotourism activities, for better understanding of the forest by wildlife enthusiasts who visit forests out of genuine love for it. This would motivate them to make more visits to Sundarbans and in turn, that would help the forest department to spread the glory of Sundarbans. Nonetheless, that would also create alternative source of income for poor forest dwellers. Mere visit by general tourists may give forest department short-term gain, but such tourists may not always appreciate the true nature of the forest. In fact, during my trip, many of my co-travellers complained that they felt cheated, as they *"didn't see any tigers"*.

In West Bengal, people like Riddhi Mukherjee ensured the inclusion of local villager like Samar Joardar as the nature guide in his team. The man, who knows every nook and corner of Sundarbans is a master spotter of animals. Riddhi succeeded in engaging wildlife photographers and nature lovers in Sundarbans and subsequently spreading the glory of the swampland.

Unless wildlife photographers and naturalists of Bangladesh do not take the lead in Sundarbans exploration, the purpose of Sundarbans conservation would remain defeated. It is not that Bangladesh does not have such people, but evidently, it is difficult for them to take charge. Shahadat informed me that Khulna based syndicate runs the entire tourism in Sundarbans and no one else is allowed to enter into business. Therefore, it is not an easy task for my Bangladeshi nature conservationist friends, Foridi Numan, or Sadat Amin Khan, or Imdadul Islam Bittu to become a "Riddhi Mukherjee" or "Samar Joardar".

CHAPTER SIX: The Tiger Economy

As per an article written by investment adviser James Chen in *Investopedia*, *"commoditization is the process of converting products or services into standardized, marketable objects"*.

Possessing tremendous diversity in climate and physical conditions, the Indian subcontinent has a great variety of fauna, numbering 92,037 species, of which insects alone include 61,375 species. Besides that, there are around 410 species of mammals, 1300 species of birds, 518 species of reptiles, and 472 species of amphibians.

Ecotourism, especially the wildlife photography focussed ecotourism in the subcontinent, is largely unorganized. The sector is mostly operated by businesspersons who are not formally trained in biodiversity or wildlife sciences. They are people with varied academic and socio-economic background, trying to make ends meet. They are thus not inclined to include such varied range of faunal diversity in their ecotourism offerings, which is largely designed to cater to the entertainment needs of affluent folks.

Hence, the sector was in need of a "standardized, marketable object".

According to James Chen, the perfect commoditization is when a product or service gets converted into an interchangeable and marketable item. A commodified item should be standardized enough to be purchased as a transaction rather than be customized.

Bengal Tiger as a wildlife photography subject or ecotourism object perfectly fits into this category. The same tawny-coat with black stripes majestic beast can be found in various landscapes – sub-Himalayan foothills, river flood plains, tropical, deciduous and rain forests, mangroves, and Himalayan high altitude.

Irrespective of its varied landscape, its shape, size, colour, and behavioural pattern remains unchanged. The landscape of its habitat may vary, but the Bengal Tiger is always found as apex predator in its habitat.

If you make several visits to various subcontinental forests, then you indeed have a fantastic probability to see a tiger in its natural habitat. It's a large animal with bright and contrasting colour combination, which makes spotting, and even shooting, easier. In the subcontinental ecotourism sector, there is no other species besides the Bengal Tiger, which can be appropriated, "standardized" and made "interchangeable".

If you do not spot a tiger in the sub-Himalayan landscape, then you can always try your luck in the

North-East Hills of India; if you do not see it in Western Ghats, then luck may favour you in the Central Indian landscape. This vast landscape (market!) makes this single species an interchangeable commodity at almost the same price and in a similar tourism package. The tiger tourism in this geography does not need any "customization".

Therefore, the human eater incarnation of Bengal Tiger could be an unfortunate natural reality[3] but it does not help the ecotourism sector in selling their "commodity". This explains why none of the crew and photographers of our Indian Sundarbans exploration team, spoke publicly about, or posted any images in social media of the "accident".

The sector would rather prefer an amusement park environment with a tag of tiger tourism, regardless of whether such an environment generates even a remote possibility of tiger sighting. As long as the "tiger tourism" tag itself is capable of drawing thousands of tourists every year, it serves the purpose of this sector. That is why Bangladeshi Sundarbans receive an average of 250,000 visitors annually, despite a feeble chance for tiger sighting.

When the buyers invest on any commodity, they expect a return as promised by the sellers.

---

[3] Natural reality includes entities and properties that came into being through the purposeless processes of nature or that came into being through the purposeful intentions of human beings. (*Ref. Naturalism and the First-Person Perspective by Lynne Rudder Baker*)

I witnessed this expectation of tiger tourists in forests of Corbett Park, the park which is closely connected with tiger hunter turned conservator Jim Corbett and his legendary novel *"Man-Eaters of Kumaon"*.

But I also witnessed such expectations at forests, where it was least expected.

Until my trip to the Sundarbans of Bangladesh, I explored tiger habitats of this subcontinent mostly with other wildlife photographers. Bangladesh was an exception.

Four years after my Nagarhole-Bandipur-Periyar trip, I started my second phase of explorations in Western Ghats, as a solo ecotourist. This time I chose a forest that was unique, and infrequently visited by wildlife photographers and ecotourists – BRT or BR Hills.

The Biligirirangana Hills, commonly called BR Hills, is a hill range situated in southeastern Karnataka, at its border with Tamil Nadu (Erode District) in south India. The area is called Biligiriranganatha Swamy Temple Wildlife Sanctuary or simply BRT Wildlife Sanctuary. Located at the confluence of the Western Ghats and the Eastern Ghats, the sanctuary is home to ecosystems that are unique to both the mountain ranges.

The BR hills links the Eastern and the Western Ghats allowing animals to move between them and facilitating gene flow between populations of species in these areas. Thus, this sanctuary serves as an important biological bridge for the biota of the entire Deccan plateau.

Abhinandan, the nature guide of *Jungle Lodge and Resorts* (JLR – my accommodation at BRT), informed me that there were 55 tigers, 65 leopards and around 255 species of birds in BRT. Our first safari of the first day started at 4:00 pm, with nature guide cum driver Narayan, and continued until 6:30 pm, with some typical "tiger drama" at the end.

At the beginning of the safari, we saw a few regular birds like paradise flycatcher, blue headed bee-eater, common hawk cuckoo, and jungle owlet. We spotted a lot of elephant dung, but not the big mammals. Few birds of prey spotted were – crested serpent eagle and oriental honey buzzard. In the latter part of the safari, we saw a couple of giant squirrels and a relatively uncommon bird in Western Ghats – a black stork. In the following days, we saw the black stork several times and we must admit that the population of giant squirrel, common hawk cuckoo and grey wag tail were quite high.

When we were planning to exit, the driver of another safari gypsy told us a tiger was spotted near Battargatte waterhole, which was the place where we had been an hour ago and had spent about ten minutes observing the oriental honey buzzard. The usual and familiar excitement erupted in our gypsy. In the morning, on my way to JLR, another driver Nagesh told me about a recent leopard sighting, but tiger sighting in BRT is certainly big news!

All the co-passengers screamed in excitement and driver Narayan got the message instantly, and shouted, *"Hold tight!"*, as he drove his gypsy like he was in a formula one race over the rough and lumpy terrain, to reach the spot at the earliest. We reached there in a few minutes, and a gypsy was already waiting there. The driver was Nagesh, and he shook his head to indicate 'no'. No sign of the big cat.

There was a sigh of disappointment in the gypsy. Narayan reacted as though he had lost the will to continue living. I felt sorry for him, more than I did for myself and my fellow tourists. A veteran and learned naturalist like him continued apologizing to us, till we reached our camp. As if everything had been for naught. The two and a half hours in the forest all in vain, as if we had spent the precious hours in a broken land full of filthy garbage, not in one of the most significant biodiversity hotspots of India. As if it was a wasteland and not the biological bridge of Deccan plateau.

After arriving at the camp, as I exited from the gypsy, I thanked Narayan, and complemented him for his knowledge on the flora and fauna of BRT, and yet again he apologized for being unable to show us the tiger. It was time to intervene. I explained that there was no need to apologize. People who have some experience in the forest are aware of the uncertainty involved in spotting predators or any big mammals in the forest. People who love forest, just love the forest – the flora, fauna, terrain, waterbodies, odour, and breeze – every bit of it. Not just one species. They also enjoy the uncertainties involved in exploring the forest, and only such people keep coming back to the forest.

There were, in all, four gypsies in the forest. Tourists of only one gypsy had seen the tiger near the waterbody. There were four tourists besides the driver, in that gypsy. A couple among them was most vocal and enthusiastic about sharing their experience of sighting the tiger. Of course, when we returned to camp and gathered for a short documentary film-show on the forests of Western Ghats, over high tea, the couple received some special attention from others. They repeated their story of tiger sighting multiple times to different people, which they did with much joy and pride.

Many of the tourists who did not see the tiger that evening, considered the couple to be lucky, and were evidently envious of them. During dinner, I heard whispers from other tables, speculating tiger sighting possibilities on the safari the following morning. The noticeable fact was, besides a lawyer couple from Bangalore and myself, all the others were scheduled for their last safari in BRT the following morning, as they had booked a one-night package that included two safaris. Therefore, the morning safari was their sole beacon of hope, and if they failed, they would complain that the forest of BRT had nothing worthy of seeing. In fact, at dinner that night, a few tourists were already declaring it.

This is the general situation of commoditized ecotourism in India as far as the demand of ecotourists, the buyers of this commodity, is concerned.

On the other hand, the seller of this commodity is ready to alter their traditional ecotourism offerings to cater to this growing demand from the buyers.

Travelling as a solo ecotourist with other non-photographer ecotourists allowed me to interact with them more than I had in my previous trips. This helped me to better understand the demand.

After eight long months of break due to COVID19 pandemic induced lockdown and travel restrictions, I made my comeback to this highland of India, with a three-day trip to Western Ghats' most happening and highly glamourized forest, where apparently "anything can happen at any time". It was the most sought after ecotourist destination of Western Ghats – Kabini (part of Nagarhole Tiger Reserve). I was part of a photography bootcamp organized by a famous Bangalore-based wildlife tour company.

In the Kabini part of the 653-km² Nagarhole, separating the Kabini reservoir from the Bandipur National Park and Tiger Reserve, our fist safari started in the B zone, in the afternoon. It was the end of monsoon season. All of a sudden black rosette on yellow fur appeared out of nowhere. A dramatic and lightening appearance of a leopard and its sudden disappearance into the thickets marked the beginning of our exploration.

We then spent a couple of hours quietly roaming around in the forest. Other than few pea fowls and grey jungle fowls and plenty of babblers, we did not encounter too many birds either. Langur and bonnet macaque happily jumped between branches making occasional territorial calls. The cubs were playful as always. We also saw a serpent eagle flying across.

During the last hour of the safari, there was another dramatic appearance through the bushes on our right. The demigod of the subcontinental forest was within eight-ten feet from our gypsy.

Each time I have seen the Bengal Tiger in the forest, I have been astounded by some or the other display of their characteristic behaviour.

The mature female sniffed the tree trunk, grasses and even soil vigorously. She made a "stinky face" and rolled her tongue out. Our tour leader explained this as *flehmen* response. According to German Wildlife Keeper of the mammal department of Wildlife Conservation Society's Bronx Zoo, Dr. Erin Mowatt, *"in German the word flehmen means lip curl or curl of the upper lip".*

Flehman is a behavior that involves the curling back of the lips to expose the teeth and inhaling through the nostrils, often accompanied by a characteristic grimace or facial expression – the "stinky face". This behaviour is often seen in response to certain scents, particularly those associated with reproductive or social cues. By curling back their lips and inhaling in this manner, the tiger can draw air over a specialized sensory organ called the vomeronasal organ (Jacobson's organ) located in the roof of their mouths. This allows them to detect and analyze chemical signals, such as pheromones, which can convey important information about potential mates, territorial boundaries, or the presence of predators.

That afternoon in Kabini, the tigress named by the locals as "Temple Tiger female", displayed the flehmen response to investigate different scents left by other tigers, what Erin describes in his article, as "smelling in high definition". After two-three minutes of sniffing and making "cheesy faces", she went inside the nearby thickets. She earned the name "temple tiger", as she was often spotted lying on the roof of a 900 AD Chola temple located inside the forest.

At the end of our day's safari, we heard her roaring continuously, lasting for almost half an hour. Tigers, especially females, roar to call their cubs or to attract mating partners. Our tour leader indicated that, in that occasion, she was calling for a mating partner.

The following morning, we went to A zone of the forest. Another female tiger was reported to be spotted by a few gypsies and a couple of forest department's canters. But we missed being at the right place at the right time. The forest was otherwise calm.

The evening safari was to be the highlight with the usual tiger drama. After roaming inside the forest for an hour and a half, we heard the strong alarm call of spotted deer. Soon as we arrived at the source of the call, we found spotted deer running away and few sambars staring into the forest. We waited for some time. As we waited, we heard the alarm call of a langur from another direction and followed the call, and arrived at the tree, atop which sat langurs, looking into the distance and letting out the alarm call. After a while, though, they went quiet.

After another half an hour of wandering, we caught sight of a male tiger sitting quietly inside a narrow ditch and licking his paws. Shortly, he stood up from the semi dry ditch and walked into the deep forest. He was the subadult cub of another dominant tiger of Kabini, "Russel line male", as named by locals.

Few moments after he disappeared, another male subadult tiger appeared from the other side of the forest. As the gypsies and canters followed him, he broke into a run and disappeared in the same direction as the previous one. Incidentally, this cub was the offspring of the "Russel line male" as well.

Pseudo Ecotourism

Half an hour later, an adult male tiger was spotted further ahead, by another gypsy. By the time we reached there though, the tiger had disappeared into the bushes, evident by the roaring from the direction of the bushes.

Essentially, in the two days at Kabini, tigers popped out from just anywhere and at any time, at times with alarm call and many times without.

That's how Kabini had transformed lately. Even Tadoba of central India, known as "maternity centre of Bengal Tiger", did not offer such frequent tiger sightings.

Few months later when I visited Kali Tiger Reserve, also in Western Ghats, a nature guide informed me that in Kabini the forest department cleared the vegetation and defined the tourism gypsy track in such a way that sighting of animals become easier. That was their response to the commoditized ecotourism market.

Anyway, we waited for some time, listening to the intermittent roaring, until the forest turned dark and the safari time for tourists ended.

On our last day at Kabini, the safari started with an overcast sky and soon after we started, there was heavy down pour. The rainforest in monsoon looked pristine and lush. The spotted deer ventured into the clear areas of the forest and huddled together. We spotted plenty of such spotted deer herds across the forest. White spots on brown coat against the wet foliage of verdant Western Ghats was quite a pleasure to the eyes.

On that day, the forest department gypsy spotted two subadult cubs of "Russel Line male". None of the safari vehicles saw them. However, in each safari, conducted twice a day, there was someone who spotted a Bengal Tiger, the supreme hunter of the subcontinental forest.

Despite the so-called successful tiger tourism in Kabini, a photography bootcamp participant expressed disappointment at not sighting a big cat on one of the four safaris. I was amused.

In a photography bootcamp, the mentors/tour leaders are generally smart enough to tackle such customers. And in forests like Kabini, even if you do not see big cats, there are elephants, gaurs, and dholes to both entertain you and to meet your photography needs, which in turn satiates your desire for fame and glory.

The situation, however, becomes desperate in tiger reserves where Bengal Tigers are perceived as the only "glamorous" objects.

Pseudo Ecotourism

During the second wave of the COVID 19 pandemic in India, I visited *Tiger Den* resort of *Rajasthan Tourism Development Corporation* (RTDC) located near the entry gate of Sariska Tiger Reserve in the Alwar district of Rajasthan.

One afternoon, at around half past two, under the guidance of local nature guide Ajay Kumar Singh, we set out on our "tiger-centric" ecotourism. For three and a half hours we chased dominant male ST21 and female ST9 on route number one of Sariska Tiger Reserve.

We also saw sambar and spotted deer, plenty of northern plain langur, pair of mongoose and flocks of rufus treepie, bronze and white bellied drongo, bronze winged jacana, white breasted water hen, purple sun bird, pea fowl etc. However, in the shadow of the Bengal Tiger of the dry deciduous forest at the foothill of Aravalli, no one cared for them.

Ajay mentioned that there were around 27 tigers in Sariska, including 8 males, 6 cubs and the rest females. Of them ST9 and ST21 were the most sighted duo in the park. Thus, on the first day of the trip itself, it was quite apparent that our tiger-chasing game would continue for the remaining three safaris and in this process, we would ignore all other interesting species and ecological phenomena of the forest. In those days in Sariska, Ajay and other guides in different gypsies received prompt information of tiger movement from different parts of forest through dedicated trackers assigned for each tiger by the forest department. The tracker was responsible for keeping track of the whereabouts of the animals assigned to them and reporting promptly to the forest department. Two such trackers were Mukesh for ST9 and Kalu bhai for ST21. All guides and drivers received tips from them about the movement of these two tigers, based on which they were driving their gypsies from one corner of the forest to the other.

The third safari, the one scheduled after noon, was quite eventful. Ajay, who was disheartened as Sariska's sweethearts ST9 and ST21 had not been sighted, took me to a different zone of the reserve on the bank of Karnawas Lake. There we saw few crocodiles, migratory birds - ruddy shelduck, and flocks of painted stork. A pair of them were engaged in courtship. Ajay seemed unaffected, his heart and mind were clearly elsewhere. After a while, he insisted that we get back to the regular tourism zone known for sighting of the duo. Thereafter, we started combing the forest again – the waterholes, bushy hideouts, and steep terrain of Aravalli hills.

A strong wind blew through the forest with dust settling in a thin grey layer over my cap, camera, and lens hood. The atmosphere in the forest was indicative of an approaching dust storm. The pale light of the hour seemed to be a reflection of Ajay's mood. He was visibly upset. So were other guides and drivers. For them tiger was money, and not sighting the animals for two consecutive days was a matter of concern.

The previous year, there were hardly any tourists due to the first wave of COVID 19. This year although there was a prevailing and much worse second wave, tourists and safari conductors alike decided to ignore the risk and continue their tourism in tiger reserves. Now the momentary disappearance of ST9 and ST21 was a cause for worry.

Magic transpired in the last hour of the day's safari, at around 5:00 pm. A mellowed alarm call of spotted deer was heard from a thicket nearby, and the next moment ST21 emerged from the thicket. Within the next moment, the usual cacophony of gypsies and the clamour of people shouting and hurling abuse at each other to get a better position to see the animal began.

In fact, the same morning we had spotted fresh pug marks of both ST9 and ST21 and their impression of sitting on the soil near the same thicket from where ST21 appeared. Ajay and other guides speculated, *"ST9 must be somewhere nearby too!"*

ST21 started walking along the forest path. A moment of déjà vu. I was reminded of the road show by the subadult cub of T12 (*aka* Maya) at Tadoba.

Too many gypsies and canters in the narrow forest path of Sariska blocked ST21's way. Under the faint glow of daylight, I clearly saw him growling mildly looking at a gypsy. As though he wished to make a plea, *"please make way for me!"*

Nevertheless, tourists and guides had gone crazy upon sighting him; therefore, no one really considered what the tiger may have been looking for. Left with no choice, ST21 made a detour and disappeared again into another thicket on the other side of the forest. Soon after, we heard the alarm call of a sambar, and a female sambar leapt out from the same thicket and ran for her life into another thicket. Fifteen minutes later the tiger was spotted climbing a thorny bush clothed steep terrain of the Aravalli range and he gradually disappeared behind the rocks.

That was not the end of the drama. About half an hour later, ST9 was reportedly seen near a waterbody. All vehicles hurried towards the waterbody located close to the check post of zone one. She was visible from afar, through the thorny bushes.

With these sightings, Ajay's body language had improved significantly. Life surged back into his soul, and the economy of Sariska held prospects of revival.

To top it off, as we exited the forest, at 6:15 pm, in the faint glow of twilight, Ajay spotted a leopard standing in open and perhaps stalking sambars that were at a distance. The moment he saw us and heard the shutter click; he ran towards a thicket further away without presenting photo opportunities.

Be that as it may, by the end of the safari, everyone in Sariska was happy! Later in the evening, at the resort, a few tourists approached me for the contact information of Ajay. They all desired to embark on a safari with Ajay, so as to have experiences similar to mine.

This is what guides like Ajay seek. This is the "tiger economy" of Central Indian tiger landscape. The larger question is, does it do any good for the animal itself?

In a documentary made on Sariska (interviewer Tom Alter, and available on YouTube), ex-member secretary of tiger steering committee, Mr. Navin M Raheja, says, *"Sariska Tiger Reserve is always in news for all wrong reasons and generally wildlife enthusiasts do not recognize the park as their favourite destination"*. In fact, during my visit to the park, I was the only wildlife photographer across all four safaris spanning three days.

According to Mr. Raheja, the wildlife enthusiasts question the credibility of the park as a tiger reserve. In an attempt to improve the image of Sariska and to attract serious wildlife tourists to the park, the forest department has initiated relocation of tigers from the neighbouring, more glamorous, Ranthambore Tiger Reserve. Raheja mentions in the documentary that five tigers had recently been shifted and apparently, they had comfortably accepted their new habitat. He asserts that Sariska is still the most disturbed tiger reserve of the country and the key reasons behind that, he says, are the two key highways that run through the forest, a religious temple in the forest, and the village settlement in the fringe areas of the forest. He explains, *"Highways, religious tourism, and mining are the key issues of Sariska. But poaching is probably the biggest issue among all. Promoting ecotourism can create a compelling case to eradicate these issues."*

I agree with Raheja that ecotourism has played an effective role in tiger conservation in subcontinental forests. However, the commercial expectations associated with "tiger-centric" ecotourism, at times, also puts the animal under stress. I have witnessed this in various instances during my explorations. Drawing a line between optimal usage and over usage of this effective conservation tool known as "ecotourism" is essential. The matter of concern is that to maximize the "ecotourism" opportunity, forest departments across tiger reserves and national parks are in the race to increase tiger population in their respective jurisdictions.

A gypsy driver in Sariska mentioned that they wanted more wildlife photographers than general tourists. *"Photographers increase our income"*, he said.

Veteran wildlife biologist and a renowned expert on tigers, Dr. K Ullas Karanth, in an interview published on 15th March 2021 in the online edition of *Hindustan*

Times, stated, *"Most misguided efforts for tiger redistributions failed".*

His most interesting view on the conservation efforts leading to a higher density of tigers is, *"They are artificial and excessive, misguided manipulations of vegetation and water, which have increased prey densities to unnaturally high levels. As a result, the number of tigers has also reached unnaturally high levels. These civil works and vegetation manipulations with huge budgetary outlays are drastically altering the natural state of the habitat and animal density levels. If the park budgets are drastically trimmed, the habitat will revert to a more natural state and prey and tiger densities will also settle down to those levels.* **We are turning our tiger habitats into "Disney-lands" and the ignorant tourists think that this is a great idea!"**

In Sariska, Dr. Karanth's view on tiger redistribution and relocation issues emerged as a harsh reality. In the interview he was critical and asserted, *"It is utterly foolish to think of "redistributing tigers". They are not chess pieces or cattle to be redistributed in this manner. The distribution will happen naturally once the prey base recovers, and the dispersing animals find new habitats. Most misguided efforts for tiger redistributions across India have failed and can have tragic consequences both for locals as well as the tigers. The problem is, in the absence of any scientific inputs on tiger management, only such failed ideas are going around again and again."*

Despite the pressure induced by commercial expectations on tourism, this majestic animal continues to enlighten with its ecological significance and behavioural pattern. The visit to Sariska was no exception. After all the hustle bustle of the evening safari, the following morning saw a relatively smaller number of tourist vehicles in the reserve. We witnessed ST21 and ST9 devouring their kill, an adult male nilgai, presumably killed early in the morning before the park opened to tourists.

Our tracker Kalu bhai had spotted ST21 with the kill and based on his information we arrived at the right location. He was busy enjoying his morning meal inside the dense foliage. The sound of bone cracking was chilling and at the same time indicative of the immense power of his jaws. A study confirms that tigers have a bite force of around 1,050 psi, and they bite almost twice as hard as lions do.

After having his fill, ST21 left, and ST9 took his place to finish the remaining of the kill. She repeatedly licked the dead nilgai. Her mouth was covered with fresh blood of the herbivore which made her look even more fearsome and deadly.

Like all felines (including the domestic cat), the Bengal Tiger's tongue is covered in small, hook-shaped growths called papillae, which point towards the back of the mouth, and are used as a brush to separate flesh from fur and bone, particularly when the cat is feeding on a humongous kill (nilgai, sambar, spotted deer etc.) – in the case of smaller prey items (rabbits, rodents, bird etc.), the carcass is devoured whole, with only a few or no bone splinters left.

After she completed her meal, she came out of the thicket and sat on the open ground for some time. Then she walked into the waterbody, submerging herself. She roared intermittently. The guides explained that she was calling out to ST21 to join her. ST21 might potentially be her future mate, once he becomes an adult.

Sariska's beloved tiger duo was back in action, as was its "tourism" and "economy"!

CHAPTER SEVEN: The Great Indian Tiger Show

Dr. Sophie Raine, a PhD in English Literature from Lancaster University, wrote in one of her articles titled *What is Commodity Fetishism?* *"According to Karl Marx's Das Kapital (1867), in a capitalist society, a commodity appears as if by magic to the consumer. This miraculous appearance, crucially, is divorced from the labour which produced it. This process is what Marx calls commodity fetishism.".*

Sophie explains that fetishised commodities are not viewed in terms of their utility but rather its value is determined by the economic and social relationships which provide these commodities their exchange value.

Fetishised commodities create an illusion of their magical qualities. Consumers, despite being aware that it is an illusion consciously consume these commodities.

Sophie explained this with the help of American economist and social scientist, Thorstein Veblen's *The Theory of the Leisure Class (1899)*. In this book, Veblen refers to 'conspicuous consumption', which describes *"the purchasing and displaying of commodities to indicate social status. Conspicuous consumption also extends to all types of lavish spending that is done to ostentatiously exhibit one's wealth."*

When consumers buy luxury clothes, they are aware that despite its ornateness and cost, the dress remains no more than an assemblage of materials. Commodity fetishism however elevates the value of the outfit to an indicator of wealth and status.

"Far removed from the materials or labour that produced it, the dress takes on this mystical quality under capitalism, granting the wearer esteem among their peers. As Veblen points out, the dress is a 'spiritual need' not a practical necessity."

This commodity fetishism was so far predominantly applicable to newly launched smart phones, expensive cars, electronic gadgets etc.

The ecotourism industry has also created their own illusive commodity – the Bengal Tiger. Like other fetishised commodities of capitalism, Bengal Tiger itself is not an illusion. It, however, has a mystical quality (created by the industry) that grants ecotourists and wildlife photographers a certain esteem among their peers.

Conservationists, Wildlife Biologists, and forest dwellers may see the real "use value" of tigers as apex predators and protectors of forests. Ecotourists and wildlife photographers are aware of this real use value, but their spending decision on tiger is largely influenced by the illusion of magical qualities that create opportunity for them to display their wealth (advanced photography gears) and elite status (expensive tiger tourism package, personal nature guide, and "rare images" of tiger among others).

Possessing this commodity with magical qualities, named the Bengal Tiger, then, is a foolproof way to achieve fame and glory for urban affluent ecotourists and wildlife photographers. The success story of this commodity fetishism is scripted in the flourishing ecotourism industry in the heartland of subcontinental tiger landscape – the Central Indian landscape.

Ranthambore Tiger Reserve was India's most profitable wildlife park in the financial year 2017-18. According to the forest department statistics, Ranthambore Tiger Reserve has been ranked first with a revenue of Rs 30 Crore ($ 3.6 million). Member of *Rajasthan State Wildlife Board* and wildlife enthusiast, Valmik Thapar, said in a news report published in *Times of India's* online edition, *"Ranthambore is a shining example of what wildlife tourism can do to a small district like Sawai Madhopur. The district earns over 350 crores ($ 47 million) each year from wildlife tourism with direct impact on local economy, on tens of thousands of people right down to the vegetable seller. There are 2,000 hotel rooms and 1,200 tourist vehicles in the district."*

One early winter I visited the richest tiger reserve of the subcontinent. Rain was forecasted, which was unusual considering the time of the year.

Contrary to the forecast predicting heavy rainfall, the following morning was pleasant with an overcast sky.

We witnessed avian activities of woolly necked storks, yellow footed green pigeon and grey francolin perching on branches and pecking on grounds in different parts of the forest. The search for the tiger was of course the main agenda; and thus, no one had time to stop too long for other species.

Our guide Sunil opined, *"Forest Department should remove T124, aka Riddhi, the celebrity tigress of Ranthambore, from the tourism zones two, three and four. That would encourage the other female tiger, Arrowhead, to return with her cubs and provide more photo opportunity to tourists. In turn that would attract more tourists to the park."*

As if there was dearth of tourists in Ranthambore. The more pressing question at the moment though was, *who is Riddhi?* And why is she so famous in Ranthambore?

In Ranthambore, almost every tiger has a special reputation and legend associated with it. To know Riddhi, we must begin with another legendary tigress known as "Lady of the Lake", Machli (T16). She would perhaps be remembered as the most famous tigress of Ranthambore, who loved to pose for tourists and photographers. Her soaring popularity among tourists and wildlife enthusiasts saw her featured in the national award-winning movie, *"The World's Most Famous Tiger"*. She even found mention in the book, *"Three Ways to Disappear"*, by Katy Yocom. Unfortunately, tigress Machli, the most photographed tigress in the world, died on 18th August 2016. Sundari (T17), the daughter of Machli, was another famous tigress of Ranthambore National Park. However, she passed away well before her mother, in October 2011. Arrowhead (T73) was the daughter of Sundari's sibling, Krishna. Born in 2012, she was known for her shy nature and was mostly spotted in an area of the park known as Kachida Valley. In 2019, Arrowhead mothered two cubs.

T124 *aka* Riddhi, the fearless and adventurous great granddaughter of Machli, one of the two cubs of Arrowhead, is the latest buzz of the forest. Sunil's comment on relocating Riddhi from zone two, three and four is an indication of her territorial dominance over her mother Arrowhead.

Possessing an adventurous spirit since cubhood, tigress Riddhi had the sheer audacity to clash with her mother tigress Arrowhead over territory. She is said to be bold like her great grandmother, Machli, once was. Perhaps it's true when they say that genes skip generations. Cubs Riddhi and Siddhi remained with their mother for some time but this joyous mother-daughters family scene was fleeting. While both possess immense courage, Riddhi's power and adventurous spirit is one of a kind. She established her territory within her mother's territory. She can toss tourists with her bold looks as she wanders like a queen between zone three and four, around Padam Lake, Raj-Bag, Malik Lake and the Mandoob area. This territory is the heart of Ranthambore where Machli ruled for years, followed by her daughter Sundari and then her daughter Krishna. Krishna's daughter Arrowhead continued the legacy of dominance until she was dethroned by her daughter Riddhi.

I heard these stories of Ranthambore tigresses from local guides, gypsy drivers and veteran participants of our bootcamp who have been visiting this park for a decade. The stories mostly spread by word of mouth, and some were captured in wildlife bloggers' sites. These stories undoubtedly establish the love of tourists for the tigers, but this is also a biased love for tigers and tigresses who were "bold" enough to come close to tourist vehicles and "pose" for photographs. The wildlife photographers are thus the key contributors in spreading this *love* for select tigers and tigresses of the park. It is understandable then, that the people who make their living out of this park – gypsy drivers, nature guides, hoteliers, forest department staffs, tour operators and even wildlife photography mentors –want every tiger-lover headed to Ranthambore National Park to take home with them a happy tiger story.

Therefore, the entertainment package of tiger-tourism in this park includes not merely sighting the majestic beasts, but a tiger story in the style of *"Game of Thrones"*.

These Bengal Tiger stories undoubtedly brings them on par with the human emperors whose glorious stories we read in History books. As a result, personifying the tigers through their lineage and battles for succession is delightful indeed. At the same time, this entertainment package somehow disparaged the almighty and apex predator image of Bengal Tigers created by Sy Montgomery and Jim Corbett respectively, in their stories.

On the very first day of our scheduled three full-day and two half-day safaris in India's richest tiger reserve, we had our customary sighting of T124, at around 9:00 am near Padam *talab* (lake). Incidentally, she was moving from zone four to zone three marking her scent afresh to attract male tigers for mating. The rain from previous day had washed away her scent marking. She thus remarked her scent. In the absence of rain over the next few days, there was high probability of seeing her in movement. Afterall, she had to cover a large territory with her scent marking.

In a full day safari, typically, the day in the park begins at 6:30 am and ends at 5:30 pm, with a couple of breaks in between – one for breakfast at around 10:00 am and then for lunch at around 1:00 pm, together lasting about two hours. This amount of time spent in a forest like Ranthambore creates immense opportunity of tiger sighting.

With intermittent drizzling, the afternoon on our first day of safari was gloomier than the morning. In the last few hours of the safari, we saw a busy ruddy mongoose running here and there. The notable bird species were a pair of alexandrine parakeets, few flame back woodpeckers, common hoopoe, greater thick-knee, open billed storks, and lot of greater cormorant perching on trees, popping out of waterbodies and on different branches of tall canopy.

The vegetation of Ranthambore is certainly different from that of Sariska. The vegetation in Sariska is arid and dry deciduous. Ranthambore is a mix of moist and dry deciduous forest with open grassy meadows, which reminded me of Kanha. The park has an area of 1,334 km^2. It is bounded to the north by the Banas River and to the south by the Chambal River. The park is named after the historic Ranthambore Fort which lies within the park.

As per weather forecast, the next morning was to be overcast with some sun light. The day, however, started with heavy downpour. The rain was so heavy that our raincoats failed to protect us. The plastic sheets we placed on gypsy seats to keep them dry, started collecting rainwater, that made our pants and undergarments completely wet. It became difficult to explore the forest under such circumstances. The high point of the rain-washed day was sighting T124 again, near Raj-Bag. We watched as she chased a wild boar. The local guide of our bootcamp team, Hansraj, suggested that she might have already finished eating her kill, as crows waited on tree branches, perhaps to finish the remaining part. The chasing appeared to him as a mock one.

The rumour of translocating Riddhi to Sariska was very strong in those days. The safari guides, drivers and even photographers were talking about it and expressing their concerns. Absence of T124 in the forest of Ranthambore would impact tiger sighting and photo opportunity for visitors. It is not that we did not see other tigers or tigresses in the park besides Riddhi, but most of them were shy and disliked human presence.

As per the blog called *Ranthamborenationalpark.com*, the fierce tigress Riddhi is said to have killed a tiger cub T102 in the Tamba Khan area of Ranthambore National Park. Forest officials had seen her chasing down T102. The blog mentions that due to these incidents and the conflict of Riddhi and Siddhi over territory, the tigress Riddhi will be shifted to Sariska Tiger Reserve. The blog further states that the cat population is rising at Ranthambore Tiger Reserve due to which there is a lack of space and a fear of territorial fights. To reduce this pressure Riddhi will be moved out of Ranthambore on her new journey.

Many believe, though, that the Hotel and Resort lobby of Sariska, with the objective of enhancing tourism in their park, is influencing the Government to take such a decision. The previous summer when I was in Sariska, safari guides complained about not having enough wildlife photographers visiting the park, thus not generating adequate income.

What was cause for delight for Sariska could be dismay for Ranthambore. However, not every guide of Ranthambore was disappointed with this possible translocation. Sunil was of the opinion that relocation of T124 would create opportunity for her mother T17, *aka* Arrowhead, to regain her territory. That would enable tourists to see a female tigress with cubs. Rumour was rife that T17 had borne a few cubs.

The heavy rain in Ranthambore forced us to suspend the safari and return to the hotel. We decided to resume after lunch at around 1:30 pm. Our tour leader received news from a trusted source that, that morning T12, *aka* Maya, (the Tadoba equivalent of T124 in terms of celebrity status) had killed a lady forest guard, Swati Dhumane. Dhumane was on foot with three labourers for the All-India Tiger Estimation (AITE) exercise when the incident occurred. They were conducting a transect survey in a patch of forest near waterhole number ninety-seven. T12 was resting in a bush and did not notice their movement. Therefore, she was surprised and attacked in her defence. As per the news report, it was a first-of-its-kind incident, but our tour leader told us that it was her fifth human attack in the recent past.

Based on the news report of 21st November 2021 in the online edition of *Times of India*, Tadoba field director Jitendera Ramgaonkar has suspended the enumeration exercise as well as the movement of tourists in gypsy in the area. According to Ramgaonkar, Dhumane and team had started walking around 7 am. After four kilometres, they noticed Maya sitting on the road, about two hundred metres ahead of them. The team waited for around thirty minutes and when the tigress did not budge, they decided to take a detour through the forest. The tigress then attacked Dhumane and dragged her into the forest. Maya's sudden aggressive behaviour has surprised those who have followed her life. Incidentally, T12, *aka* Maya, is the first Bengal Tiger I sighted in the wild.

Many raised the question as to why the forest department staff were unarmed while walking in tiger zone. Perhaps over humanization of tigers and tigresses of Indian forests convinces us into believing that they can be treated like pets of human households. The reality remains that they are the apex predators of subcontinental forests.

Rain finally subsided by the afternoon of our second day. Diffused sun light caressed the lush green forest. Water puddles were drying up and news came in from zone one, that a tigress had killed a sambar. At around 2:30 pm, we reached the site hoping that the tigress would come back to her kill. It would not be possible for her to drag the kill further up. The tigress incidentally had cubs, so if we were lucky, we could see her and her cubs devouring the sambar.

The foul smell of dead and rotten carcass assailed our nostrils. A few tourists quickly covered their nose and mouth with handkerchiefs. There was however no sign of the tigress. From the beginning of our bootcamp, our team was divided into two groups on two gypsies. Local guide Hansraj led one such group, and on that day, I was part of his group. Hansraj did not want to waste time waiting there and suggested going further in search of the tigress. Sure enough, after fifty meters we found fresh pugmarks of a female tiger, and we followed the track. After a kilometre or so the track disappeared into dense undergrowth and we decided to turn back. When we were halfway through to the point where the carcass was lying, we met the other group. They informed us that a male tiger (T101) appeared out of nowhere and dragged the kill further up into the dense foliage. T101 was known for his dislike of safari gypsies.

The photographers in the gypsy got decent shots of T101. We hurried back to the site only to catch a quick glimpse of him through greyish green bushes as he disappeared into them. Sadly, a missed photo opportunity.

To be at the right place at the right time – the secret of tiger sighting in the wild. This was not the first such instance in my exploration experience. Wildlife enthusiasts understand this, but tourists who have already become the commodity consumer do not, and that gives a lot of stress to the gypsy drivers and guides. And they transfer this stress to the tigers.

We then headed towards zone three, the territory of T124. On the way, we got some nice shots of scops owl and brown fish owl. When we arrived at Raj-Bag, she was already on the move.

Hundreds of tourists gathered on the bank of Raj-bag in ten canters and around twenty gypsies, erupted into joyful and excited noise. It was an early winter sunny Saturday afternoon. Families with children enjoyed "the great Indian tiger-show" in the richest tiger reserve of the subcontinent.

T124 slowly walked along the bank. A marsh crocodile lay busking. Startled by the sudden appearance of T124 it jumped into water with a huge splash. That caused the decibel level to rise even higher. Her great grandmother was famous for killing crocodiles. The atmosphere was akin to a cricket stadium. Riddhi scored boundaries and over-boundaries with each move, entertaining the crowd.

She was slowly inching closer to us. Expert guide Hansraj with the help of driver Mahender parked the gypsy in such a way that we had the best possible angle and light to shoot her. Soon she was in a position where she was surrounded by tourist vehicles. This particularly annoyed her and she snarled at a gypsy nearby, displaying her magnificent fang.

The crowd roared further, as if she hooked another sixer. Photographers were delighted as they captured their "lifer" image of the angry tigress's expression. Wildlife enthusiasts, guides and tour operators were winning.

Only Riddhi was losing as everyone overlooked her stress. But she has learnt to live with human pests in her kingdom. After all, she is the great granddaughter of Machli. She found her way between tourist vehicles and took a narrow forest path. It was not possible for the big twenty-seater safari canters to enter such a narrow path. Gypsies carrying non-photographer tourists stopped following her, as the passengers had lost interest and considered it as end of show.

The photographers though are a different breed altogether. Their greed for better images never ends. Moreover, the all-knowing guides and drivers of the park (against exorbitantly premium payment) always accompany them. Two of our bootcamp gypsy drivers anticipated from where she could appear again and positioned the vehicles accordingly. Within half an hour, T124 was just head on with us and walked towards us. As photographers, we were delighted with this sudden head on appearance. But in all honesty, I could feel a chill through my spine. This sudden appearance was a stark reminder of the Sundarbans experience. The recent report from Tadoba of Maya's attack on a human flashed through my mind for a fraction of a second. However, the photographer's instinct emerged as the victor, as I indulged in capturing some best "head-on" shots of the Bengal Tiger of the Indian subcontinent.

After walking straight towards us for some time, she was distracted by a herd of spotted deer and took a detour into the dense foliage.

Neha Jain in her article published on 28th October 2019 in the online edition of the journal *Mongabay* says, *"Ever wondered how tigers feel in response to hordes of vehicles ferrying tourists eager for the thrill of a perfect close-up encounter? Now, a study examining stress hormones in tiger scat collected from two popular central Indian tiger reserves has revealed that these iconic carnivores suffer from high levels of physiological stress due to wildlife tourism and a large number of vehicles entering the parks. Prolonged stress can adversely affect both survival and reproduction."*

The article quotes senior author Govindhaswamy Umapathy, a principal scientist and project leader at the Laboratory for the *Conservation of Endangered Species* (LaCONES) at *CSIR-Centre for Cellular and Molecular Biology* (CCMB), Hyderabad, *"If it continues it will have a definite impact on the population in the long-term."*

This is the impact of commodity fetishism on Bengal Tiger. The real conservational use value of the species is ignored, and only the illusion created through biased social and economic evaluation prevails.

Neha mentions in her article, *"Interestingly, a previous study by the authors, published in 2015, showed that tigers introduced in Sariska Tiger Reserve in Rajasthan failed to reproduce, probably due to stress elicited by human disturbances."*

A matter of concern for Riddhi, as very soon she could be on her way to Sariska to be greeted by the cheers of her crazy fans waiting there. In fact, during the safari Hansraj told us that we were perhaps seeing her for the last time in Ranthambore. The translocation team was all set and had it not been raining the last few days she would have been tranquilized by now and well on her way to Sariska.

The third day in Ranthambore was all about following T124. We sighted her first at 6:45 am, even before we entered the main safari zone. We spotted her on the road. We watched as she came down from an uphill hillock, crossed the cemented road in front of our gypsy and descended further down, disappearing into the dense forest.

Again, we saw her roaming from zone four to three and scent marking trees and bushes. This is an important behaviour of the tiger, and is key to their survival as far as natural history is concerned. Tigers inform each other of their whereabouts through complex scent markings that contain pheromones. Scientific studies say that marking is most intensive when tigers are establishing territories, and animals on adjacent territories appear to mark in response to each other. Females mark intensively just prior to oestrus; this behaviour is reduced during oestrus. Males marked more frequently when females were in oestrus than during other stages of the females' cycle.

In the last few days T124 had marked her territory intensively, an indication perhaps of her pre oestrus status. The local guides of Ranthambore told us that T124 was once seen mating with a male tiger T120, but she might not have conceived. According to them, her pregnancy was the only way to suspend her relocation. They kept their fingers crossed.

Later that morning we went to tourism zone six to search for another female tiger who was apparently nursing her cubs. But, besides a lot of chinkaras and sambar we didn't see much else. And that was our first chinkara sighting in Ranthambore.

In the afternoon our guides received news of a fully-grown male tiger, T120, sleeping in zone two. We rushed to the spot and found him sleeping under the cool shade of trees and shrubs. As full day safari tourists, we had the privilege to enter the park fifteen minutes before the regular tourism hour began. Once it started, hordes of tourists arrived in canters and gypsies in the narrow forest path to see T120. They completely choked and blocked the path and created enough clatter waking the animal up.

He woke up and looked directly at us, giving us a fabulous opportunity to shoot a tiger portrait. T120 is undoubtedly a beautiful male tiger. He yawned and licked his paws. Perhaps he intended to move. But the presence of so many tourists made him reluctant to do so. Besides, it was nearly impossible for him to escape through the clutter of canters and gypsies. Therefore, he lay there till the last hour of safari time. At last, at around 5:15 pm, he emerged through a different route, one full of thorny bushes, from the opposite side to where he was lying. Cats generally prefer to walk through plain forest path because of the padding they have on their paws. But the assembly of visitors forced him to walk on the thorny forest path. Anticipating his movement towards the thorny path of forest, the smart gypsy drivers also moved their vehicles towards that direction. Therefore, when he came out on the clear path, he again was amidst chattering crowds. All the tigers of Ranthambore had by now probably learnt how to dribble through safari vehicles. T120 also did so and went on to disappear into the distant dense forest of zone two. Our guides assumed that he was perhaps on a mission to find T124 and was heading towards zone three.

When we were exiting the forest for the day, we heard the bellowing of spotted deer's alarm call from afar. Through the haze of twilight, we watched T120 pass by a herd of spotted deer, without paying much attention to them, while the panic-stricken deer looked on as he melted away in the foliage of the Central Indian tiger landscape.

Our bootcamp ended, and the evening was all about celebrating "successful tiger photography tourism" around the campfire lit by our hotel staff. We discussed the close proximity between tigers and visitors in the park, thus creating great photo opportunity.

The discussion brought back memories of an article written by Priya Ranganathan in 2019. The article was published in the online journal *The News Minute*. Priya says, *"No longer is wildlife tourism simply a chance to observe animals in their natural state. A recent report from Rajasthan's Ranthambhore Tiger Reserve reveals the dark side of tiger tourism in India, where a tour guide pelted stones at a sleeping tiger in Ranthambhore's Safari Zone six so that his guest could get the "perfect action shot"*. In the article, Priya also highlighted the fact that *"Tigers are treated as a commodity on safaris, where guests tip drivers depending on the number of successful sightings and call-in favours to get seats on jeeps booked for zones with known tiger sightings or high tiger densities."*

I do not think mere relocation of tigers from one park to another can reduce pressure on the animals, unless there is some large-scale endeavour to make the tourists "wildlife safari literate".

Although our bootcamp had ended, we still had the entire day to spend on our last day at Ranthambore, as our Bangalore bound flight from Jaipur was scheduled to depart at 6:30 pm. Therefore, two other Bangalore based photographers and I did another additional regular safari in zone one, in the territory of T101.

After a couple of hours of scouting through the forest, we got a tip from another safari gypsy on the whereabouts of T101. We had to be extremely cautious to locate him, as he is not known for being "tourist friendly". At around 8:30 am, fellow photographer Rajesh spotted him hidden in the undergrowth, his large face visible through the grass. We got a few minutes to shoot him before he stood up and disappeared deep inside, clearly displaying his displeasure for human sighting.

We got images of him where his face was obstructed by foliage. In photographic parlance, this foliage is called "clutter" as it "spoils the image".

Jim Corbett said in his legendary novel *"Man-Eaters of Kumaon"*, *"Those who have never seen a leopard under favourable conditions in his natural surroundings can have no conception of the grace of movement, and beauty of colouring, of this the most graceful and the most beautiful of all animals in our Indian jungles."*

The same concept is applicable to any animal in its natural habitat. I have always failed to understand why we wildlife photographers perpetually must go for clean images, which are at times "unnatural"?

The wildlife photographers and ecotourists, who look only for a commodity to consume on their journey towards fame and glory, become passive towards the real use value of the commodified species in ecosystems.

Dr. Sophie Raine of Lancaster University in her article *What is Commodity Fetishism?* writes, *"The passive nature of the consumer makes it all the easier to sell them products they do not need. In capitalist societies, typically all of our basic needs (food, water, shelter) are met; in order for capitalism to continue thriving, the consumer industry converts 'wants' into 'needs'. The consumer places vital necessity on unnecessary products. For example, advertising may show a new sports car and indicate that this may present the image of success. This is illusionary as no car can make someone successful. However, as this image of the car and its relationship to success has been disseminated via mass media throughout wider society, it becomes accepted that the commodity (the car) has this magical property. As it is accepted, the illusion becomes real."*

The real consumer of the ecotourism industry would have been satisfied with sighting the majestic Bengal Tiger in its natural habitat. But under the influence of the fetishist spell cast by the commodity market (tiger tourism) they have become passive, isolated, and immobile and then turn to the Bengal Tiger as a way of connecting with a sense of community, action, and self. The social media postings of Bengal Tigers' images are examples of how they connect with wildlife enthusiasts' community, wildlife enthusiasm related actions and self. This is also an indication of their passiveness towards the real use value of the species in forests.

To them there is no materialistic difference between a model in the fashion industry and a tiger in the subcontinental forests. Both are commodities after all.

Four months after my Ranthambhore exploration, I visited the subcontinent's "maternity centre of Bengal Tigers" – Tadoba Andhari Tiger Reserve (TATR), for the second time.

Five years ago, it was at this very tiger reserve that I had my first so-called "successful tiger safari", sighting the Bengal Tigers in the wild for the first time, a winter in pre-pandemic era. Post-pandemic, I returned to this tiger terrain in the scorching summer.

The first safari of my second trip to Tadoba on a hot March Day, started from the Telia zone of Moharli gate, exactly where I ended my previous trip on a chilly winter morning of January.

The area continues to be ruled by T24, *aka* Sonam, just as it was five years ago. Although she is now the mother of three tiny cubs.

Apart from the change in climate and Sonam's family status, this trip was much like the previous one, as far as tourists and tourism in this park was concerned. The photography bootcamp participants are typically white-collard Corporate Technology professionals from Bangalore. We were six photographers in the bootcamp, three of who accompanied me in the gypsy on the first safari. All three were Techies from Bangalore,

Our nature guide Kajal was an enthusiastic and conversational young woman.

"What do you want to see?", she asked.

"Tiger!". A unanimous response in a matter-of-fact tone from my three companions.

Of course, Kajal was not surprised by the response. She was fully aware – photographer or non-photographer; all tourists come with a singular wish – "tiger".

The safari started with high expectation of tiger sighting, an expectation established by none other than our tour leader and mentor himself. Upon our arrival at *Pugmark resort* he announced that the previous bootcamp batch spotted 10 tigers in a single safari one morning. Across eight safaris of the bootcamp, the participants sighted a total of 17 individual Bengal Tigers, including adult males, females, and cubs.

My fellow photographers, thus, cannot take the blame for expressing their expectation to Kajal.

Incidentally though, we were not as fortunate as our predecessors'. On a safari spanning four hours, we did not spot a single tiger. In fact, I did not click a single picture.

Regardless of how hard we try to commoditize the apex predator of an ecosystem to fame hungry consumers, we mustn't forget that they are real living beings belonging to nature. The concept of production on demand does not really work here.

Nonetheless, Kajal tried to show few birds of prey such as mottled wood owl, white eyed buzzard etc. She was keenly aware, though, that these species did not deserve a place in her "ecotourism menu". But when you do not see tigers, you fill the void by seeing the other species.

You keep your camera busy by shooting them, when you do not shoot the tiger. And try as you may, your spirit remains low.

On this particular safari, we combed the forest between Pandharpauni and Telia lake and I felt quite nostalgic. In my initial days of exploration *in the shadow of the Bengal Tiger*, I explored these areas with a lot of energy and with a hope of getting a glimpse of this majestic animal in the wild. In those days, my exploration expectation was heavily tiger-centric. I started my wildlife photography not just for achieving fame and glory, but also due to my interest and admiration for this animal, and Tadoba did not disappoint me. Near the watchtower of Pandharpauni, Vedavyasa and I had seen, T12 *aka* Maya. In those days of crazy tiger-chasing adventures, this animal taught me how to fall in love with nature and why it was important to respect every non-human life form, irrespective of their apparent value (in this case being photogenic) to human life form.

That afternoon on my ongoing bootcamp, as we approached Pandharpauni watchtower, all previous sightings in TATR flashed through my mind, and I enquired about a subadult male, Bhola, I had seen on my previous visit. Bhola was born to Maya in her second litter. Kajal was aware of Bhola' whereabouts. She spoke of a fight between Bhola and T54, *aka* Matkasur, as a result of which T54 fled from the Pandharpauni area. Bhola however, failed to hold his ground after repeated attacks from T54 made him leave the territory. Kajal had lately spotted him near Navegaon gate of the park.

I was glad to know that Maya was still the undisputed queen of Pandharpauni. As none of her female cubs survived, there was none to claim her throne.

The area was now frequented by four strong male tigers – Rudra (T103), Balaram, Mowgli and of course Matkasur. Of the four, Maya was sighted with Rudra several times in the past few weeks. In fact, the participants from the previous safari had seen them together a couple of times, and a possibility of mating appeared to be on the cards.

The possibility of shooting the mating ritual of Bengal Tigers in wild raised the excitement and expectation among photographers. Nonetheless, the "tiger sighting score" dropped from ten to zero, within a span of a few hours between the morning safari of the previous batch to the afternoon safari of our batch.

That was the harsh reality of forest and biodiversity exploration. We humans, photographers, and non-photographers alike, should never be ignorant of this.

Our luck did not change over the next couple of safaris. In the last thirty minutes of the third safari, there was marginal improvement as we spotted Sonam with her tiny little cubs, barely three months old. They were visible from a distance through the tall grass in Telia lake. In the last rays of the sun, Sonam looked gorgeous. On my previous trip to Tadoba, I caught a glimpse of her through the grass of Telia. On the current safari, we watched as a mother calmly and protectively guided her tiny cubs to the safety of thick bushes.

After three safaris in the core zone, we moved to the buffer zone through Agarzari gate. This zone had plenty of waterbodies which allowed for abundant avian activities. Over the four days, I spotted and identified around forty species of birds. I was mighty pleased with myself. The courtship display of Indian male peafowl, the mating of Indian rollers and the osprey swooping to catch fish - what a spectacular display!

But like I said earlier, these were just stop gap arrangements in the *tiger* reserves of the subcontinent.

Birds aside, even other predators are no match for the majestic tiger, as far as photographic preference is concerned. Tadoba is home to three sympatric carnivores - tiger, leopards and wild dogs or dhole. Of the three, dhole, like the tiger, is also endangered. The animal that is so agile, hunts in packs and is quite successful at taking down prey, is facing extinction, with less than 2500 of them remaining in the world. Their count is much less than the number of Bengal Tigers that exist on Earth.

They are dogs that do not bark. Instead, they make whistle calls for long-distance communication - such as getting the pack together after a hunt or waking members up from mid-day naps. They show a remarkable behaviour trait for a wild animal by allowing the youngest member of the pack to eat first.

We saw a pair of dholes on one of our morning safaris. A solitary male dhole, kept his eyes on a sambar on one of our afternoon safaris in the buffer zone. Spotting this animal in the Central Indian Forest is a stroke of luck.

But of course, we were in no mood for a dhole. Afterall, we were in search of the tiger!

On one of our afternoon safaris we were accompanied by nature guide, Bharat. From the beginning, he was trying hard to spot tigers, escorting us to all the remote and difficult to access areas of the Junona zone of the buffer zone. He said he was searching for a female tiger, popularly known as "W".

But three hours of his relentless effort went in vain, leaving a fellow photographer furious. He declared that "W" was a useless tigress as she did not pose to be photographed like Sonam or Maya. Besides, her territory was full of bushes and clutter, and even if we had spotted her, it clearly would not have been a camera worthy sighting, he complained.

In the gentleman's view, there was no point wasting time on "W". He also made snide remarks against Bharat, suggesting he was equally useless with no understanding of photographers' preferences. He further added that Bharat should stick to "general tourists" who merely want to see tigers, and are not inclined towards photography.

This was revelatory. Not just birds, other mammals or even other predators were less camera worthy compared to the tiger, but even among tigers, not all were equally "useful".

In the eight safaris during our bootcamp, we saw twelve fascinating species of mammals, including tiger, dhole, sloth bear, gaur, nilgai, ruddy mongoose, langur, barking deer among others. Despite that, most participants considered the entire trip quite "dry". Even sighting of Sonam and her cubs through the grass was not seen as significant as it provided no photo opportunity.

I admit that I was disappointed too, for not having enough tiger sighting in Tadoba, the so-called "maternity centre" or "breeding ground" of Bengal Tiger. But at the same time, I was also relaxed, experiencing the forest for what it was.

In an exploration in another part of India, I met a fellow photographer, an ENT specialist (Doctor of Eye, Nose, and Throat), Dr. Gopal Belokar, from Nagpur. He was proud of Tadoba because of its high success rate in tiger sighting.

In a conversation with him, I once told him *"Tadoba has become nothing but a zoo!"*

Dr. Belokar was clearly unhappy with the comment, but said nothing. At the end of my second Tadoba trip though, I was glad that the forest proved me wrong. Tadoba is like any other natural dry and moist deciduous forest of the subcontinent, where sighting big cats is all about being at the right place at the right time.

Tadoba was certainly not a zoo.

We set out on our last safari, to the core area through Mohorli gate. A fellow participant, Ananda, said that he normally does not target a particular species, but he signed up for this bootcamp particularly for tigers.

"Now I am going without any expectation and will shoot everything in this forest.", declared Ananda at the onset of the last safari in Tadoba. He was my roommate at Ranthambore the previous winter. Ananda had arrived at Ranthambhore without any expectation, but of course we saw tigers in every safari.

I was, yet again, reminded of the wise words of Bangalore based photography mentor, Kesava. *"Do not go to forest with any expectation and always expect the unexpected."*

If ecotourists, however, visit forests with an intention to buy a commodity, then that would be a transactional visit. Such a visit cannot be made without any expectation.

Near Telia lake at around 6:45 am, our nature guide for the day Sravan and driver Mubarak, let out a scream together.

"Tiger, Tiger!"

T24, *aka* Sonam, was stalking a herd of Sambar. The herd included an adult male, seven females and four fauns. They clearly sensed her presence and stared at a thicket on the opposite side of Telia lake. The herd, bellowed their characteristic alarm call, and moved towards the thicket.

The experienced sambar herd knew they were safer in the thicket than on a clear forest path. Tigers always find it difficult to chase their prey through thickets. Sonam realized her cover was blown. Tigers prefer ambush attack. Although she made a mock charge

Pseudo Ecotourism 223

that made the herd run away, and eventually she came out on the open forest path.

The golden light of the rising sun, made her even more beautiful and of course "photogenic".

Good for us, good for Sravan and Mubarak, the photography tour company and their leader, good for Tadoba and its tiger community, good for forest and tourism department of Maharashtra – finally the sounds of shutter clicks filled the air. Intriguingly, it sounded much like the notes being counted on a teller machine.

It was not over yet. After the "successful sighting", we got busy shooting barking deer crossing the forest road. Yes, after capturing "camera worthy" views of Sonam, we were agreeable to considering barking deer a worthy photography subject. Meanwhile, approaching gypsies informed us that Rudra and Maya were sighted together near water hole number ninety-seven.

We rushed to water hole number ninety-seven, to find some ten gypsies gathered there.

Rudra mounted Maya. He watched her, licking her neck, with occasional love bites. Maya was on her belly, forelegs fully extended and hind legs partially bent. Although fully mounted, Rudra was in a knee-bent position, to ensure he did not put too much pressure on her. He vocalised loudly a few times. When he was about to ejaculate, he let out a sharp cry and took hold of Maya's loose skin around her neck.

That exposed her neck to his bite, which could lead to instant death.

But Maya's eyes were closed, and face raised. Their sharp whiskers rubbed against each other. Maya's closed eyes assured Rudra, that she had full faith in him. She knew Rudra's bite would not take her life.

The reason for the neck bite was to ensure that both were in the correct position at the time of climax. There have been instances where a mistake by an inexperienced couple has led to death.

As he dismounted, Maya responded by growling and jumping up to dislodge him. She tried to slap him, and Rudra jumped back escaping her paw. Though superficial, a slap such as that may at times be quite severe, inflicting scratches.

Both, Rudra and Maya, vocalised loudly. These otherwise quiet animals were at their noisiest during lovemaking. That alerted a sambar deer. He hollered the frequent alarm call near water hole number ninety-seven.

We watched for around thirty to forty-five minutes and in that duration, they mated thrice, with a gap of ten to fifteen minutes each time. They were exhausted, and laid down on the forest floor. Rudra's massive head rested gently on Maya's soft belly.

We left the forest after witnessing a fundamental, yet rare to sight, natural phenomenon, letting the satisfied couple enjoy their moment in the lap of nature.

Pseudo Ecotourism

As I left Tadoba and boarded the Bangalore bound aircraft from Nagpur, I saw several posters promoting tourism by Maharashtra Government at the Nagpur airport. The posters featured a close-up shot of the Bengal Tiger and a map of Nagpur district. The posters proclaimed Nagpur as the tiger capital of the world. The three tiger reserves - Tadoba, Pench and Melghat are located in and around Nagpur district. Of the three, Tadoba contributes heavily in Nagpur's confident claim in being the tiger capital of the world.

Many photographers, conservationists and ecotourists are likely to disagree with the above claim, and hold Bandhavgarh as the tiger capital of the world.

Irrespective of which claim holds true, the reality is that it is nothing but a promotional strategy of the tourism department. The success of this promotional strategy hugely depends upon increased tiger sightings. Higher the tiger density, higher the rate of tiger sighting. The detrimental effects of high tiger density are well known to ecologically conscious people.

As per the report published on 19th May 2020 in the online edition of *Times of India*, there are 115 tigers in TATR core and buffer area, and this number is increasing. During my visit to the park that summer, I learnt that tigress T24 (Sonam) had borne three small cubs, T19 (Lara) three slightly older female cubs, and T127 (Madhu) two cubs. T12 (Maya) and T103 (Rudra) mated a few times in our presence, so it was likely that soon she may be expecting cubs.

This is undoubtedly promising news for tiger-centric ecotourism, wildlife photography and the path towards a successful economy for the national park. However, in TATR there is a trend among subadult or weaker males to risk their lives by leaving the forest to escape attacks from stronger adult males. The territorial conflict triggers such an exodus.

Just two days after I concluded my second TATR exploration, I read a disturbing news article published in the electronic version of *Nagpur Today*. The article included the gruesome image of a fully-grown tiger's swollen dead body floating on water. The big cat reportedly died of blood poisoning caused by injuries due to its defunct radio collar. The following day saw yet another news of a mysterious death of a subadult tiger, raising eyebrows of the conservationist community. The news published in the online version of *Times of India*, reported that a male tiger was found dead under mysterious circumstances in a small irrigation canal on Bawanthadi River, near Bapera village in Nakadongri forest range of Tumsar Tehsil.

The tiger was between 15-18 months old, and according to sources, death may have been caused by territorial fight. One of the paws of the animal was found broken and there was a deep injury in the leg.

In the editorial of the monthly newsletter *"Tadoba Diaries"* published by the *Tadoba-Andhari Tiger Reserve Conservation Foundation*, the Chief Conservator and Field Director of TATR, Dr. Jitendra Ramgaonkar, sighted the lack of space as a problem for the growing tiger population in Tadoba. In the January 2022 edition he mentioned, *"It is well known that tigers are territorial animals and require vast areas for breeding and exhibiting their range of behaviour. In fact, tiger-bearing capacity is a function of good prey density, extent of area available for establishing territories and extent of human disturbance."*

Dr. Ramgaonkar, in his editorial, emphasized on Government's endeavour in relocating human settlement outside of tiger territory to provide more space to tigers. Providing more space is the only way to sustain high tiger density in reserves like Tadoba. According to him, around 750 families of five villages have voluntarily relocated since 2007, vacating 482 ha (4.82 km^2) of land within the tiger reserve.

As per the 17th December 2021 news report in the electronic edition of *Times of India*, *"In a major victory for tigers and people, the Supreme Court has paved the way for relocation of Rantalodhi village from inside the Tadoba-Andhari Tiger Reserve. After this relocation, Tadoba will get another 175.26 hectares (1.75 km²,), equivalent to 433 football fields of inviolate forests."*

Clearly, there is a silver lining in anthropocentric versus eco-centric conservation conflict, and environmental justice at times does go in favour of non-human life forms.

During my first visit to Tadoba, I must admit that I got carried away by the excitement of my first ever tiger sighting in the wild. Thus, I failed to notice the obvious loopholes in their tourism approach. One of them was the use of mobile phones by tourists, guides, and drivers to exchange the information about tiger movement.

I remember how hundreds of gypsies gathered in no time, upon receiving the sighting-information of Bhola and Maya, near waterhole number seventy-nine at Nawachila and in the thickets of Ayanbodi area, respectively. Communication through mobile phone made that possible, in the process creating havoc and disturbing the animals.

During my second visit, I saw significant change. The use of mobile phones in core and buffer zones was banned. However, banning of mobile phone usage was yet to be strictly enforced in buffer zone. Tourists, gypsy drivers and guides sometimes look for opportunity to secretly use mobile phones. Based on a newspaper report in the 28th March 2022 edition of *Lokmat Times*, the TATR administration has warned that entry gates from where such drivers and guides operate would be closed for a year in the event of violation of mobile phone ban rule.

Disciplined tourism and ecological consciousness among tourists (both photographers and non-photographers) may serve to establish TATR as the real "Tiger Capital of the World". Nevertheless, it would be interesting to compare how the other contender for this title fares in terms of conservation and tourism.

The premier wildlife photography tour operators of the country leave no stone unturned in using the tag line "Tiger Capital of the World" in selling their Bandhavgarh tour package. One such tour company mentioned the following on their website, *"At the heart of Wild India, Bandhavgarh National Park has come to be known as one of the best havens of our national animal. It is the tiger capital of the world. Here, the tiger is not merely a wild cat. It is an obsession that resonates in the mind of locals and visitors alike. It is the very spirit of the place, and it lives in every pore of the jungle and every heart that dwells around it."*

To be part of this "obsession" I headed for the other tiger capital of the world, again with the same Bangalore based tour company for yet another bootcamp.

"Kajari with cubs seen in Tala!"

"Dotty with four cubs seen today!"

"Dhabhadol female with 2 cubs spotted!"

"Mahaman male seen today!"

"Jamhol male today!"

"10 tigers were seen today in Magdi zone alone!"

It goes without saying that Kajari, Dotty, Dhabhadol, Mahaman, Jamhol etc. are tigers named by locals (read guides, gypsy drivers and photographers).

The above anecdotes were posted by the tour company on social media to entice the participants to enrol in such bootcamps.

What happened during my five-day bootcamp at Bandhavgarh one spring season? – *"It rained tigers"* true to what was posted by the tour company on social media.

In the dusty and sweltering 44°C days at Bandhavgarh, we went on four morning safaris, three afternoon safaris and one night safari. Morning safaris in Bandhavgarh are long, starting at 6 am and continuing till 11 am. Afternoon safaris start at 3:30 pm and end at 6:30 pm. Essentially, we stayed in the park for almost eight hours a day.

Over a span of four days, we spotted 22 different tigers, including adult males, adult females, subadults, and a few cubs.

During our first safari in Tala zone, we saw ten-year-old Spotty along with her two-year-old subadult cubs, numbering three.

The same afternoon, in Khitauli zone our gypsy driver Salim almost ran over two subadult cubs of Dabhadole. Rash driving within the forest was typical

Pseudo Ecotourism

of Salim. As we sped by in his gypsy, we noticed that the herbivores of the forest fled not merely because of the presence of predators, but also after spotting Salim's gypsy.

Several times, we saw herds of spotted dear and wild boar run for dear life as Salim's gypsy raced furiously on the bumpy forest path.

Coming back to the "rain of tigers" in Bandhavgarh, that afternoon on the same safari we saw an adult tigress Tara and an adult tiger Chhota Bheem.

Over the next four consecutive safaris in Magdi zone, we caught a glimpse of Dotty and spotted Dotty's four cubs, Dabhadole's male subadult cub and Jamhol, a subadult male cub of Dotty, from another litter.

On our last safari in Khitauli we captured the so-called *most desirable tiger shot*, known as the "head-on shot", of Tara.

In Bandhavgarh we saw tigers when we were least expecting to see them. Five tigers including adult male, female and three cubs were spotted in the glare of the gypsy's headlights during our night safari, in buffer zone four. I must add that this was the shortest safari of all.

That's not all. We saw tigers when were not even inside the park. On the second day as we exited from Magdi gate in the evening, and were heading towards buffer zone four for the night safari, an adult tigress, Chaabni, charged fiercely at a motor bike and subsequently, the roaring female crossed the road with three huge leaps. She was waiting at the edge of the road and the presence of too many vehicles on the National Highway annoyed her.

On the last day, as we concluded our trip and made our way out of Khitauli gate and took NH 45 towards Jabalpur airport, we had to come to a halt caused by a traffic jam right in front of the Khitauli gate.

Trucks, passenger bus, motor bikes, taxis, auto rickshaws and even a police van were part of the roadblock.

"Bajrang was seen!", people were shouting in ecstasy.

Bajrang, the adult male tiger was hiding in the bushes and his head, popping out from the bushes, was visible from the National Highway, connecting Bandhavgarh and Jabalpur.

To sum up, well literally, since my first Tadoba trip until right before my trip to Bandhavgarh, my total count of tiger sighting in the wild across six different tiger reserves (out of a total of twelve reserves visited) of India was 23. Post my five-day trip to Bandhavgarh the number spiked up to a stellar 45.

Now, I will leave it to you, my reader, to decide whether Bandhavgarh is truly the "Tiger Capital" as claimed by various tour operators and the tourism department; or if it is one of the "Disneylands" as expressed by Dr. Karanth.

Bandhavgarh arguably has the highest tiger density per square kilometre, with 124 tigers spread over in 1536 km^2, as per 2022 data. Years ago, the forest suffered a huge set back due to superstition and false sense of pride of the ruler of that land. It was the favourite hunting ground of Baghel rulers, who had a target of killing at least 109 tigers a year. As a result, Maharaja Gulab Singh shot 83 tigers in 1923 while Maharaja Martand Singh shot 100. Despite extensive hunting, the area continued to support a large tiger population thanks to the park's rich biodiversity and restoring capacity.

The wildlife map of this park is also changing dramatically. Earlier it was home to gaurs but all of them died after contracting contagious diseases from cattle. In 2012, as many as 50 gaurs were relocated to Bandhavgarh from Kanha National Park. In year 2020, there was news of wild elephant sighting in this forest. Apparently, due to food shortage, a herd of 38 elephants entered the park from Chhattisgarh and began breeding.

I heard this story when I made a short visit to the park one monsoon for a jungle survival training. During my recent visit in summer, we did see a few wild elephants in the park. In fact, during our night safari, we saw a group of local tribal people on the highway going through the forest, with fire torch and stick in their hands. They were there to chase off an elephant which was apparently sighted near a village.

Later we saw a terrified elephant and her cub standing in the cover of trees on the side of the road.

Elephant intrusion in Bandhavgarh perhaps created an additional competition for Bengal Tigers in the race for space in this forest with high tiger density.

In January 2021, there was a news article published in the online version of *Times of India*, about an apparent cannibalization of a male tiger in Bandhavgarh. The carcass of a one-year-old cub, almost severed in two, was found in Manpur forest area of the tiger reserve. Male tigers kill cubs, which are not their own lineage. But cannibalization is unheard of.

There was another equally weird but a diametrically opposite story that we heard on our visit.

In the Jamhol waterbody area of Magdi zone, we regularly found Dotty's four female cubs. They were born to Dotty and the dominant male of the area, Mahaman. Dotty however was mother to another male cub from her previous litter, named Jamhol male. This offspring of another male tiger is now a subadult. Now to the weird part of the story. All seven of them live together. Not just that, on several occasions the Jamhol male was found "babysitting" his "half-sisters" when both Dotty and Mahaman were out hunting or attending to other matters.

Jamhol male never tried to attack Dotty's four cubs, in fact the cubs appeared to have bonded with him. Most astonishingly, Mahaman did not kill or drive away Jamhol male from his area, despite not being his biological father. Apparently, Mahaman did attack him a few times, but on each occasion Jamhol male submitted to him.

Are the tigers of Bandhavgarh learning key lessons in "importance of family life" from the elephant intruders? Certainly not.

Can this change in behaviour be attributed to the pressure of high tiger density in the park? Be it Cannibalism or Family living – both are atypical of tigers.

Capitalism has turned the real consumer with a true need for a necessary commodity into a "ready to spend a fortune" passive and immobilized consumer, spell bound by the illusion of an unnecessary commodity. At the beginning of this book, I talked about the emergence of another commodity called neo-liberal sustainability to counter the effect of radical environmentalism.

David Nelson and Linley Tulloch of University of Waikato, in their article titled, *"The Neo liberalization of Sustainability"* state, *"As sustainability's 'self-declared champion', neoliberalism 'defends itself against critique'. As an outcome, not only is the radical ecological movement effectively marginalised, but more environmentalists are satisfied and relieved that 'something is being done' because sustainability is now a mainstream project."*

Marginal and oppositional "radical environmentalism" which was once positioned against capitalism has now moved from the margins to the centre, and the struggle to save the environment then, becomes very straightforward, non-ideological activity. With great ease, individual citizens perceived this struggle to be all about meeting targets, changing attitudes and being responsible consumers. The effect of development over ecosystems, which was an ideological debate, appeared to be a non-issue.

Once this hegemony called neo-liberal sustainability takes over the hearts and minds of urban affluents, whose desire for fame and glory continues unabated, commodity fetishism completes the cycle.

Commodity fetishism did not just delude consumers about the magical qualities of neo-liberal sustainability as the only means to save the environment, it also offered ecotourism and wildlife photography as alternate means of being part of the environmental movement. Commodity fetishism then produced another standardized, exchangeable commodity called The Bengal Tiger as part of the ecotourism/wildlife photography commodity, as a means of achieving fame and glory for the urban affluents.

The intersection of these three commodities (neoliberal sustainability, ecotourism/wildlife photography and Bengal Tigers) creates the dominance of a single species in subcontinental forests, ecotourism activities, wildlife enthusiasm and photography.

This hegemony has not just transformed ecotourism and wildlife photography into tiger-tourism and tiger photography respectively, it has transformed the whole wildlife enthusiasm into a mere tiger enthusiasm.

Besides this hegemony is not consistent and constant across all tiger reserves. Through my ecotourism as well as tiger-tourism activities I bear witness that this hegemony is biased towards a few tiger reserves of this subcontinent.

As discussed earlier, commodity fetishism is not just about material or real use value of the commodity, but it is also a derivative of social evaluation of the commodity. Similarly, Bengal Tiger in this subcontinent, especially in India, among tiger tourists and tiger photographers, is perceived not just as an apex predator of the forest. To them, tiger is an emotion. The level of this emotion often defines the status of various tiger reserves in India.

Eminent tiger scientist Dr. K. Ullas Karanth in an interview published on 19th February 2023 in the electronic version of *The New Indian Express*, eloquently stated, *"Science, not emotions, is needed in managing wildlife"*.

In the interview, Dr. Karanth mentions that only 4% of the land in India is reserved for wildlife and in his view, India can potentially harbour 10,000 to 15,000 wild tigers. He also mentioned, *"We have only 3,000, but we cannot increase tiger numbers without expanding more protected areas."*

Therefore, at some point perhaps, there is a need to anthropogenically control the tiger population. In a media report dated 19th January 2023, by *The New Indian Express*, noted Indian ecologist Madhav Gadgil, the chairman of the *Western Ghats Ecology Expert Panel*, favoured the idea of culling of the big cats in Wayanad and suggested there should be licensed hunting outside India's national parks.

Although Dr. Karanth was not supportive of such drastic measures, but he opined that the misplaced sentiment and misguided kindness of urban animal lovers need to be altered. *"Wildlife conservation is very different from animal rights or loving individual animals"*, said Dr. Karanth.

Dr. Karanth further elaborated in this interview, published on 19th February 2023, *"Tiger population has increased over time because we have protected the prey base well in a few areas. In fact, there is one thing that has gone out of hand."* In Karanth's opinion, all forests have a natural tiger density and a prey density. When Project Tiger started, the goal was to maintain what is natural for that area. But over time, excessive zeal, and the desire to spend money, has led to problems over excessive 'management'. For example, lack of water holes is a natural stress that regulates prey populations periodically. When there is a lack of water in dry year cycles, there is greater mortality of prey species. The natural prey density is around 20-30 deer sized animals per square kilometre, but their number in these overmanaged reserves is 3-4 times higher.

He further mentioned, *"This leads to a rise in population of two common species, spotted deer, and wild pigs.* **A supermarket for tigers has been created.** *Normally, a tigress will be able to bring up 1-2 cubs in a litter of 3-4. But with this kind of super-abundance of prey, we are repeatedly seeing 3-4 cubs reaching adulthood.* **The density of tigers, which should be 5-6 per 100 sq km, is now 15-20 in some overmanaged reserves.***"*

There is another interesting aspect of this conservation conundrum. The tiger tour operators, tiger tourists and tiger photographers alike, are always vocal in claiming their contribution to tiger conservation.

However, if we move further to the east of Central Indian tiger landscapes, we hardly see these claimants.

One summer afternoon, at around 12:40 pm, after a drive of five hours from the Hyderabad airport, I arrived at India's largest tiger reserve, Nagarjuna Sagar Srisailam tiger reserve of Andhra Pradesh state. It was my very first visit to the Eastern Ghats. In the peak summer of India, the afternoon temperature was around 40°C.

As per my ecotourism package booked in Nallamala Jungle Camp Bairluty, run by Andhra Pradesh Forest Department, a gypsy safari to the core area of the tiger reserve was scheduled that afternoon. But apparently a Panchayat (village administrative unit) road construction related work became a hindrance to enter the forest. Therefore, the safari was cancelled, and the manager of the camp, Ismail, arranged an alternative bushwalk near the forest department base camp, inside the plantation forest of the buffer zone.

The walk, scheduled to start at 4:30 pm, after repeated follow ups, started well after 5 pm, with my gypsy driver, Malik. Most of the urban ecotourists and wildlife photographers would not tolerate such "ecotourism unprofessionalism" in other popular tiger tourism destinations where they generally claim their contribution to tiger conservation.

The bushwalk started, and I realized that I had underestimated the ecotourism potential and biodiversity of this forest. I also undermined Malik's knowledge of local flora and fauna.

Within fifteen minutes, he pointed out different bird species. The most astonishing sighting was Indian pitta. I had never seen Indian pitta from such proximity and for such a long time.

I regretted not carrying my camera to the walk. I did have my binoculars with me.

In the seventy to ninety minutes' walk, we saw birds like black napped monarch, oriental magpie robin, white breasted kingfisher, white-rumped shama, Indian pitta, rose ringed parakeet, black drongo, tree pipit, red vented bulbul, orange headed thrush, common tailor bird and a male rufus morph of Indian paradise flycatcher. Within the confines of the camp, we saw flocks of green imperial pigeon and brown headed barbet. A giant squirrel hung upside down from the branch of a teak tree. The camp was also frequented by various troops of bonnet macaque.

Next morning, it was finally time for the much awaited "tiger safari" in the core area of an Eastern Ghats tiger reserve. Malik was the driver. We started at 6:30 am and continued until 8:30 am. We saw plenty of birds such as jungle babbler, spotted dove, rufus treepie, Indian pea fowl, red jungle fowl, Jerdon's leafbird, and Indian cuckoo shrike. In all twenty-two birds were spotted over two days. While exiting the forest, we saw a spotted deer crossing the forest path. Otherwise, we did not see many herbivores.

From the watchtower of Pangidi West beat, in the faraway forest of Nagarjuna Sagar, we saw a yellow shape with black stripes, popping out from the bushes. For about fifteen minutes we watched the motionless shape through the binoculars. Even through binoculars the shape was so small and indistinguishable from its surroundings, that it was difficult to infer what it was.

"It looks like a tiger!", Malik exclaimed after observing through my binoculars for a few minutes.

After a while, the shape shrank, becoming even smaller. As if it was sitting on its front legs earlier, but later lay down completely.

I had my 70-300 mm Nikkor lens mounted on D500 Nikon camera. But nothing conclusive could be captured in those gears.

The question, then, remained unanswered. Was this my first tiger sighting in Eastern Ghats, and in the largest tiger reserve of India?

The reserve spreads over five districts - Nandyal, Prakasam, Palnadu, Nalgonda and Mahabub Nagar. The total area of the tiger reserve is 3,728 km^2. The core area of this reserve is 1,200 km^2. The tiger count in the reserve as per the census of 2022 was 75. Which means around 49 km^2 per tiger, or roughly two tigers per 100 km^2. This was significantly less than Dr. Karath's recommendation of healthy tiger density of 5-6 tigers per 100 sq. km, as mentioned in his interview.

For tiger tourists, tiger tour operators and tiger photographers, chasing tiger in this forest would be like finding a needle in a haystack. Precisely why they do not visit the park to claim their "contribution to tiger conservation".

Nagarjuna Sagar is endowed with a rich floral diversity comprising of trees, shrubs, herbs, and climbers. The faunal diversity documented here is also phenomenal which includes various species of mammals, birds, reptiles, amphibians, fishes, butterflies, moths, beetles, dragonflies and damselflies. Despite having tremendous potential, ecotourism has not flourished at the pace it should have as the possibility of tiger sighting is very bleak.

"A railway track passes close to the Gundlabrahmeswaram (GBM) Wildlife Sanctuary (part of this reserve) which enables timber mafia to indulge in the illegal wood collection. There are around 15 villages inside the core area of reserve with a high dependency on this reserve for fodder, fuelwood, and bamboo. Illegal fishing in the backwaters of the multipurpose dam on river Krishna is a concern," experts opined in a report, as published in a news report on 5th August 2019 in the online version of *The Times of India*.

These hindrances to tiger conservation are far beyond the reach of tiger tourists, tiger tour operators and tiger photographers' in providing any resolution.

In a separate interview published in the electronic edition of *Frontline*, on 4th May 2023, Dr. Karanth, answered the question related to wildlife tourism industry's claims in helping save the tiger. Dr. Karanth said, *"The tourism industry usually arrives on the scene after a tiger population has recovered following decades of hard work by forest officials and conservationists."*

However, he also substantiates, *"In some cases, a few thoughtful tourism operators have subsequently assisted local people and small enterprises to prosper alongside them. But this is far from enough."*

A 10th April 2023 article written by U Sudhakar Reddy in the online version of The *Times of India*, narrated such involvement of local people and their economic prosperity through tiger conservation.

This tiger conservation story was from Amrabad tiger reserve of Telangana state, the second largest tiger reserve of India, situated just adjacent to Nagarjuna Sagar Srisailam tiger reserve.

As per the article, Amrabad Forest divisional officer, Rohit Gopidi explains, *"Improvement in protection strategy through deployment of Chenchu tribals and upscaling infrastructure by procurement of boats and vehicles helped us reduction in number of poaching cases, tackle forest fires and reduce illegal fishing."*

The forest department also focused on health outcomes of tribes through a health clinic to build trust with local tribes. *"Improving the protection strategy through staff, infusion of technology and infrastructure, along with other community-building activities helped enhance trust with local communities, leading to more cooperation,"* said Gopidi.

The health clinic built within Munnanur jungle resort of the tiger reserve, with support from Apollo Hospitals is among the first things I noticed, when I visited the tiger reserve. The interesting aspect of visiting this tiger reserve was meeting a couple who ran a resort in the buffer zone of Amrabad.

Akhil and his wife Shweta, a Telugu speaking couple in their early 40s, have dedicated their entire life in forest conservation and building sustainability awareness among the local Chenchu tribe. For the last

23 years they have been associated with various forests of India in conservation work. Since 2022 they have been working with Amrabad forest division of Telangana Forest Department. Akhil and Shweta took a conscious decision to not have kids as their contribution for sustainable living.

I explored the forest twice, in two different ranges. One evening, in the three hours long safari in the core area of Amrabad, we spotted seventeen species of birds including Indian pitta, coppersmith barbet, jungle owlet and streak throated woodpecker among others. We saw four species of herbivores - spotted deer, sambar, nilgai and wild boar.

The following day, early in the morning, we went on a moderate trek of three hours in the Amrabad range of the forest. We trekked up to the highest point of the tiger reserve from where the city of Hyderabad was visible. During the trek Shweta and Akhil enlightened me about various floral diversity of Amrabad and their usage in the daily life of the Chechnu tribe.

Akhil and Shweta were very passionate about nature and forest conservation. During the trek we saw about eleven other species of birds, including common iora, white browed bulbul, plum-headed parakeet, oriental honey buzzard and a suspected saheen falcon.

In my two-day long trip in the Amrabad tiger reserve, I saw one burrowing frog and four types of reptiles, including a spectacled cobra, rescued by Akhil from the driver's room. The other reptiles we spotted included Jerdon's snake eye, fan tailed lizard and couple of rock agama.

Although I did not see any, Akhil and Shweta told me about frequent tiger, leopard, and sloth bear sightings. On our trek we saw fresh scuts of sloth bear and palm civet. Akhil mentioned that several times he had spotted the elusive rusty spotted cat in the fringe area of the forest.

Like Nagarjuna Sagar, the floral and faunal wealth of Amrabad is equally diverse. Yet Amrabad is one of the low-profile tiger-reserves of the country. There are around 20 tigers as per the 2022 census data in one of the largest tiger reserves in India that extends about 2611.4 Km^2 over Nagarkurnool and Nalgonda districts of Telangana State. This implies, there is 130 km^2 of forest available for each tiger.

How, then, can tiger tour operators establish their business in this tiger reserve?

Being so low-profile, creates a backlash on the conservation process. The National Highway (NH-765) passes through the lush green forest of Amramad, taking pilgrims from Hyderabad to Srisailam. Akhil told me there were several attempts in recent times to re-carpet and make it a four-lane highway. This would cause over speeding of vehicles, which in turn would increase the number of animals killed in road accidents. According to Akhil, even now on an average 40 such road kills of various animals are reported every month.

Pseudo Ecotourism

In addition, there was a proposal for uranium exploration on 83 km² area which falls under Amrabad and Nudigal Reserved Forests of the 'core area' of the tiger reserve.

Mineral exploration or highway construction could not be thought of in Tadoba, Bandhavgarh or Ranthambore. Urban tiger lovers would create havoc against any such proposal. But Nagarjuna Sagar and Amrabad only has the voice of forest dwellers, ground worker conservationists and well-meaning politicians.

Clearly fetishism of any of the three commodities mentioned earlier – neo-liberal sustainability, ecotourism, and Bengal Tiger – would cast its spell on fame hungry consumers, only if there is assurance of return on investment. As this assurance varies from reserve to reserve, so does the segregation of tiger reserves into elite and ordinary class.

The merchants of this commodity, called tiger tourism, like most of their counterparts of other commodities, are prepared to go to any length to ensure their return on investment for the commodity fetishism struck tiger tourists and tiger photographers.

American political theorist and philosopher Jane Bennett, once said in her article titled *Commodity Fetishism and Commodity Enchantment*, "*Consistent with Marx's critique of commodification is the environmentalist position that the intensive and excessive consumption typical of middle class is ecologically disastrous....such consumption practices are indeed part of a system that tolerates a deplorable level of economic inequality....they promote greed and, eventually, military adventurism among administrations;*"

In case of tiger tourism, if not the "military adventurism", the unethical practices are shamelessly accepted or tolerated. During my Bandhavgarh photography bootcamp, one morning we did not get a single tiger shot in the first hour of our safari. This was not considered "Bandhavgarh standard" by our mentor cum tour operator and a few fellow participants. To reiterate, it was the bootcamp where we saw 22 different tigers over five days.

The disappointment of not meeting the Bandhavgarh standard was promptly communicated to our local guide and driver. As a result, our influential local guide (who was apparently also a local village level political leader) had a talk with the forest departments' mahout. Once their conversation was over, our photography mentor cum tour operator, without any hesitation told us he was going to give some extra money to the mahout, and in return he would create some "favourable situations" for us to shoot tigers.

I was not sure about other participants, but I did not quite understand the real meaning of "favourable situation". However, I realized that everybody was in agreement with the arrangement.

After a few minutes we were asked to wait near a huge thicket, where apparently a subadult male tiger was hiding. In a few minutes, the mahout appeared from a distance on the back of a forest department's elephant.

The picture was clear to me by then. For the next thirty minutes the elephant charged towards the thicket, and running in and out was a helpless, confused, and traumatized subadult male tiger.

As per *Section 9* of *The Wildlife Protection Act, 1972 (of India)*, hunting of wildlife (the species specified in any of the four schedules of the Act) is prohibited unless permitted by Chief Wildlife Warden for any specific purposes. These specific purposes are also mentioned in the Act. Wildlife tourism and photography are of course not listed as specified purposes.

Now, the tiger tour operators and tiger photographers may well argue that chasing of the tiger by an elephant, was clearly not with an intention to hunt the animal.

However, it does not matter how you and I define the word "hunting". All that matter is how law defines it.

The *Section 2* of the Act clarifies this explicitly. As per the act the word *"hunting"* should be used *with its grammatical variations and cognate expressions, includes – capturing,* **coursing***, snaring, trapping,* **driving,** *or baiting any wild or captive animal and every attempt to do so.*

I am ashamed that, that summer morning in the forest of Bandhavgarh, all seven of us (three participants, our mentor, guide, driver, and the mahout) committed something grossly unethical, to satisfy our commodity fetishism.

Additionally, during the incident our mentor warned us several times to keep the mahout and his elephant out of our camera range.

CHAPTER EIGHT: The Under(-Rated-) Story!

In Buddhadeb Guha's novel *"Madhukari"* (The Honey Gatherer), the protagonist Prithu was attracted to an uneducated, bohemian - singer, dancer, sex worker, named Bijli, who lived her life at her own will. A free bird, not controlled by anybody. She slept with multiple men to make her living, but never surrendered her freedom permanently to a single man called husband.

Prithu believed she had all the freedom in the world. The freedom that he had lost to his legally married wife, Rusha. In the novel, he ends up in the hospital with amputated legs due to a bullet injury caused by a notorious dacoit, Maganlal, while attempting to save Bijli's life. Risking his own life for a sex worker, was beyond imagination to a foreign-returned affluent engineer like Prithu. He was left contemplating whether confronting Maganlal was an act of bravery or stupidity.

Prithu was confused because his materialistic lifestyle taught him not to sacrifice the comfort he enjoyed for any reason. He realized that Bijli would never sacrifice her freedom to embrace comfort. This made him envious of her. His attraction to her was but the expression of envy. As he lay confined to his solitary hospital bed, he felt dejected and declared that, *"Freedom is not for the so called educated and modern, civilized people".* He felt helpless as he found himself caged in comfort.

In the same novel, Guha introduced another character - a bohemian forest dweller, Baiga, who lost his village to nature's fury. Baiga held Prithu in high esteem. But at the same time, he was also sympathetic towards Prithu. Baiga wondered that when nature had provided abundantly to allow for survival of all life forms, then why was it that only the human chased after comfort at the expense of peace.

Prithu failed to achieve the freedom he desires, as he failed to sacrifice his materialistic comfort. In a desperate attempt to achieve fame he confronted dacoit Maganlal and in the process became crippled, and subsequently, regretting his act of breaching his comfort.

Both commoditization and neo-liberal sustainability; and their resultant force – ecotourism, *aka* tiger tourism, has created many victims in the form of desperate tiger tourists and tiger photographers. They are fame hungry but not ready to give up comfort. In the event that they do give up their comfort, they, like Prithu, go on to regret it.

Vedavyasa, my childhood friend, is one such Prithu. He hated the comfort provided by his married and professional life, but did not have the courage to leave. He tried to leave his marriage when he found a girlfriend. But eventually that turned out to be transactional as well. Comfort in which love, sex, emotional and material support are assured, in exchange for love, sex, emotional and material support. He also parked his profession aside to make time for nature exploration and wildlife photography. He knew that his profession would never fulfil him, and thus he needed to continue his wildlife photography, to prevent him from losing his mind. However, soon he realized that he needed his profession to support his hobby. He chose to give up the quest for his version of freedom and settled for another transactional relationship - profession vis a vis hobby.

The market of commodity and neo-liberal sustainability not just understands this various comfort based transactional relationships in human life, but essentially thrives on it. Therefore, this market engages in massive propaganda to project comfort as an essential human need.

During my wildlife photography in various tiger reserves, I discovered how this comfort blended seamlessly with commodity fetishism. The business of tiger tourism and tiger photography are nothing but business of comfort.

However, it is very difficult to recognize this blending of comfort and commodity fetishism unless you get out of this comfort zone or at the very least make an honest attempt to do so. You may not spontaneously be able to make that first attempt, unless you are in a situation which leaves you no choice. The challenge to my comfort zone came in the form of the Indian monsoon.

Under a sky veiled in tar-black, colossal clouds drift, initiating a gentle tapping upon lush green canopies, gradually evolving into a soothing pitter-patter. Concealed puddles within the undergrowth commence a soft plinking as the rain intensifies, while a silvery-white curtain of rain traverses over the evergreen trees, its droplets drumming against the canopies. Eventually, the clamour diminishes, and the drops transform into a melodic chime, accompanied by the earthly scent of moist soil and the harmonious orchestra of cicada, crickets and frogs. The full impact of the protection offered by Bengal Tigers to Mother Nature remains incompletely understood unless explored within the rainforest. And the true beauty of the rainforest cannot be fully appreciated without venturing into its' depths on a monsoon night. Bengal Tiger maybe the apex predator, ardent protector, and supreme hunter in the subcontinental forest, and he plays a pivotal role in carrying on the cycle of life in his kingdom, which in turn has earned him the status of demigod.

The splendour of a monsoon-night in his forest rests on some relatively ignored and misunderstood creatures living in the darkness of the forest under growths.

Pseudo Ecotourism

After several years of intense tiger-centric exploration, I had to shift my attention from our demigod to these ignored creatures of his kingdom. The shift, though, did not happen naturally. It was evident that Vedavyasa was close to giving up his pursuit of dedicated nature exploration, I was thus left with just myself. That was only one part of the reason. This shift was equally an outcome of the situation created by the Bangladesh Train incident wherein I lost my upgraded version of DSLR and telephoto lens. I was now left with a second-hand Nikon D3100, and a macro enabled Sigma 70-300 mm lens.

Lack of a companion and advanced photography gears forced me to rethink the ignored non-human life forms.

My first venture of a night-walk in the rainforest during monsoon, was with a Bangalore based organization, *Darter Photography,* in the rainforest of Agumbe. I was part of a professional wildlife photography group on a tour organized by a tour company which was not just a tiger-tour company but also has special focus on undergrowth and nocturnal life forms.

Herping is the act of searching for amphibians or reptiles. The term, often used by professional and amateur herpetologists, comes from the word "herp", which comes from the same Greek root as herpetology (herpet- meanis "creeping"). Herping was another key agenda of this exploration; therefore, I joined mentor M.V. Shreeram, and five other

Bangalore based wildlife photographers. Herpetologist Gowri Shankar was the host of this exploration team. We stayed in his research camp at *Kalinga Centre for Rainforest Ecology* (KCRE) in Guddekere, located at Agumbe, in the midst of Agumbe Reserved Forest and Someshwara Wildlife Sanctuary.

After an overnight bus ride from Bangalore, I reached Guddekere just before 7 o'clock in the morning of an early monsoon season. Shreeram and other fellow explorers reached ten-fifteen minutes before me, by another bus and awaited my arrival at the bus stand. The eight of us and Gowri's Man Friday and snake rescuer Prashanth, got into two cars and headed towards camp. It was a twenty-minute ride through narrow and raw forest path of Someshwara Wildlife Sanctuary. The five-acre field site (camp) is nestled in the heart of the rainforests of Agumbe.

Shreeram did not want to waste any time. Immediately after breakfast and a briefing about camp and ground rules, we started our exploration in the nearby area, towards the southwest. A shallow and greenish pond created by rainwater was our first stop, where we observed few species of frogs - golden frogs, cricket frogs and skittering frogs, different types of damselflies and dragonflies. We slowly advanced through the dense forest, with multiple halts to take photographs, and to understand the biodiversity of the rain forest. Shreeram was continuously issuing instructions, asking us to try different angles and composition, making us lie down in mud and on bushes, and intermittently checking our shots. In the very first interaction with him during exploration, I realized that he was a passionate teacher and an ardent wildlife enthusiast. He hand held each of us and taught us both photography and rainforest ecology.

It was my very first experience in some serious macro-photography (using macro-enabled lens to capture larger than the life size pictures of herpetofauna), the first time I engaged in wildlife photography out of the comfort zone of a safari gypsy or boat. I must admit Periyar was a hard trek as well. Yes, it was. But it did not involve any intense photography of insects and amphibians which involved frequent lying down on mud or stepping into marshy land. Challenges at Periyar were anchored in terrain and weather.

Those days I was regularly training for marathon and mixed martial arts, and so was at the top of my fitness level. But repeated lying down on mud to capture "eye-level" shots of frogs and insects and then again standing up to hike through uneven, steep, muddy, and not so explored forest path, and then again, a sudden squat in front of a lower branch of a tree to shoot a rubber fly, was making me tired and dehydrated. Along with the other firsts, I also realized what it meant to leave my comfort zone to achieve genuine fame in the field of ecotourism/wildlife photography.

Since Vedavyasa hung his boots, I was looking for a passionate and knowledgeable mentor. M.V. Shreeram stepped into the role. I have since worked with him in numerous nature explorations in various forests of this subcontinent.

Shreeram had an incredible pair of keen eyes in spotting amphibians and insects in the dense rainforest of Agumbe. As days progressed, we encountered numerous stunning examples of this. Once he instructed us about the species he spotted and how to shoot it, he would advance further to check for other species that were out there, while we busied ourselves in applying his lessons.

On one such occasion, when we were busy with a golden frog, we heard Shreeram shout from afar – *"Pit Viper!"*

We rushed towards the source of shout; and there on the huge trunk of a Punnaga tree, in the shade of its broad and lined leaves, lay a Malabar pit viper - completely immobile, perhaps resting and preparing for its nocturnal activity. We spent almost thirty to forty-five minutes observing and capturing the species. The intensity of light was insufficient to take any clear images though. Besides, it was 12:45 pm, and we were hungry and tired after the overnight bus journey. We decided to head for lunch, and return later, perhaps at night, with torch and tripod, when chances of seeing it active would be higher.

The following day after our exploration in the morning, followed by a break for lunch, we walked uphill within the campsite. Shreeram was a little ahead of us, and then, as before, we heard him shout. This time it was a brown vine snake. Shreeram was highly excited, as apparently the species was spotted in Agumbe after ten years. It was quite a rare sight in the wild. We observed it moving from one branch to another and eventually disappearing into one of the upper branches of a tree. Brown vine snake is a diurnal and arboreal species, which is active throughout the day at low to moderate heights. Its colour may vary from grey to brown with a yellow underside. Spotting the well camouflaged brown vine snake among the tree branches is not an easy task. Another brilliant work of spotting by Shreeram.

After lunch, we went on a short walk around the campsite, this time towards the northeast. We spotted few forest calottes, grasshoppers and saw a huge giant squirrel jumping from one branch to another atop a tree. However, the biggest moment of the day was yet to come. After a nice shower, as I was resting in my tent and considering reading about vine snakes in J. C. Daniel's *The Book of Indian Reptiles and Amphibians (published by Bombay Natural History Society)*, I heard fellow photographer Kaustubh, call for me. I stepped out of my tent. He mentioned that there was a call for a snake rescue from a house from the local village of Sringeri, thirty kilometres from the campsite. We were to accompany Gowri and Prashanth on the rescue mission. We started around 7:30 pm, and after a drive of forty-five minutes on the State Highway, we arrived at the house. A few local people and a forest department representative had gathered around.

Gowri cleared the site and asked people to stay away from the window and door. As a first response to such a situation, before reaching the rescue site, he generally asks people to close the door and window of the house where the snake is spotted. Thus, when we reached, we found all windows and doors of the house closed. Reportedly, the snake entered the house at around 4:30 pm, and was sleeping quietly under the bed. Gowri entered the said bedroom with two snake-catching hooks. The rest of us waited outside in anxious anticipation. A couple of minutes passed with no sight of him or the snake.

There was complete silence among the spectators gathered around the house.

And suddenly we heard *hisssssss...*

Gauri emerged from the bedroom, walking backwards with his extended right hand holding the bottom of the snake catching hook. His left had was holding the second hook.

He dragged the snake out through the door into the open ground in front of the house. It was dangling from the other end of the hook, from its "U" shaped bend.

It was an eight feet long young king cobra, with a raised hood, making spine chilling hissing sounds in its defence.

Gowri dropped the second hook on ground and caught the tail of the dangling king cobra with his left hand. He tried to put it inside the catching bag, fitted with pieces of PVC pipes, directing the snake with the hook towards the bag. The bag was kept ready, before he started his rescue operation. In the first attempt, the snake refused to be bagged and attacked Gowri. However, an expert snake rescuer, Gowri managed to put it inside. The entire rescue operation took less than five minutes. The next task was to release the snake, and as per protocol, it had to be released away from the village, but within 5 km^2 area from where it was rescued. This ensures it remained in its natural area of movement. We returned to the campsite at around 9:30 pm. I was pleasantly exhausted after the activities through the day. The rainforest of Agumbe had in a single day, enriched my knowledge and experience manifold.

Agumbe and, particularly the herping experience with Shreeram and other photographers, taught me the importance of humility when living in nature with non-human life forms. The gypsy safaris somehow, failed to be as effective.

Prior to this trip, my nature explorations and wildlife photography trips were designed to subscribe to a certain elitist attitude. It wouldn't be incorrect to say that both Vedavyasa and I, did so intentionally as both of us sought glory outside our professional arena.

However, working among other photographers, I learnt what it meant to be grounded in nature, literally, as I lay down on the forest floor for better images of reptiles, amphibians, and insects. The shots required going down to their eye level, and this implied relinquishing your arrogance. This brought on a sense of harmony and peace, and I slowly let go of my pride of elitism, and felt lighter and more relaxed. Although I was proven to be a novice in this hobby, strangely I didn't feel inadequate, but rather a sense of awe and wonder at the intricacy of the natural world, and a deep appreciation for the beauty and complexity of life.

Following morning a kukri snake decided to pay us a surprise visit. It is an active little snake, mainly diurnal and seen most often during the rainy season. When alarmed, it inflates its body to a remarkable degree. Some specimens also flatten the posterior part of the head, making the head more apparent than when its normal. After spending some time with this little reptile, we headed to the spot where we had seen the brown vine snake the previous afternoon. This time we spotted a green vine snake, besides a few treehoppers and forest calottes. The snake was nicely camouflaged among green tree twigs and leaves. As always, Shreeram was the first to spot it, and challenged us to spot it to earn our breakfast. Surprisingly, I was the first in the group to succeed. Later, in a herping workshop at Bangalore, Gowri mentioned that green vine snake is the only species of snake which has a "binocular" vision like us – humans.

My new ecological – photographic relationship with *Darter Photography* continued as I joined Shreeram, again, for another rainforest biodiversity exploration in Western Ghats.

The destination was Chorla Ghat, a nature destination located at the intersection of the borders of Goa, Karnataka, and Maharashtra. The Chorla Ghat forests are part of the Mhadei Bio region. This area is home to tigers, leopards, gaur, spotted deer, sloth bear, critically endangered bats and scores of other species, and serves as a crucial corridor between the Bhimgad Wildlife Sanctuary and its reserve forests, and the Mhadei Wildlife sanctuary of Goa. The sanctuary is an area of high biodiversity and is the potential 55th tiger reserve of India under Project Tiger, owing to the presence of resident Bengal Tigers.

The monsoon season was at its peak in the Western Ghats. The sky was gloomy, and the land vibrant. The ponds and waterfalls were in full splendour, flowing vividly through the forests and infusing life into entire ecosystem. The monsoon in India truly gifts us with some of the most breathtaking natural landscapes. Rivers rush with full vigour, their currents painting a picture of wild vitality. The mountains, long dormant, awaken from their slumber, their peaks adorned with fresh greenery and mist. The entire panorama of Chorla Ghat stood testament to the transformative power of monsoon.

It was a celebration of wildlife and wild lands, when I reached at Swapnagandha resort of Chorla Ghat, with mentor Shreeram and seven fellow wildlife photographers. We were the guests of eminent herpetologist of Goa, Nirmal Kulkarni, for three days. In the span of three days, we spotted and identified around eight different types of frogs including endemic Malabar gliding frogs and Fejervarya; we saw six different types of snakes including venomous saw scaled viper, Malabar pit viper (two different morphs), non-venomous Travancore wolf snake, montane trinket snake, eight different individuals of green vine snake and one juvenile python. The python was rescued by Nirmal from one of the cottages and eventually released in a nearby area.

The Malabar gliding frogs naturally like humid surroundings but do not tolerate water. On our second night, a group of three frogs, sitting on bamboo shoots, filled the air with their calls. Foam nests were attached to vegetation some meters above a water body. The following day just before dusk, we saw two Malabar gliding frogs resting on the same tree nearby. It was raining intermittently, and the forest was alive with the song of cicadas. During daytime the frogs usually rest on leaves with their legs gathered and body flattened, the forefeet folded underneath their body, and pupils contracted to tiny slits. This posture coupled with their green leaf colour rendered them almost invisible among the leaves of Malabar black mouth trees. Nirmal's and Shreeram's sharp vision helped us in locating them, and Nirmal was, of course, aware of a few precise locations of their nests.

Besides amphibians and snakes, we also recognized around eight different species of lizards, including endemic Prashad's gecko and Goan day gecko; and seventeen different species of insects and aquatic creatures. The species we encountered were primarily nocturnal, as exploring during the night was a key focus of our trip. We spent two nights in the dense rainforest, where our collective nocturnal explorations, amidst heavy downpours, totalled more than eight hours.

Western Ghats rainforest is home to different kinds of insects, arthropod, spiders, bugs and flying insects. The species we most spotted were tiger centipede, pill bug, forest crab, toe biter, millipede, cicada, rock crabs, dark mantis and fishing spider among others. Some of these small but dangerous species have the ability to kill large mammals using their sharp sting, bite and venom.

Before my Agumbe and Chorla trips, making list of birds and mammals used to give me a sense of achievement. As I made a similar list of herpetofauna from Agumbe and Chorla explorations, I felt the same sense of achievement.

On one of our night walks, we sighted the spot where a male Bengal Tiger was photographed in a camera trap. This helped us conclude that Mhadei Wildlife Sanctuary was certainly a worthy claimant for the status of tiger reserve, and as an important tiger corridor in Western Ghats. Drivers of trucks plying along the route said that tiger sighting was common and that they spotted the big cat at least twice or thrice in a fortnight. In fact, it is worth mentioning that prior to the onset of monsoon in 2016, the images of two tigers and around four cubs were captured from the area. This prompted the Maharashtra government to make plans to convert the region around the water reservoir into a wildlife sanctuary. This has sparked a glimmer of hope for the development of the area as a habitat and corridor, by providing long-term conservation of the Western Ghats region.

The prospect of a potential encounter with a Bengal Tiger in the pitch-dark monsoon-drenched thickets of Chorla filled me with a sense of unease. How do you feel when you walk through a forest path knowing there is a tiger hiding somewhere and watching you silently? That night in Chorla, I may have let my imagination run wild, influenced by the mystic darkness of monsoon. However, I was reminded of an incident I experienced one winter morning bushwalking within a core forest of Kerala.

I trekked for a couple of hours in Parambikulam Tiger Reserve of Kerala, with a local tribal guide. In the two hours, we could spot and identify around nineteen different bird species, including Malabar whistling thrush, Malabar starling, vernal hanging parrot, Asian fairy blue bird, lesser flame back woodpecker and one of the flagship birds of Kerala, Malabar trogon. We saw seven different species of mammals including Nilgiri langur, Western Ghats palm squirrel, spotted, sambar and barking deer, wild boar and gaur.

Throughout the trail, there was evidence of tracks and signs of tiger, elephant, gaur and sloth bear. The most spine-chilling discovery, though, was that of a freshly killed sambar, assumed to have been hunted down by a tiger. There was no smell of rotten flesh, nor a single fly around the dead sambar - both indicative of the freshness of the kill. As we drew nearer, we saw blood oozing from the hip of the sambar. The predator perhaps started eating it, then left the place for whatever reason. There were sharp puncture marks and clotted blood around the neck of the sambar, clearly indicative of how it died. The sambar breathed its last, with punctured windpipe, under the massive force of powerful jaws accessorized with fierce canines. Surely, dholes did not kill it, as the carcass was quite neat apart from the exposed flesh and bone at its bottom. Leopards generally don't attempt to kill huge herbivores like sambar. Therefore, we zeroed down to the tiger and assumed the animal saw us coming from afar and left the kill to return later. If this inference was true, it was hiding somewhere within twenty-thirty meters radius of the kill, with its eye on us.

This was first time I had encountered such a fresh (non-human) kill presumably of a tiger, standing in a dense tiger reserve. The possibility of being in proximity to the apex predator of this subcontinent, made me shudder. Our tribal guide Sathish prayed for the tiger not to appear. Almost immediately, the incident from the Indian Sundarbans flashed before my eyes, with the tiger dragging the fisherman to the mudflat between Peerkhali and Lebutala. We hurried towards the exit of the forest. I noticed that despite being tired, we were walking unusually fast.

Such experiences are priceless for adventure tourists but counterproductive for tiger photographers.

However, the night exploration in the fringe areas of Mhadei Wildlife Sanctuary, adjacent to Chorla, were uneventful. One morning, at 8:00 o'clock, after breakfast, Nirmal led us to another unique ecosystem on the Goan side of Western Ghats – the plateau ecosystem called "Sadas". Nirmal and his colleagues have been studying the ecology of the plateau focusing on herpetofauna and their relationship with these plateaus. Goa's plateaus, many of them now occupied by sprawling industrial hubs of economic activity, harbour microhabitats with unique floral and faunal biodiversity. In the dry season, the plateau seems dry, rocky, and desolate in patches, in comparison to the surrounding lush green forest. However, the red dust comes to life after monsoon. Streams appear in rocky beds and the ground is covered in a thick mat of vegetation. The high density of species observed during our monsoon walk on the plateau was fascinating. In three hours, we spotted around twenty different amphibians, reptiles, arthropods, and aquatic species – water scorpion, different centipedes and millipedes, and few endemic species, like Fejervarya CEPFRI and Dobson's burrowing frog.

Nirmal mentioned that the plateau is the habitat of cobra, Malabar pit vipers and saw scaled vipers, and that the possibility of spotting saw scale vipers in the monsoon season was high.

He said one could spot them by lifting the medium to big sized rocks lying on the plateau. He cautioned us to keep a safe distance, as some of the snakes are found on the edge of such rocks, and are incredibly agile in striking.

Saw-scaled vipers are relatively small snakes. All members of this genus have a distinctive threat display, which involves forming a series of parallel, C-shaped coils and rubbing them together to produce a sizzling sound, rather like water on a hot plate. The proper term for this is stridulation. These snakes can be fierce and will strike from the position described above. When doing so, they may overbalance and end up moving towards their aggressor (an unusual behaviour for snakes).

Shreeram and Nirmal led our pack; Nirmal stopped intermittently, bending over grass and at times lifting rocks to search for saw scaled vipers.

We followed them, maintaining a gap of eight-ten feet. Each time he lifted a rock, our excitement peaked.

Beneath one such rock was a Fejervarya CEPFRI, sitting quietly; and under another was a tiny burrowing frog, embarrassed and confused by the sudden exposure; but we had no luck with the saw scaled viper.

This continued for a while. Meanwhile we captured images of the surrounding landscape. A hazy and moist background marked by intermittent rain and changes in brightness with repeated appearance and disappearance of the sun.

Suddenly the shout we eagerly awaited for, *"Saw Scaled Viper!"*

We rushed towards Nirmal. The viper lay coiled on moist ground, as Nirmal removed the rock covering her. An alert little snake, extremely capable of quick movement when necessary.

We observed, for thirty minutes or so, the stridulation behaviour and a sudden strike on the nearby rock, a sign of aggression. Nirmal identified that she was pregnant. Her swift readiness to strike at the slightest provocation, coupled with a few rapid strikes on the nearby rock, under which she was hiding, made her appear to be a very dangerous reptile. Nirmal put all of us on alert.

Although rain forest of the Chorla Ghat is also known for its spectacular avifauna, heavy rainfall over three days, prevented us from spotting any major bird species. Couple of significant and worthy of mention sightings include the speckled piculet, the smallest woodpecker in India, and a lone brahminy kite gliding against the backdrop of the magnificent, silvery, and gigantic twin Vajrasakla waterfalls.

Once I stepped out from the comfort zone of gypsy safaris in the tiger reserves of subcontinental forests, in just two explorations I recognized the power of proximity to nature and non-human life forms.

The metamorphosis had begun. From being obsessed to possessing the perfect image of the tiger, to compassion for every living form of nature. In my innermost being, the seed of bio-spherical egalitarianism was sown.

Undoubtedly, I am not the only wildlife photographer who started off with the hobby of tiger photography and then transitioned to herping as the more interesting aspect of this hobby. Many have undergone this transformation before me, and there would be many more in the days to come.

Sadly though, in the commoditized market of ecotourism this transformation is limited.

Research on the tourism industry by *Allied Market Research*, values the ecotourism market size at $214.6 billion in 2022, and projects that it would touch $785 billion by 2031, registering a compound annual growth rate of 15.5%. Not just that, according to a consumer survey conducted by *GlobalData*'s in the quarter four of 2016, 37% of the survey participants were likely to book ecotourism holidays. The survey finds that millennials are the generation most interested in ecotourism, along with high net income individuals.

All the above market research carried out by reputed global organizations clearly indicate the popularity of ecotourism across the globe. The big question is - what do these ecotourists prefer to see during their ecotourism holidays in the renowned global ecotourism destinations?

Let us understand the response from the World's most sought-after ecotourism destination – Africa.

In an article titled *Wildlife Viewing Preferences of Visitors to Protected Areas in South Africa: Implications for the Role of Ecotourism in Conservation*, authored by P. A. Lindsey of *Wildlife Conservation Network and others*, published in May 2007 in *Journal of Ecotourism*, a preference analysis of ecotourists in African Game reserve was carried out.

The graphical presentation of the result of this preference analysis sourced from the article is given below:

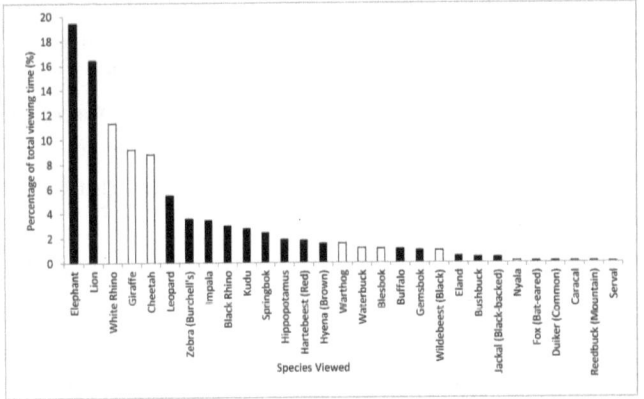

The most preferred animal is the elephant, followed by the lion, then the white rhino, the cheetah and so on. We can summarize then, that the larger the size of the animal higher the percentage of total viewing time (or viewing preference). Out of 30 species listed in this graph, besides reptiles, amphibians, and insects, not even a single species of bird made it to the ecotourists' viewing preferences.

This is not just statistical data in a graph; I personally experienced similar viewing preferences among my fellow ecotourists when I visited Kruger National Park of South Africa.

On our three-day safari, we saw plenty of lions, elephants, zebra, giraffe, wild buffalo etc. On our last safari, we saw a huge bird of prey, with dark brown coloration on the dorsal side, head and upper chest, with slightly lighter edging to these feathers. The ventral or underside were feathered white with sparse but conspicuous blackish-brown spotting, and the underwings were dark brown. It was a martial eagle. This endangered bird is known for its remarkable and extremely keen eyesight (3.0–3.6 times human acuity), partly due to their eye being nearly as large as a human's eye. It was a rare sight bird, as mentioned by our local South African nature guide.

For obvious reasons, I requested him to stop the safari vehicle to capture compelling images of the majestic bird. I was ridiculed by my fellow ecotourists, albeit in a lighter vein. How could I stop the vehicle for a mere bird, when everybody was eager to see the "big mammals" of African savannah?

A typical ecotourism situation in Africa, and elsewhere.

As per *Nat-Geo* and *Travel Triangle*, the top eight ecotourism destinations in India are the national parks of Ranthambore, Jim Corbett, Kaziranga, Kabini (Nagarhole), Gir, Periyar, Satpura, and Sundarbans.

Clearly no further explanation is needed here – these destinations are predominantly tiger reserves, and the national park Gir, is the only home in the world for the Asiatic lion.

How popular are these places in India? We find the answer from the commercial success of these places, as per the 2021-22 data collected from *CEIC Data Global Database.*

In the year 2021-22, Ranthambhore generated an average annual ecotourism revenue of Rupees 30 crore ($4.1 million), and the entire district of Sawai Madhopur of Rajasthan, where the reserve is located, generated Rupees 350 crore ($47 million).

Similarly, Corbett generates an average annual ecotourism revenue of Rupees 10 crore ($1.2 million); and Sundarbans generates Rupees 7.2 crore ($970,000).

Evidently, each rupee invested in an Indian tiger reserve yields a return of Rupees 2,500 ($33.6).

Kaziranga, where the flagship species is the one horned Rhino, earns on an average Rupees 7.8 crore ($940,000) in 2022-23. Due to COVID in 2020-21, this fell to Rupees 2.22 crore ($298,000).

Indian state of Karnataka, where Kabini forest is located, and the flagship species are elephants, Bengal Tigers and leopards (specially the black leopard), set a target of Rupees 500 crore ($675 million) as ecotourism revenue in the year 2021, and eventually made Rupees 679 crore ($819 million).

Lastly, in Gir, despite the COVID19 pandemic, in the year 2019-2020, the lion safari generated a revenue of Rupees 10.78 crore ($14.5 million).

This huge ecotourism economy can also be termed as tiger economy or big mammal economy in this industry.

Nevertheless, bearing the viewpoints of natural history and conservation of natural resources, the fundamental question that arises from the commercial success of these sanctuaries and national parks, then, is – *Does this Ecosystem belongs to only big mammals or big cats?*

My journey in the *Shadow of the Bengal Tiger* was to seek the answer to the question, *"Why is the tiger the most desired object (or photography subject) in the wild, and why is it perceived as the demigod of the subcontinental forest?"* Thus far in this journey the question has led to several other questions, the most existentially challenging among them being the one related to the so-called supremacy of big mammals or big cats over all other lifeforms in the ecosystem.

This question also relates to the detrimental effects of the single species supremacy in ecotourism, and the perilous impact of commodity fetishism on Bengal Tiger and its habitats.

However, every problem is an opportunity in disguise. Agumbe and Chorla showed me, that to find the remedy to our current problem of "Bengal Tiger commodity fetishism", we need to look down, literally.

The remedy lies in the understory of the forest. The most ignored part of the forest but the most significant, from an eco-restoration perspective. The species in the forest undergrowth are seriously misunderstood living creatures although this undergrowth of tropical rainforests play an immense role in the nourishment of the forest, which in turn provides nourishment to all other species, including the big mammals.

Therefore, to further understand the importance of herpetofauna, I embarked on my next herping expedition during monsoon to a mid-elevation hill station with tea and coffee plantations, surrounded by the evergreen forests of Western Ghats. I headed to a private reserve forest, considered as sacred grove, known locally as *Devara Kadu*, situated adjacent to the *Parvathi Valley Coffee Estate* of Coorg or Kodagu district of Karnataka. The concept of this *Devara Kadu* has immense impact in conservation history of this Indian highland. Felling, lopping, clearing of fallen branches, plucking of weeds, pruning, or burning of trees is prohibited in *Devara Kadus*. It is believed that offenders will be punished with death by the folk deity. Such granting of sacrosanct status to forests dates back to the Indus Valley civilisation.

The scared groves were a 1000-acre forest situated in an area which receives a high amount of rainfall. These groves have abundant variety of life, especially with regard to the numerous species of amphibians and reptiles, many of them being endemic to the area and found nowhere else on Earth. The area is also amazingly rich in bird life and boasts over 300 species including the beautiful Malabar trogon, orange minivet, hill myna, Asian fairy bluebird and various species of woodpeckers, flycatchers, and raptors. Mammals found in the area include, leopards, barking deer, wild boar, and an amazing array of nocturnal life such as mouse deer, various species of lesser cats, flying squirrel and porcupines. During my visit, I was delighted to see the fascinating and colourful birds of Western Ghats such as Malabar grey hornbills, Malabar parakeet, plum headed parakeet, yellow browed bulbul, black throated munia, golden leaf birds, white cheeked barbet, red whiskered and red vented bulbul.

The highlight of the visit though was not the commonly seen avian fauna, but the endangered undergrowth floral and faunal species. These include seven different frog species, numerous different insects (including five different species of spiders), five different fungi, three different blue morph individuals of Malabar pit viper and plenty of wild flowering plants, mosses and ferns.

During monsoon, Coorg or Kodagu (which translates to 'dense forest on steep hills') is brimming with tourists. The tourism industry added yet another dimension further adding to the load of this nature destination's already exceeding carrying capacity. The blooming of a flower of *Strobilanthes kunthiana*, locally known as *Kurinji* or *Neelakurinji* in Malayalam and Tamil. Nilgiri Hills, which literally means the blue mountains, got its name from the purplish-blue flowers of *Neelakurinji* that blossoms only once in twelve years. Another strictly endemic angiosperm of Western Ghats that I discovered during my visit to Coorg, was *Impatiens*. The Impatiens found in Western Ghats are endemic to this region. Western Ghats is the hub of tea/coffee plantations and tourism. The growing demand of these two activities are now the biggest threat to survival of this species. Based on a blog called *happybotanist.com*, all the *Impatiens* species present in the Western Ghats are either endangered or critically endangered as their environment is changed by humans.

Flowering plants have many reasons to attract attention of humans, although for the survival of the species it is more important to get attention of birds and insects that help in pollination. There is another undergrowth species that lies between plant and animal kingdom, and is often ignored. The Fungi. They grow well under moist and warm conditions, in the presence of suitable nutrients. Most of them are saprotrophic, that is, they obtain their nutrients by growing on animal and plant remains, and that makes them one of the most important contributors in maintaining the vigour of the habitats for all species, including our beloved Bengal Tiger.

Fungi break down plant and animal matter and recycle important elements like carbon and nitrogen back into the natural environment. The rainforests of the Western Ghats provide ideal conditions for the occurrence of a wide diversity of remarkable fungi. Among the five different types of fungi I spotted on my exploration in Coorg, one was *Coprinus sp*. As these are saprotrophs, they decompose wood, dung, and forest litter. Their spores, when dissolved, form a black, inky substance that can be used as writing ink. Hence, the common name – ink cap fungus. Other species of Fungi in Coorg were *Stereum* and *Foitopsis* bracket fungi. An additional astonishing insight from my "macro-photography" in *Parvathi Valley Coffee Estate* was the display of mycelium network of *Schizophyllum* (bracket fungi). Mycologist Paul Stamets, in his book titled *Mycelium Running: How Mushrooms Can Help Save the World*, mentions, "*...mycelium is the neurological network of nature. Interlacing mosaics of mycelium infuse habitats with information-sharing membranes. These membranes are aware, react to change, and collectively have the long-term health of the host environment in mind. The mycelium* *stays in constant molecular communication with its environment, devising diverse enzymatic and chemical responses to complex challenges."*

If the health of the forest is taken care of by the undergrowth flora, then the rejuvenation of the forest is done by the undergrowth fauna.

In the forest of Madikeri range of Kodagu district, as we immersed ourselves in fungi and flowering plants, the iconic sound of cicada served as our background score. Subsequently, under the dim lit canopy cover, as we busied ourselves with a blue morph of the Malabar pit viper, the sound of cicada was subdued by the pitter-patter of light rain. Gradually the pitter-patter transformed into the whoosh and splash of heavy down pour, which immobilized us for a good thirty to forty-five minutes. The musical ensemble constituted by these undergrowth faunas, accompanied by all the onomatopoeia of rain fall, beginning with pitter-patter and ending with whoosh and splash, marked the transition from day to dusk. The pitter-patter, was accompanied by a varied range of orchestra, from the tick-tick of Wayand bush frogs, to the high-pitched whirring of bicolour bush frog, and the deep bonk of common tree frog. Darkness soon engulfed us, and along with an array of sounds emanating from numerous unseen insects, amphibians and reptiles, the rainforest came alive.

With the flash of hand-held and head torches in the few nights at Coorg, we sighted species of *Indosylvirana* (golden frog), bicolour bush frog (Malabar frog),

Waynaad bush frog, Coorg yellow bush frog, small gliding frog, a species of Fejervarya and *Raorchestes ponmudi*. Of them except the golden frog and Fejervarya, all others are endemic to Western Ghats. The Coorg bush frogs were quite distinctive because of their colourful appearance. They are mostly found in disturbed habitats, near coffee plantations adjacent to primary forests and waysides, often on leaves or stems of shrubs about one meter above the ground. Male frogs start calling at dusk, first under the leaf litter and then ascending to the vegetation. A beautiful blue ring around their pale-yellow elliptical eyes gives them a mesmerizing look like "the frog prince" from Grimm Brothers' fairy tales.

The *Devara Kadu* of Kodagu is the habitat of many of these entrancing undergrowth species. The small gliding frog is declared as an endangered species, nevertheless in those couple of days we spotted at least ten of them in the forest. The folklore of forest deity indeed plays a significant role in conservation and that is how science and mythology come together. I witnessed this before in Sundarbans, where respect for Bengal Tigers was anchored in the stories of Bon Bibi.

On the day of our final exploration, at around 10:30 pm, as we were leaving the forest, we spotted two pairs of fine and long antennae, protruding out from underneath a large leaf of Arabica coffee plant. When we went closer, we recognized them as a pair of mating cicada. The key vocalist of the daytime concert in the forest of monsoon caressed Western Ghats, was engrossed in the process of bringing new life and spreading love for all the jewels of Mother Nature. Fascinating diurnal insects, these cicadas are. They are able to produce ear-shattering sounds because they possess an organ that is almost unique among insects, the tymbal organ. Cicadas also have air sacs that have resonant frequencies comparable to tymbal vibration frequencies, thus amplifying the sound and producing the crescendo of high-pitched buzzing that is the characteristic sound of Western Ghats' monsoon.

That very night at the sacred grove of Kodagu, the soft emphatic whistle of a slender loris also joined the nocturnal orchestra of the rainforest, emphasising the significance of "inherent value" of all life forms on Earth.

The admiration for undergrowth ecosystem and effort to uphold this "under-(rated)-story" in the shadow of the Bengal Tiger does not end here. The story of undergrowth ecosystem is even more vivid and enthralling when it is brewed in the land ruled by the demigod itself.

The Annamalai hill is easily the most biodiverse and rich habitat in the Western Ghats. It is located in Valparai (originally known as Poonachimalai) Taluk, a hill station in the Coimbatore district of Tamil Nadu, and consists of Annamalai Tiger Reserve (earlier known as Indira Gandhi Wildlife Sanctuary and National Park, and prior to that as Annamalai Wildlife Sanctuary). My night walk in *Anali* and *Sheikalmudi tea estates* of Valparai were towards the end of the monsoon season in Western Ghats. Nevertheless, I was not disappointed.

Near our bungalows in both the estates, we spotted some fascinating night crawlers like the entirely nocturnal and rather rare Ferguson's toad, and other amphibians like golden frog, Wayanad bush frog, Jayrama's bush frog, ponmudi, quite a few damselflies, ampurella snails, slugs, forest cockroaches, orb web spiders, huntsman spiders and an unidentified spider, which could be a wolf-spider of *Hippasa* genus. Not just herpetofauna, while exploring in patches of Anamalai tiger reserve around *Anali tea estate*, in the high beam of torch light we saw a pair of porcupines, and rare sighting species like mouse deer and brown palm civet. Successful eco-restoration indeed converted this land into a captivating ecotourism destination for many.

The herpetofauna or undergrowth species, I found in Agumbe, Chorla, Coorg and Valparai have been conventionally categorized as forest pests for ages. But the role of some of these species can have a profound effect on large areas of anthropogenically-impacted forests.

Consider the life cycle of an amphibian, a tadpole feeds on algae and when it becomes mature it starts feeding on invertebrates. They are herbivorous to omnivorous and serve as prey for both invertebrates and vertebrates. Adult amphibians are the best biological pest controllers. We hardly find such examples of ecological contribution in big mammals.

Speaking of spiders, their presence limits the habitats open to insect pests. Spiders threaten insect pests with various foraging strategies. In addition to consuming large numbers of insect pests as prey, they also kill all insects living in their territory. For this reason, spiders are a favourable biological control agent in the ecosystem and can be successfully used to check pest population in the forest floor. No big mammals can be as effective as spiders in this role.

Talking about snakes, they play an integral role in maintaining balance in the ecosystem. In most systems, snakes can be both predator and prey. When a large prey population attracts and sustains a large snake population, these snakes become prey for birds, mammals, and even other snakes. On the other hand, Bengal Tiger is only the apex predator; nobody dares to prey upon it.

Indeed, nature has much more to offer than tiger for her as well as for the animal itself, to ensure protection of both. If Bengal Tiger is credited with protecting the forest, then there are tiny little weird folks who keep this chain of protection uninterrupted by contributing through all stages of their life cycles.

However, there is no denial of the fact that lot of emphasis on tiger conservation in Western Ghats in turn has ensured conservation of these ecologically significant undergrowth species as described above.

Because of tiger conservation programmes these important zones comprising Agumbe-Chorla Ghat-Coorg-Valparai are also protected. As a result, these zones, despite not being the mainstream ecotourism destinations enjoy some attention of nature enthusiasts and wildlife photographers. This approximately 1000 km stretch along the west coast of India has become frequently visited herping hotspot of Western Ghats by the urban wildlife photographers. All these four herping hotspots are situated either at the buffer zone or distributed through the corridors of six tiger reserves of four states – Tamil Nadu, Karnataka, Kerala and Goa. Valparai is located in the protective coverage of Mudumalai, Anamalai and Parambikulum tiger reserve; Coorg (Madikere forest division) is adjacent to Bandipur and Nagarhole tiger reserve; Agumbe is not far from the buffer zone of Bhadra tiger reserve; and Chorla Ghat is bordered by the dense forest of Kali tiger reserve on the south and Mahdei Wildlife Sanctuary on the northeast.

But in spite of having such magnificent and diversified conglomeration of flora and fauna with so many endemic species, these four forest areas are not really considered as mainstream ecotourism destinations of India. Even among wildlife photographers, these places are certainly not top priority.

Whenever Shreeram planned for any macro-photography bootcamp at Agumbe or Chorla, no more than five or six participants signed up for it. On the other hand, photography mentors and tour operators, who specialized in tiger photography, were required to hire two to three safari vehicles to accommodate all the participants for every batch of their wildlife photography bootcamps whether at Ranthambore, Tadoba, Bandhavgarh or Kabini.

Again, comfort is the key element based on which ecotourism (or at least tiger tourism) is built. The hardship involved in shooting herpetofauna sometimes becomes an impediment for many photographers. Macro-photography demands them to get out of their comfort zone, as it requires you to get up close to your subjects, to lie down on mud or water-puddle in leech infested forest floor on rainy days of monsoon, to venture out in the darkness in the odd hours of night, to risk possible insect bites or to put up with crawling weird nocturnal creatures on your body. That way, shooting big mammals or big cats is much safer from the protection of a safari gypsy with telephoto lens in hand. The preference, thus, for the so-called glamourous and photogenic species is obvious.

But what would happen to these glamorous big mammalian species if the understory of their habitats is not sustained?

What would happen if there were no undergrowth species in the ecosystem?

There would be a pile of dead things on the forest floor – dead trees, animal carcass – as decomposition process will be much slower in the absence of these creatures. They are Mother Natures' ecosystem engineers, and they are the key pollinators, who initiate new life forms on Earth. If they disappear, then so will the forest along with the Bengal Tigers, the elephants, the leopards, the deer. And us.

If my fellow wildlife photographers are reading this book, I would humbly request them to become an inclusive photographer with no bias for any species as their photography subject.

If my general tourist friends are reading this book, I would really urge them to include ecotourism in their next vacation plan. I would insist also that you find such a destination which does not focus solely on big cats or big mammals.

At the end I would like to make a plea to both photographers and the tourist community, with folded hands, to not consider undergrowth species as pests. To conserve your beloved big cats, you need to conserve undergrowth ecosystem and for that you must leave behind your commodity fetishism for the Bengal Tiger and comfort of the gypsy and boat safari.

However, like any other commodity fetishism created in the capitalist market, this one is also not just dependent upon buyers (wildlife photographers and ecotourists). As I mentioned earlier, tour operators and nature guides have played a major role in creating this fetishism. Therefore, remedy of this fetishism is also largely dependent on them.

It is the responsibility of ecotour operators and nature guides to understand the fundamental principle of bio-spherical egalitarianism. The ecosystem, which is ruled by the mighty Bengal Tiger, is not fascinating just because of big herbivores, arboreal or birds of prey. Tiger as apex predator protects the ecosystems by controlling species population in its food pyramid. However, the vigour and diversity of this ecosystem depends upon a natural nourishment process.

There are many grassroot nature guides who understand this principle of bio-spherical egalitarianism in their own way.

Karnataka is one of the most successful revenue generating states of India through ecotourism activities. However, out of five tiger reserves of the state, ecotourists' favourites are Nagarhole (Kabini), Bandipur, and Bhadra. Because it is an established fact that big cat sighting probability is very high in those three reserves. The other two reserves Dandeli and BRT are relatively ignored by ecotourists and photographers.

During my trip to Dandeli, my nature guide Dutta was well aware of this fact. Therefore, while roaming inside the rainforest of Dandeli, instead of chasing tigers he drew my attention towards a female black wood spider, in her vast web on a large bush. I was particularly excited about this sighting. Dutta was equally excited and made a great ecologically significant statement, *"Forests are not all about just tigers and leopards"*.

Despite being a trained environmentalist and practicing sustainability consultant, I would have never picked up any interest in these so called "forest pests" had Vedavyasa not been reluctant in wildlife photography and nature exploration.

The life changing moment in my nature exploration was the Agumbe trip where I had the good fortune of meeting M. V. Shreeram.

"You need to lie-down to get a different perspective of your subject. That's how creativity in wildlife photography starts." That was the first lesson I learnt from Shreeram on my first ever herpetofauna photography trip at Agumbe.

That first lesson did not just change the way I was doing photography, it changed my whole perspective towards life as an environmentalist.

The wellbeing of human and non-human life on earth is of intrinsic value irrespective of its value to humans. This is the first principle of Deep Ecology, coined by Norwegian environmentalist and philosopher, Arne Naes. I recall reading this as a student, but I had forgotten it conveniently.

Shreeram's first macro-photography lesson reminded me of this principle with a long-lasting impact.

CHAPTER NINE: The Silver Lining

"Mass production of economic goods necessitates the mass production of environmental bads" Allan Schnaiberg and Kenneth Alan Gould, Environment and Society: The Enduring Conflict, St. Martin's, 1994, p. 25.

The mass production of tiger tourism and photography has the potential to create more conservational bads than any benefits. Evidently, tiger tourism is unlike production of economic goods. At least the intention behind tiger tourism or any ecotourism was not the creation of any form of economic goods or commodities. But anthropocentric conservation theories are built on the concept of integrating economy and ecology. The demand of materialism transforms this integration into a process of economy dominating over ecology. Thus, tiger tourism or most of the other forms of ecotourism (along with wildlife photography) favours economy over ecology. Therefore, as outcomes of neo-liberal sustainability, tiger tourism and photography are commoditized and have become new forms of economic goods.

The strongest counter-force to this side effect of embracing neo-liberal sustainability is – bio-spherical egalitarianism – the principle of equal rights for all living forms.

For the very first time, I witnessed the possibility of upholding this principle in the domain of ecotourism and wildlife photography, in another very popular tiger reserve of Karnataka.

Bhadra Wildlife Sanctuary and Tiger Reserve take its name from the Bhadra River, its lifeline. Popularly known as Muthodi Wildlife Sanctuary, after the village on its periphery. After Kabini, this is another tiger reserve whose flagship species is not the tiger. In Kabini, the flagship species may not be Bengal Tiger, but it is at least another member of "Big Cat" family – the Black Panther or black leopard. But here in Bhadra, it is not even a mammal. It is an avian species that is considered as the flagship species of this reserve – the river terns.

It is a great place to sight and observe many other mammals, reptiles, and more than 250 species of birds, many of which are endemic to the Western Ghats. October to March is the best time to visit this 892.46 km^2 area of forest, like any other tiger reserve in India. However, in reality the "commercial peak season" for this reserve is April to June. During summer the backwaters of Bhadra River recedes, and many small islands emerge, thus providing a safe nesting ground for thousands of river terns. At the onset of monsoon in Western Ghats, water level rises,

Pseudo Ecotourism

and these islands start submerging again, which makes the river terns leave their nests only to come back again the next season. Wildlife photographers and nature enthusiasts across the world come to see one of these largest congregations of river terns in the uphill of Western Ghats.

Although my pre-summer Bhadra trip was a specifically designed photography bootcamp for the World's largest congregations of river terns, but when you are with M.V. Shreeram, you need to work in "two shifts". Day for birds and mammals; and night for herpetofauna.

Our river tern photography workshop was not an exception, and during night-time herping, within the River Tern Lodge of JLR, we spotted some two different species of frogs; two species of gecko; some four-five species of spiders, including a tarantula; one collard cat snake, resting on dry twigs right across the path towards cottages; and many other insects. However, the most special one initially appeared as a refrigerator magnet. It was the size of a lapel pin, resembling a metallic dark-coloured object. This crawling-multi legged-clawed lapel pin may easily be mistaken as an accessory to your Halloween costume. A Halloween décor dropped on the forest floor by a forgetful co-tourist.

This night-creature shone in light of the torch, as it fed on millipedes.

Later Shreeram with the help of his naturalist friend from JLR, identified it as nymph of the sub-family

(Ectrichodiinae) of an assassin bug, that specializes in feeding on millipedes.

Post the trip, in one of his *Instagram* posts, Shreeram asked all nature enthusiasts and wildlife photographers, *"Do you walk around wildlife lodges and resorts to look for wildlife when you are not on safaris? If not, please start doing that. There are so many things that'll blow your mind."*

Reputed wildlife photography mentors should not just limit themselves in teaching photography. Enticing their mentees towards natural history and significance of "so-called insignificant life forms" is also part of their noble job.

But when something is commoditized to respond to the need of market-economy driven materialism, then such noble thoughts of a noble job become irrelevant.

The hegemony of pseudo conservation converts ecotourism into pseudo ecotourism. If the tiger-centric ecotourism (which is now a commodity fetishism) is this pseudo conservation's worst victim, then photographing herpetofauna or "macro-photography" is the first one to be disdained by this hegemony induced pseudo ecotourism.

The pseudo ecotourism created by this hegemony is largely centred on tiger chasing in subcontinental tiger reserves as well as fascination for big mammals. However, being ignored by this pseudo ecotourism industry, the herpetofauna ecotourism/macro-photography has created an opportunity for an alternative ecotourism. An ecotourism which is at relatively less risk from getting shamelessly commoditised.

The reflection of bio-spherical egalitarianism in ecotourism and wildlife photography, that I witnessed in river tern photography at Bhadra (including the night walk within the JLR property), could also be recognized in fragmented shola forest among acres of tea estates and vast eucalyptus plantation in one of the popular hill stations of the southwestern Indian state of Kerala. Another destination for alternative ecotourism.

Munnar, which is believed to mean "three rivers", referring to its location at the confluence of the Mudhirapuzha, Nallathanni and Kundali Rivers, is a popular tourist destination for honeymoon couples, fun loving young tourists looking for selfie opportunities and for tourists with small and large family. The tea estates and spice garden owners of Munnar provide opportunity to the tourists from various part of the world to visit their places as part of their tourism activities.

Based on an article *Agriculture now moves into the field of tourism*, written by Madhvi Sally and P.K. Krishnakumar, published in *Economic Times (ET)*, the *Kanan Devan Hills Plantations (erstwhile Tata Tea) tea estate* of Munnar feel tourism can be a good source of income in the long term. Kerala government's decision to permit the use of 5% of plantation land for tourism and allied activities has inspired farmers to diversify. The article mentions, that with 23,000 hectares of tea plantations spread over Munnar, *Kanan Devan* is the largest tea corporate in south India with production over annual 20 million kg. The company had a plan to invest around Rs 100 crore ($12 million) by 2016 to give thrust to tourism. By tying up with a hospitality company, it intended to manage 21 bungalows, many of which were built by the British when they started tea estates that were subsequently bought by the Tatas. As per the article published in ET, *"With the Kerala government's decision, we plan to build additional cottages in Munnar. In the past two years, there has been a steady increase in flow of tourists to our bungalows,"* pointed out Tharani Tharan, head of hospitality division of the plantation company. This agrotourism concept is of course highly inclined towards fulfilling materialistic needs of the market economy. But it is astonishing to note how nature turned this agrotourism into an agroforestry ecotourism opportunity in this tea country.

During daytime these tea and spice gardens are busy in welcoming their farm visiting guests. After dusk these agroforest plantations are frequented by herpetofauna lovers like Shreeram. He is accompanied by local folks, Sebinster and Augustin, who run a tea café which serves the best tea from the tea estates of Munnar to their day tourists. With night fall in monsoon season, they become nature guides to offer their extensive local knowledge of amphibians and reptiles to their night visitors.

On one such monsoon night, I was part of a herpetofauna photography workshop led by Shreeram. Sebinster and Augustin were our local naturalists. As I said earlier, working with Shreeram means being on the field in two shifts. Our day started at 8 am, after breakfast, and continued until midnight, with a couple of breaks for lunch and an early dinner in the evening.

In three days Sebinster took us to various tea estates and plantation forests in and around Munnar; and to Meesapulimala forest range, situated around thirty-five kilometres from Munnar town. The phenomenal part of our exploration was that in just three days in the tea estates and plantation forests of Munnar we found twenty-one species of frogs, and barring one or two, the rest were new species I had ever seen. All these twenty-one species are endemic to Western Ghats.

Frog species we saw in the tea estates were - green-eyed bush frog, Sushil's bush frog, griet, and resplendent shrub frog which are critically endangered as per IUCN *(International Union for Conservation of Nature)* conservation status; Kodikanal bush frog which is a vulnerable species as per IUCN; and critically endangered Anamalai flying frog or false Malabar gliding frog, a very special frog as it is found both in lower canopy and understorey vegetation and on the ground. Besides these we also found other species such as dancing frog; blandus; Jayaram's bush frog; yellow-bellied bush frog; ochlandrae; and

Beddomii's bush frog. Except Beddomii's bush frog all are relatively newly discovered species (between years 2000 and 2014). All are bush frogs, except resplendence or resplendent shrub frog which are found in shrubs of high-altitude region. We found quite a few individuals of resplendence near Meesapulimala peak. The list does not end here. The other interesting frog species we found in Munnar, and surrounding areas were Indian golden-backed frog; western tree frog; starry eyed tree frog; meowing night frog; sali; and Anamalai dot frog. Few other endangered frog species we found were Kalakad gliding frog; Wayanad bush frog; and Indirana. Like their names, these species are just as fascinating in their appearance, call and behaviour.

The tea estates and plantation of Munnar severely destroyed the natural shola forest of this part of Western Ghats which had led to significant species destruction. Despite such destruction there remains much diversity which is enough to draw the attention of wildlife enthusiasts.

Although tropical forest ecosystems around the world have been modified and fragmented by agroforests planted to produce commodities such as coffee, rubber and areca palm, amphibian communities can survive in these transformed landscapes — if the agroforests are managed to support biodiversity. That's the conclusion of a new study led by *Penn State's* wildlife ecologists who surveyed frog populations in the Western Ghats. As per the survey, researchers at the *Centre for Wildlife Studies*, led by Dr. Krithi Karanth, Dr. Shashank Dalvi and Vishnupriya Sankararaman, a doctoral student in the Ecosystem Science and Management program at *Penn State*, searched for amphibians on 106 agroforest tracts across a 28,500 square km area.

The study analysed amphibian populations and land management in coffee, rubber and areca palm — three of the largest commodity agroforests in the Western Ghats. Researchers found that "microhabitat availability" — the presence of streams, ponds and unpaved service roads — had a major influence on amphibian numbers and species distribution. Sankararaman said, *"Amphibian populations are declining around the world, and they need protection. They provide huge ecosystem services to landowners — frogs are natural pesticides that consume more insect biomass than almost any other animals,"* she said. *"They have real financial significance and allow us to eat more organically, using fewer chemicals in crop production. But beyond that, these creatures have evolved over millions of years, and they have immeasurable value in their own right."*

Research conducted by Sankararaman and *Penn State's* wildlife ecologists' make it abundantly clear as to why Munnar has become a heaven for amphibians and a sanctuary to many critically endangered, endangered, and vulnerable species, which are also providing ecosystem services of pest control to tea estate and spice garden owners across the region.

If there are frogs, there will be snakes. We were delighted to spot four fabulous species of snakes in Munnar. These include Gunther's vine snake; Thackeray's cat snake; the venomous large-scaled pit viper; and the purple-red earth snake. All four are endemic to the Western Ghats.

I should not forget to mention three amazing lizards we found in those three days. The vibrant coloured Anamalai spiny lizard - Elliot's forest lizard, is a species of arboreal, diurnal, lizard; and the Indian day gecko or Nilgiri dwarf gecko. A bright coloured Indrella ampulla, a tropical terrestrial air-breathing gastropod mollusc was crawled on a tree stump on a rather rainy mid night in the tea estate of Munnar.

Twenty-one frogs, four snakes, three lizards and one mollusc. All endemic to Western Ghats. It is a rather long list of endemic species listed above, considering just three days of visit in a few plantation patches of Munnar and Meesapulimala hill. I could not help but list them down, as that is what Munnar's nocturnal herpetofauna life has to offer to wildlife enthusiasts.

This transformation of agrotourism to agroforestry ecotourism is not just limited to "God's own country" – Kerala, but is equally evident in two more popular agrotourism destinations of Western Ghats – Coorg and Valparai.

When I was in Coorg, I witnessed how *Hornbill Nest homestay* transformed their *Parvati Valley Coffee Estate* into an agrotourism destination and gradually into a wildlife photography bootcamp station for serious wildlife enthusiasts.

In Valparai, the agroforestry ecotourism attractions are not just centred on herpetofauna. Birding is indeed the other attraction for ecotourists. The wildlife enthusiasts and photographers visit the tea estates here and surrounding hills to capture dream shots of stunning and exquisite great hornbill in flight. An article *"My love letter to the Great Hornbill"*, written on 20th May 2021 in the online edition of *Nature in Focus*, by Prakash Ramakrishnan and Nikhil Sreekandan, mentions that *"As natural habitats of Great Hornbills continue to shrink at an alarming pace, these majestic birds are now frequenting plantations and other disturbed areas which once they called home. Today, Valparai, an area of 220 km² which has nearly 40 rainforest fragments of varying sizes ranging from 0.3 to 300 ha remains one of the last strongholds of the Great Hornbill."*

There are around 56 tea estates in Valparai. Gaurs and elephants from adjacent Annamalai tiger reserve of Tamil Nadu and Parambikulam tiger reserve of Kerala frequent all of them. Leopard sighting is also not so rare in these tea gardens.

In April 2023, National Geographic released a documentary titled *"Secrets of Elephants"*, on the OTT platform *Disney plus Hotstar*. In episode four of this documentary, narrator Natalie Portman mentions that farmers of Western Ghats have stopped applying chemical herbicides to kill weeds in their tea estates. Instead, they leave them out for visiting elephants to mulch. As a result, it has turned into a win-win situation for both farmers and elephants. Elephants get their food and much needed resting places, and farmers obtain tea yield which is completely organic. Besides, ecotourists and wildlife photographers have the opportunity to see and shoot wild elephants.

The flagship species of Valparai is Lion Tailed Macaue, locally known as LTM. Close to *Monica Garden bungalow* there is a village called Puduthodam. The village is home to a big troop of LTM. I was surprised to see how an endangered species survived and thrived in proximity to human settlement by partially scavenging on human food waste. The other mammal species we spotted in these tea estates were bonnet macaque, Nilgiri langur, Malabar flying squirrel, Indian giant squirrel, Western Ghats palm squirrel, black napped hare, wild boar and striped necked mongoose.

During my four nights - five days stay at Valparai, I understood why in addition to lion tailed macaque and elephants, the avian ecotourism is a big attraction. During our visit to the tea estates, we captured splendid portrait and aerial shots of the great hornbill. We were also delighted to sight other feathered friends such as Malabar whistling thrush, chestnut bellied bee-eater, rufus babbler, black eagle, crested serpent eagle, Malabar parakeet, Nilgiri flower pecker, oriental white-eye, ashy drongo, scarlet minivet, spur fowl, jungle fowl, plenty of oriental magpie robin and the only parrot of India – the vernal hanging parrot.

Bird photography in Valparai, was carried out by walking through valleys and tea plantations, and a few steep hikes along Annamalai tiger reserve and by crossing river streams. Real nature exploration with hard work on ground.

When you put such physical effort to see the beautiful avifauna of the forest, you do not think about your so-called dream shots. Rather, you immerse yourself in nature and experience the spectacle presented.

The proximity to nature is the key here. More aligned you are with nature further away you are from the materialistic thoughts of achieving fame and glory. That's how you keep the commodity fetishism for one single species at bay. That's how Shreeram's principle of lying down, connects with the principle of deep ecology.

We humans never intended to allow the nature control over us, therefore we coined the term sustainable development – which essentially promotes development and keeps radical environmentalism under control. *"Development that meets the needs of the present, without compromising the ability of future generations to meet their own needs"*. Humans should not fail to meet their needs at any cost. If nature and other non-human life forms need to pay the price for it, as per neo-liberal sustainability, it is completely acceptable.

Even ecotourism was not spared from this human endeavour of meeting their needs. The sole purpose of ecotourism was exploring nature and being rejuvenated by nature. But it has now been transformed by humans as a way of possessing a trophy and achieving fame to stand out from other fellow humans.

Prithu, the protagonist of Guha's novel *"Madhukari"*, thus utters in his hospital bed, with sorrow and revulsion, *"No escape for modern, educated and so-called rationalist human like me, as we have sacrificed our freedom to materialistic needs of the world."*

The protagonist of my quest for an alternative to *Pseudo Ecotourism* in the *Shadow of the Bengal Tiger*, Shreeram, once said, *"There is no end to chasing money, therefore that is not my goal. I agree money is important, as everything we do in our life revolves around money we earn. But we need to realize that with every penny we earn or spend, there is an impact on natural resources. Therefore, there is no harm in putting a limit on this earning and spending."* On another occasion he said, *"The goal of my life is being part of this quest and experiencing various elements of nature, rather than stocking loads of money."*

Shreeram went to two premier academic institutes of India during his undergraduate and post graduate study, *BITS-Pilani* and *IIM-Bangalore*. He then worked for corporates for over four years. Eventually he turned down all the possibilities of creating wealth and followed his passion for nature and wildlife to make his living. He is convinced that as long as he is able to meet his basic needs, he does not need to be part of any materialistic rat race.

This is why Shreeram not only turned down a corporate career, but also, keeps tiger tourism aside from his photography bootcamp's regular itinerary. He knows not doing more tiger photography bootcamps means lesser income from his passion turned profession. But he believes that admiring nature needs a wholistic approach. *"I go to forests with a goal to learn what that place has to offer in its entirety. I would like to provide similar perspective to my bootcamp participants as well, so that they can also learn what nature as a whole has to offer. Not just a single species. In Bhadra of course I went for river tern. But if I had sat in my room, relaxing in the evening, then I would have never known that there was a species of assassin bug which only feeds on millepedes. This is the joy of wildlife photography, derived from such small moments."*

The ecotourists, including wildlife photographers who do not care for this delight in small moments, that nature offers, are pseudo ecotourists.

CHAPTER TEN: The Wonder Wasteland

To counter commodity fetishism centred on pseudo ecotourism - tiger tourism and photography, it is essential to recognize the wholistic ecotourism opportunity in ignored ecosystems of this subcontinent. Although pseudo ecotourism is the bi-product of commoditizing sustainability, the concept of wholistic ecotourism could be useful to decelerate this commoditization process.

As witnessed, agroforestry ecotourism emerging in tea and coffee estates of Western Ghats as alternative ecotourism, creates opportunities for sighting, admiring and photographing herpetofauna, other agroforestry based avian species, big as well as small mammals, and a variety of botanical beauties.

However, agroforestry ecotourism is not the only form of alternative ecotourism. I was astonished to discover that the most neglected parcel of lands known as wastelands also have similar potential. The *Merriam-Webster* dictionary defines wasteland as a barren, uncultivated land or an ugly often devasted or barely inhabitable place or area. Clearly, an anthropocentric definition which measures value of everything from the perspective of human usability. But many are unaware that Indian wastelands are a neglected ecosystem despite being home to around 56 different species notified in different Schedules of *Wildlife Protection Act* of India, including some of the most threatened species like black buck, great Indian bustard, lesser florican, Indian rhinoceros, snow leopard, Nilgiri thar and wild buffalo among others. These species are distributed across various wastelands including grasslands and deserts – dry grasslands and hot deserts of north and western India; cold deserts of western and eastern Himalayas; tropical short grass plains of western, central India and deccan; wet grasslands of Terai and northeast India; and shola grasslands of Western Ghats.

Wildlife photography mentors like M.V. Shreeram and others, who encourage their participants to focus on wholesomeness of any ecosystem as the subject of their exploration and photography, cannot work alone to create this alternative ecotourism in these ignored wastelands. These wastelands, habitats of endangered and vulnerable wildlife, are major grazing areas and a source of rural economy of this nation. As per the *Report of Task Force on Grasslands and Deserts*, published by Government of India in 2006, around 50% of the fodder for the livestock in India, home to more than 500 million livestock, comes from wastelands. This report highlights the urgent need for a National Grazing Policy to ensure sustainable use of grasslands and biodiversity conservation. However, to the best of my knowledge, as on date, we have no defined national policy on this.

Administrative intervention has always created multi-faceted conflicts in Indian forests. Why just Indian forest? There is more than two hundred years of global history of battle between foresters, forest dwellers and environmentalists on the issue of forest right and conservation. *"Liberty and forest laws are incompatible"* – *An English country vicar, c. 170* – as quoted by environmental historian Dr. Ramchandra Guha in his book *"How Much Should a Person Consume?"*

I witnessed the extreme form of this conflict in a famous tiger reserve of Eastern Ghats, that is arguably losing its tiger population due to this conflict. In an article published on International Tiger Day of 2023 in the online edition of *Odhishatv.in*, *"Similipal Tiger Reserve, which is well-known for black tigers and is the only place in the world that houses the source population of the melanistic tigers, loses 75 tigers in 12 years."*

One winter, I visited Simlipal Tiger Reserve, located in the Mayurbhanj district of Odisha state, covering 2,750 km^2. From Bhubaneshwar, the capital of Odisha, it was a six-hour drive to *Kumari Nature Camp* of Simlipal, located in the core area of the tiger reserve. The following day, I had a prebooked full day safari in forest department's twelve-seater vehicle. Needless to mention, I was the only passenger in the huge jalopy!

This was one constraint in Simlipal. Only twelve-seater vehicles were available for booking on the website of *Ecotour Odisha*.

In Simlipal, the forest department's drivers and guides are not as trained and enthusiastic about conducting a safari. Safari driver Narahari Mahato, reached the camp at around 8:30 am, instead of the scheduled departure time of 7:30. Then he took his own sweet time to finish his free breakfast provided by the camp. A happy and jolly fellow, he appeared to be on a picnic, and his contagious mood persisted the entire day, gradually transmitting to me as well.

Serious ecotourists and photographers will certainly be disappointed with this approach to tourism.

During our safari, we visited few pre-determined viewpoints such as Uski waterfalls, Jorandha and Baheripani ranges of tiger reserves and waterfalls located within these ranges, and the Chahala range. Chahala range is the only core area included on this safari route and a potential hotspot for animal sighting. However, we only saw a barking deer *en route* to Chahala range and herds of spotted deer around a human made salt pit near a watchtower. Otherwise in a span of ten hours of forest exploration we hardly saw any wildlife. I recall spotting a few oriental magpie robin, grey wagtail, black necked stork, and drongo. The mammals we saw were rhesus macaque, common langur, spotted and barking deer.

The route was a mix of dense forest and green pasture. The forest patches were segregated by agricultural land, grazing ground, and human settlements. This type of forest fragmentation has certainly impacted the wildlife sighting potential of the forest.

In Simlipal, humans and animals live in close proximity. Sometimes forest dwelling tribals are engaged in poaching activities. Based on a newspaper report in *Indian Express*, published on 24th May 2023, as a first such case, a forest guard Bimal Kumar Jena was shot by a group of people carrying a live barking deer. Narahari claimed to have seen an arrow-struck spotted deer near Kumari camp, a few days before I arrived.

According to him there are around 60 villages within the tiger reserve, with a total population of about 22,000 people, 97% of whom are tribals. As per an article *"Relocation of tribal people living around Similipal Tiger Reserve forceful, claim locals"* published in *Mongabay-India. 2020, retrieved on 12th January 2021, "In December 2013, 32 families from the Khadia tribe belonging to two hamlets of Upper Barhakamuda and Bahaghar were relocated outside the Tiger Reserve as per the guidelines set by National Tiger Conservation Authority. The village of Jamunagarh was relocated in September 2015. Following the relocation, tiger sightings in the core area has gone up. There are two villages, Kabatghai and Bakua, still present in the core area of Similipal. The Forest Department, wildlife NGOs and local administration have initiated talks with these villages on their relocation. However, the tribals alleged these relocations to be forced and wished to claim their rights under the Forest Rights Act"*.

Presence of tribal settlements within core and buffer zones of Simlipal, is undoubtedly a disturbance for wildlife sighting, and the whole purpose of ecotourism is defeated. However, this is an age-old unresolved dispute between tribal rights and forest conservation. It is obviously unfair to expect the tribals to vacate the forest lands that have been their source of livelihood for centuries. It also seems to be a biased approach that the urban affluent folks can come and stay within the forest for ecotourism while tribals cannot make their living of the forest through agriculture and livestock grazing. This triangular human civilization – nature - tribal rights conflict, also has political dimensions. Narahari mentioned that in 2018, local Maoist rebels attacked many ecotourism huts within Gurguria, Baheripani and Jorandha nature camps, located in Simlipal Tiger reserves, to protest against tribal relocation from forest lands.

Narahari Mahato and other forest department staff appeared to be empathetic to Maoists, as the complete relocation would lead to loss of their livelihood against some meagre compensation. The tribals of various tourist camps are provided alternative sources of income through ecotourism. Their income is seasonal, depending upon tourist footfalls. There is no assurance of regular income from the Government through ecotourism activities.

The tourist footfall is evidently related to the potential of wildlife sighting and the opportunity to explore and learn biodiversity. In Simlipal, the fragmented forest reduces the chance of wildlife sighting. Absence of trained nature guides hinders the promotion of awareness and the enrichment of incoming tourists' knowledge.

This vicious cycle can only be broken if the local community and forest dwellers develop an interest in wildlife, becoming effective nature guides. No premier-institute trained wildlife biologist can rival the indigenous knowledge they possess about their forest. Embarking on such an initiative would require as a pre-requisite, interim initiatives that allow for the local population to provide for their families.

Conserving India's socio-politically disturbed forests and other wastelands for biodiversity and alternative ecotourism is not an easy task. Also, it is seemingly unfair to expect the marginalized forest dwellers of third world country to sacrifice their livelihood for the sake of conservation.

What sustainability are we talking about, if it does not allow a peasant to make his living?

However, the wonder wasteland of western India surprised me with a response to this dilemma. Few years before I visited Simlipal, one winter afternoon I landed in the pink city of Jaipur and travelled around two hundred and ten kilometres to reach Tal Chhapar sanctuary located in the fringes of the great Indian Thar deserts. As per the environmental portal of Rajasthan Government, nearly 50% of wildlife species in this state is found outside the traditional protected area network. The communities in this state have volunteered to conserve wildlife and its habitat in these areas. Tal Chhapar, supposedly is one such classic case of "community-based conservation" in Indian wastelands.

One such conservation volunteer turned ecotourism guide from the local community is Anand Prasad Bhadrawal, *aka* Mahender ji. After a four-hour drive from Jaipur airport, at around 9 o'clock in the evening, I arrived at *Raptor's Paradise guesthouse*, built in 2016 by Anand Prasad. The guesthouse is located at the edge of the black buck wildlife sanctuary of Tal Chhapar. It comprises of three small rooms, a kitchen, and a small dining area, along with a front yard that measures 3 meters by 3 meters and shares a common boundary with the sanctuary.

One of Anand Prasad's key value propositions to his guests is that they can see the black buck from the guesthouse itself. This was proved right the following morning at around 7 o'clock, as I was getting ready for my first safari in the sanctuary.

In a four-and-a-half-hour safari, I saw hundreds of black bucks - male, female and calves; plenty of nil gai and some amazing winter migratory and indigenous birds of grassland ecosystems. Isabelline wheatear, southern grey shrike, sand grouse, greater short toed lark, lesser grebe, grey and black francolin, flocks of common crane and a rare migratory bird Stolikza's bush chat were some of the mention worthy avian species I spotted with the help of Anand. The Stoliczka's bush chat is also known as white-browed bush chat. The alternative name is after the discoverer, geologist and explorer Ferdinand Stoliczka. This deserts specialist has a small, declining population because of agricultural intensification and encroachment, and has been qualified as vulnerable.

This ecosystem is truly a raptor's paradise. Among the winter visitors, noteworthy raptor sightings were laggar falcon, lesser kestrel, steppe and imperial eagle. I was delighted by the presence of vulture population as for the first time I saw the much talked about cinereous vulture. This bird, also called the black vulture or monk vulture, is one of the largest flying birds and one of the iconic subjects of wildlife photography in this ecosystem. Two other commonly found species were griffon and Egyptian vultures. This was the first time I was sighting majority of the vulture species in any ecosystem I had visited thus far, and I was delighted to capture them in my camera.

The credit goes to local villager turned nature guide Anand. Several generations of Anand's family have lived in the Dewani village (a village adjacent to Chhapar) located in Sujangarh tehsil of Churu district, since its establishment. His forefathers' forefathers settled here as livestock grazers and Anand carried the legacy, with his wife, two daughters and two sons, until about fourteen years ago, when he met a Delhi based birdwatcher, Kajol Dasgupta.

Dasgupta inspired Anand to study the behaviour of migratory birds and wildlife photography. Around four-five years prior based on his advice, Anand leased the forest department's ecotourism rest house located within the sanctuary. He ran the rest house for nearly five years and that helped him in further sharpening his skill in spotting wildlife in this dry grassland ecosystem as well as learning more about wildlife behaviour.

Working closely with the forest and tourism department of this part of Rajasthan, also helped in expanding his network, which turned out quite handy when he started his own ecotourism business. Acquiring a plot located near the fence of a wildlife sanctuary to build a guesthouse is not easy, after all. Therefore, once the lease of the forest rest house expired, he started his own ecotourism service to cater to the requirements of nature lovers, bird watchers, and wildlife photographers who visited Chhapar, Jorbeer and surrounding biodiversity hotspots. It is a completely family run business, his wife serving as the main cook. She treated me to palatable and authentic Rajasthani cuisine during my stay. Anand's older son, Ravinder, is responsible for day-to-day management of the guesthouse. He also doubles up as a nature guide cum wildlife photographer.

This passion for nature and wildlife was not limited to Anand Prasad's family. He inspired other villagers in Chhapar, Dewani, Ramnagar and Guleria villages of Sujangarh tehsil, who eventually took up ecotourism over livestock grazing and farming, to make a living. Such community wide dependence on ecotourism as mainstream profession in this part of Rajasthan created massive awareness about wildlife and ecosystem in these villages.

Our afternoon safari began at 3:00 pm, as I struggled to control a strong desire for an afternoon nap after devouring a sumptuous Shekhawati spread with *bajra roti* (local bread), *gatte ka sabjee* (local curry made of lentil), and *chutney* (sauce made of mint, garlic and red chili), by Anand's wife.

The safari continued till 6:00 pm, the time when the bumblebee-butterscotch yellow of *Motha Cyperus rotundus* sedge of the sanctuary bathed in the magical vermillion rays of the setting sun. Like all other wildlife photographers, I made a few attempts to capture the customary image of a black buck silhouette against the backdrop of sunset. The afternoon safari was a memorable one. Chasing and shooting painted and black francolin, sighting of

Montague's harrier, and the most significant and rare sighting of desert cat. The desert cat was protecting its den, hidden in dry sedges, and Anand was aware of its location. Therefore, spotting the animal and obtaining decent shots were effortless.

The following day, based on Anand's advice, I witnessed yet another initiative of community-based conservation in Chhapar, known as *gaushala* (local name for cow shelter). The original idea behind establishing such a community run cow shelter was to give shelter to stray livestock that created menace in human settlements. In the process, however, the vast grazing land became a rich ecosystem for indigenous as well as endangered and migratory species.

The gaushala, named Ramshankar gaushala, is located within two-three kilometres of Anand's guesthouse. He also served as the president of the gaushala.

At the gaushala, we searched for another frequent winter visitor - spotted creeper and resident raptor tawny eagle. But instead, we were delighted by other migratory birds like variable wheatear, black redstart, chestnut shouldered pretonia and desert wheatear. Raptors like laggar falcon, long legged buzzard, ground bird red napped ibis and a nicely camouflaged spotted owlet were other bird species noticed in this land.

Despite being identified as "neglected ecosystems" of this subcontinent in the *Report of Task Force on Grasslands and Deserts*, the Tal Chhapar wildlife sanctuary of dry grasslands ecosystems of Rajasthan has done phenomenally well as far as biodiversity conservation is concerned. Community participation is undoubtedly one of the key reasons for it.

The report also pointed out that there is no law in India, that makes it mandatory to conduct environmental impact assessment of grasslands and deserts before transforming them for other developmental purposes. This ecosystem known as savannah and Serengeti of India, covers around 24% of India's total geographical area and is often considered as wastelands, on which either tree plantations are carried out or the land is repurposed for other uses. No body owns this ecosystem, neither the forest department, nor the agricultural or animal husbandry department. There is no single agency under which grassland conservation falls and most of the states have excluded the grasslands and have not identified them as deemed forest.

It is evident that ecosystems get their due attention when they are protected under Indian laws, for instance *Wildlife Protection Act* or *Indian Forest Act*. For this law to hold, an ecosystem must be home to one or more endangered or vulnerable species, which is of photographic significance for wildlife enthusiasts and ecotourists.

An excellent example of such a conservation and an important ecosystem is the Desert National Park or DNP, situated on the western border of India within Jaisalmer and Barmer in Rajasthan. It is one of the largest national parks, covering an area of 3162 square kms. It is the only place where the state bird of Rajasthan - the Great Indian Bustard, the state animal - Chinkara, the state tree – Khejri, and the state flower - Rohida are found naturally.

A year after I met Anand Prasad of Tal Chhapar, I met another community folk turned naturalist in the Desert National Park of Jaisalmer.

Musa Khan did odd jobs around DNP. In 2013, a chance encounter with Gururaj Moorching, a famous wildlife photographer, changed his life. He drove the photographer and his friends through the park and spotted a few birds. A turning point in his life. And later in 2015, when the forest department organized training for tourist guides, Khan became a top performer.

Over the last six years, he has become a sought-after guide at the park. Serving as a link between the forest department and the villagers, he has helped to create awareness about wildlife among the locals. Musa Khan is now a popular name amongst birdwatchers. He is in great demand during winters, particularly between November and March. A lot of people rely on his expertise to plan their trips to Desert National Park. Therefore, they make bookings only when Khan is free. I started talking to him five months before my visit.

I was Musa's guest for five days during my exploration of the Thar Deserts. We spotted around sixty avian species in the Indian deserts. Some very special sightings were raptors like Merlin, Eurasian sparrowhawk, common and long-legged buzzards, laggar falcon, Eurasian kestrel, tawny, imperial, and short-toed snake eagles, four types of vultures like Himalayan and Eurasian griffon, cinereous and Egyptian vultures, some special lark species of deserts such as bimaculate lark, crested lark and greater hoopoe lark, trumpeter finch and various wheatears such as Persian, isabelline, variable and desert wheatears.

However, the most mention-worthy sighting was two different species of bustards. Great Indian and MacQueen's bustards. Hugely supported by ornithologist Salim Ali, the Great Indian Bustard (GIB) was once in the running to be crowned as Indian national bird. It lost the title to the Indian peafowl, largely due to the possibility of its name being misspelled, as outlined in an article written by animal rights and environmental activist Tamanna Sengupta in the online magazine *youthkiawaaz.com*.

Thanks to Musa Khan, in three days, we saw five individuals of GIB, one adult male, two adult females, one subadult male, and one juvenile. They were mainly found foraging within the park and in the surrounding grasslands of the Sam and Salkha villages near the park. The grazing ground was surrounded by several hundred gigantic windmills.

MacQueen's bustards on the other hand are winter migratory species to the Thar Deserts. These Mongolian birds leave the wintering areas in Afghanistan and Pakistan from mid to late March and arrive at their breeding grounds after about two months of flying, taking a path that avoids the high mountains of the Himalayas. Their migrations have been tracked using satellite transmitters. In fact, we noticed tags and radio collars attached to the legs of the two adult birds we spotted.

Today wildlife enthusiasts, ecotourists, and photographers from all over the world visit Desert National Park to catch a glimpse of and take dream shots of these two bustard species. Musa Khan keeps track of these birds' movement with the help of local nomads and shepherds who frequently spot these birds while herding their livestock to the grassland for grazing. His engagement with them prevented them from hunting the birds, as everyone has now begun to understand the potential of the ecotourism economy of the Thar deserts.

Ecotourism based on the principle of bio-spherical egalitarianism must be inclusive of all species and acknowledge that each species has equal right and value. This is what I mean by wholistic ecotourism.

This inclusivity considers humans as well. The local community whose livelihood was otherwise dependent on the habitats of this ecologically important species, must be in the forefront to run the tourism activity. Their ecological and ecotourism knowledge must be enhanced. Their resources, including their home cooked food as well as home for staying, should be utilized. Urban affluent photographers' and ecotourists' fascination for fancy resorts and a multi cuisine buffet spread will clearly not find a place under this concept.

This community-based ecotourism in Indian wastelands is but environmental activism against neo-liberal sustainability. The GIB conservation serves as a classic example of this.

My colleague, biodiversity expert Dr. Arun Venkataraman, once highlighted in one of his knowledge papers, how this critically endangered species, endemic to the Indian subcontinent is now closer to extinction. A decade ago, more than 350 individuals were found across several populations in India. However, the species today is confined to three to four small pockets in Karnataka, Andhra Pradesh, Gujarat, and Rajasthan states of India. Arun further elaborated on this issue, by mentioning that the Barmer and Jaisalmer districts in Rajasthan are thought to hold nearly 75 % of the global population of the Great Indian Bustard. These districts are also valued for their extensive wind and solar energy potentials. They have experienced and continue to experience intense wind and solar energy project development. *The Wildlife Institute of India (WII)* has carried out long-term research on GIB within the Barmer and Jaisalmer districts and has obtained a comprehensive understanding of habitat utilisation across this landscape. The WII also considers overhead high-voltage transmission lines as the leading cause of mortality. Based on this research, GIB habitats in these districts have been zoned into

GIB Priority Areas with intense feeding and breeding activity and *GIB Potential Areas* used in transit across habitats. Specific mitigation planning has been suggested for each of these areas and it has been recommended that this planning occurs in consultation with the *WII*.

When states, institutions, and policy makers recognise this underlying cause and conflict between conserving GIB and promoting renewable (windmills) as part of the sustainable development agenda, there is this informal conservation activism that remains inconspicuous. That is the participation of local community turned conservationists in protecting this less glamorous but ecologically important species.

This activism challenges some of the "popular means" of achieving neo-liberal sustainable development goals and upholds the principal of bio-spherical egalitarianism to create an alternative wholistic ecotourism.

The response to Pseudo Ecotourism!

CHAPTER ELEVEN: The Wise Use of Wetland

The environmental activism that gave birth to alternative ecotourism, while challenges the neo-liberal sustainability-based pseudo ecotourism, not only embraces the principle of biospherical egalitarianism, but also ironically embraces a bi-product of neo-liberal sustainability, known as nature-based solution[4]. We can then infer that, as far as ecotourism goes, one element of neo-liberal sustainability can be used to counter the other elements of it.

It is fascinating how nature fights against her own fury in an attempt to protect her inhabitants. These protective mechanisms are collectively termed as nature-based solutions under neo-liberal sustainability. A week before my Sundarbans exploration in West Bengal, a severe storm - a strong tropical cyclone - *Bulbul*, struck Vietnam, the Indian state of West Bengal, and Bangladesh, causing storm surge, heavy

---

[4] *Nature-based solutions are defined by the International Union for Conservation of Nature (IUCN) as the sustainable management and use of natural features and processes to tackle socio-environmental issues. These issues include for example climate change, water security, food security, preservation of biodiversity, and disaster risk reduction.*

rains, and flash floods. The areas affected in India were eastern coast, Andaman and Nicobar Islands. They are all mangrove ecosystem zones.

According to meteorologists and ecologists, the mangrove forest saved the Andaman Islands and Bengal from the cyclone *Bulbul*. The Sundarbans absorbed the fury of the cyclone saving West Bengal and Bangladesh but, in the process, suffered severe damage. Reportedly, Sundarbans reduced the wind speed of cyclone *Bulbul* by twenty kilometres an hour and – at its own expense – saved the rest of southern Bengal from the fury of the storm. After the devastation by *Bulbul*, Shafiul Alam Chowdhury, the Chief Conservator of Forests of the Bangladeshi Sundarbans, in an interview with a local newspaper of the country, talked about the significance of the Sundarbans and the need for its protection. He said, *"The Sundarbans has always been like a mother to Bangladesh, protecting it from the onslaught of cyclones and tidal surges".*

In India besides Sundarbans, other large mangroves are Bhitarkanika Mangroves, India's second largest mangrove forest, located in Odisha, created by the two river delta of Brahmani and Baitarani rivers; the Godavari Krishna mangroves that lie in the delta of the Godavari and Krishna rivers in Andhra Pradesh, also under protection of Calimere Wildlife and Pulicat Lake bird sanctuary; Pichavaram mangrove, situated at Pichavaram near Chidambaram in Tamil Nadu, which ranks among one of the most exquisite scenic spots in Tamil Nadu and is home to many species of aquatic birds; and mangroves situated between Middle and South Andamans, near capital city Port Blair.

These mangrove forests have proven track record of providing nature-based solution. However, of these key mangrove forests of India, Pichavaram has a recent history of environmental activism as well as.

Based on a news report published in *India Today*, in 2013, ecologists in Tamil Nadu declared war on the State Government. The battleground was Pichavaram. As per the report, the State Government was keen on developing this magnificent forest into a tourist resort with boating, surfing, and water-skiing facilities along with cottages located in the area. The reason why Pichavaram had so many crusaders was that it is one of the few mangroves left, where the complete sequence of mangrove zonation is in evidence - from dense foliage with stilted roots on the banks to sparse vegetation at the edge.

Another recent news publication, in *The New Indian Express*, in April 2019 added another conflict to the existing concerns over this ecosystem. Based on the report, 341 hydrocarbon wells were to be drilled in Tamil Nadu by *Vedanta* and *ONGC*, while ecologists expressed concerns over environmental impacts of the drilling activities. Of the 341 wells, 67 were proposed by public sector oil major *ONGC* while the remaining 274 were by *Cairn Oil and Gas*, a vertical of *Vedanta*. The *Vendanta's* block where drilling was planned, according to records, is just 0.49 km away from the ecologically sensitive Pichavaram Mangrove Forest.

Author S. Viswanathan mentioned in his article *For a bio-shield*, published as cover story in January 29th to February 11th 2005 issue of *Frontline*, *"For instance, the Pichavaram mangrove forest, a tourist attraction in Cuddalore district, protected about 6,000 people living in six hamlets - T.S. Pettai, Vadakku Pichavaram, Therkku Pichavaram, Meenavar Colony, MGR Nagar and Kalaignar Nagar - from the tsunami attack (of 26th December 2004), according to the Chennai-based M.S. Swaminathan Research Foundation (MSSRF). These hamlets are located between 100 metres and one kilometre from the mangroves. Seawater did not enter the village and hence there was no loss of property."*

At fifteen past seven on a winter morning, I arrived at Puducherry railway station where my local cab driver, Faruk was waiting. We then picked up my ERM colleague, Arvind Mohanram (I was employed at ERM as a sustainability professional since 2008.). Arvind is a geologist who also has a passion for photography. More importantly his proficiency in Tamil was an advantage, which I would realize in the days to come. The main objective of this trip was to visit T. S. Pettai, one of the hamlets mentioned in S. Viswanathan's article. After driving through sixteen kilometres of mixed tar and mud road for about thirty-five to forty minutes from the main entrance of Pichavaram reserve forest, we arrived at T.S. Pettai.

However, before heading to T.S. Pettai, we went on a boat safari in Pichavaram mangrove forest. We hired a rowboat, which allowed us to easily navigate through narrow creeks and canals of the mangrove forest. Our boat man, Kumar told us that Pichavaram Reserve Forest (PRF) had almost twenty different species of mangroves in an area of 3000 hectares with wetland[5] area of 1100 hectare, created by backwaters of Bay of Bengal. A network of around 4400 canals intersects this mangrove forest.

The small canals were sun-flecked tunnels of roots and branches, some hanging so low that there was hardly any room to pass through. Except for the swish of paddles, intermittent commentary by Kumar, clicking of shutter by Arvind and me, sound of birds and the roaring of the sea in the distance, it was silent and still. Approximately 200 species of birds have been recorded in this forest, along with many varieties of snakes, seaweed, fish, prawns, crabs, oysters, turtles, and otters. The bird species includes migrant and local birds like snipes, cormorants, egrets, storks, herons, spoonbills, and pelicans. We saw quite a few little cormorants, common tern, western reef egret (dark morph), black headed ibis, pond herons, greater and lesser egrets; and many doves and parakeets.

The one-hour exploration in the narrow canals, where trees grow at a varying water level from three feet to ten feet (during high tide in rainy season), gave us an opportunity to experience the mangrove ecosystems up close and personal. Getting so close to this

---

[5] *These unique habitats include mangroves, peatlands, rivers, lakes, deltas, seagrass meadows, and even coral reefs.*

ecosystem of _Avicennia marina_ and _Rhizophora_, was not possible in Sundarbans.

In the article, *"Beyond tsunami: An agenda for action" (The Hindu, January 17)*, agricultural scientist M.S. Swaminathan, has mentioned, *"Mangroves are very efficient in carbon sequestration. They also promote sustainable fisheries by releasing nutrients in the water. Further, they will provide additional income and make coastal communities eligible for carbon credit."* This scientific revelation of mangrove ecosystem's significance has initiated a community-based bio-shield movement across coastal villages of Puducherry and Tamil Nadu. This is precisely why we desired to witness firsthand the mangrove conservation effort of T. S. Pettai village.

Based on a report published on 19th December 2005, in the online edition of The *Telegraph*, *"As village after village was being swept away when the tsunami struck the Tamil Nadu coast last year, a tiny hamlet stood on, defiant. Not a single house was razed in T.S. Pettai, a remote fishing village in Cuddalore district, thanks to a mangrove forest that shielded it against the sea's fury. Located 13 km from the temple town of Chidambaram, T.S. Pettai recorded only one death of a man who was grazing cattle when the waves crashed."*

A similar version of the story was reiterated by local fisherman Chandrasekhar, when Arvind and I explored the Kuchchikoluthi medu area of T. S. Pettai. Upon arrival at the village, when we enquired among a group of local villagers about the mangrove forest and the possibility of cruising through it by boat, we were informed that evening would be the most suitable time to visit. During the morning and afternoon, all the fisherfolks are occupied with their daily tasks of catching fish and shrimp.

Chandrasekhar noticed our interaction with the villagers. He followed us in his motorcycle and stopped our car. He offered to arrange a ride through the canals on a country boat. Arvind's presence came handy in conveying our expectations and arranging the trip. Within half an hour, he returned with a wooden rowing paddle, and accompanied by a young man, Yogeshwaran. Together they led us to the other end of the village where mangrove forest begins. There were small creeks that carried the back water of Bay of Bengal, and a few women catching shrimp. Couple of elderly women stood in neck-deep water, picking up prawns and collecting them in an earthen pot. Four or five boats were anchored there, and we got into one of them.

Chandrasekhar told us there were 1200 varieties of mangroves, which is perhaps an exaggeration if we go by the scientific data in different research papers available in public domain. Boatman Kumar at PRF told us there were twenty different species of mangroves. However, a total number of twelve true mangrove species are present in the Pichavaram mangrove wetland, as per the research paper *Pichavaram mangrove Wetland: Situation Analysis*, published in 2010 by *Mangroves for the future (MFF)* and *International Union for Conservation of Nature and Natural*

Resources. Among all the species, *Avicennia marina* alone constitutes 74% of the tree population and is distributed everywhere except on the banks of tidal canals and creeks.

For about two hours we explored the area on the country boat, which was a lot more unstable than the boat we used at Pichavaram reserve forest that morning. The boat oscillated precariously and with great difficulty we maintained our balance, making sure we didn't tip over. The canal was shallow, not more than seven feet deep. It was 12:40 in the afternoon, and the high tide had begun. We cruised up to an exposed sand bed on the eastern side of the forest, which separated the forest and the village from the sea. The water flowed from the sea towards the village. We were moving against the current. Given the village's close proximity to the sea, it was not difficult to envision the potential extent of a tsunami's impact.

Chandrasekhar, however, announced proudly, *"Nothing happened to our village in the last Tsunami."* He continued, *"Because of these mangroves, soil erosion is prevented, and the population of prawns has increased in the canals, which is our main livelihood."* In this village everyone makes their livelihood by fishing for fish and shrimp. This reminded me of Dr. Swaminathan's comment on the role of mangroves in promoting sustainable fishing.

The sand plane was wet, an indication that it had remained submerged in seawater, for a considerable time. We saw flocks of common tern, Pallas's gulls, brown-headed gulls, and plovers on the sand bed, feeding on small crabs and fish. There were a few Asian open bill storks, pied and white breasted kingfishers sitting on the branches of mangrove trees, keeping a close watch on the canal for prey and occasionally swooping into water on spotting one. The sand bed was also home to a good number of red ghost crabs, hurriedly clearing our path. Crabs are important component of the coastal and mangrove ecosystems and use an array of microhabitats. They feed on the leaf litter and other organic matter, and thus play an important role in recycling of nutrients. They dig into the sand which helps to aerate the soil.

A group of fishermen sorted fish from their fishing net. Human, birds, and arthropods together made their living, from the same source, in their own respective ways. Forest dweller's respect for nature and their ability to live in harmony with non-human was on display. If this was not embracing the principle of bio-spherical egalitarianism, then I wonder what would be?

After exploring for two hours, Chandrasekhar, father to a one-year-old boy and a four-year-old girl, invited us to his house and treated us to tender coconut from his own tree. People like Chandrasekhar, Yogeshwaran and many others in T. S Pettai and other hamlets near Pichavaram forests survive because of the existence of this ecosystem. Any commercial or political intent underlying the development of tourism resorts with amusement facilities or installing a drilling rig, demands an answer to this fundamental question – *Should humans strive to dominate in pursuit of their materialistic goals, or should they take a role of servitude and protection towards nature for the sake of their own survival?*

This question, however, does not apply to the mangroves of Sundarbans. Sundarbans does not need the human as its protector. They have the Tiger. Sy Montgomery conveyed this eloquently in her legendry novel, *Spell of the Tiger*, translating almost verbatim the words of local priest Phoni Guyan; *"He (Dokkhin Rai) must eat those who do not pay him respect; otherwise, people would lose their respect for the forest, and the relationships between the people and the forest – the rules by which everyone survives - would be destroyed."*

The incident I witnessed one winter afternoon in the Peerkhali area of Indian Sundarbans, was one such control measure by the demigod of the subcontinental forest.

Nature's ability to protect all life forms is unquestionable but that does not absolve the human of their responsibility in joining hands with her in protecting all life forms, particularly when human is the supreme destroyer of these life forms. Thankfully despite being influenced by neo-liberal sustainability not all humans have forgotten their responsibility.

Keoladeo National Park or Keoladeo Ghana National Park, formerly known as the Bharatpur Bird Sanctuary, in Bharatpur, is a man-made and man-managed wetland, and one of the national parks of Rajasthan. A fascinating land, which offers photographers, nature lovers, ornithologists alike a chance to be in proximity with the elements of nature in all its spectacular magnificence. Like most of the popular ecotourism destinations of Rajasthan and central India, this bird sanctuary and national park also has a history of being a game reserve for local rulers. The park was a hunting ground for the Maharajas of Bharatpur, a tradition dating back to 1850, and duck shoots were organised yearly in honour of the British viceroys. In one shoot alone in 1938, Lord Linlithgow, then Viceroy of India killed over 4,273 birds such as mallards and teals. Also known as KNP, the forest was initially a low-lying area and subject to seasonal flooding. Ajan Bund, a 3270-hectare impoundment was built here by Maharaja Suraj Mal, ruler of the state of Bharatpur in the eighteenth century, to prevent flooding and as a water reservoir for agricultural purposes. Of course, 200 years ago no one perhaps imagined that such an agricultural initiative would transform into an international ecotourism destination. The system of canals, dykes and impoundments served the purpose of flood control and created additional area for cattle grazing in dry conditions. The present ecosystem is a cohabitation of wildlife and livestock, and has developed into a fine system of freshwater marshes that attracts large populations of migratory birds.

The sanctuary is famous for being the habitat of the sarus crane—the tallest flying bird in the world—that grows up to six feet in height. I learned as a child that the Bengali word for crane is *Saras*. Now, years later, when I visited KNP with M.V. Shreeram, I learnt that the Saras, or sarus, is just one of fifteen species of cranes found globally. At an average height of five feet, these birds have a red nape (the base of the neck) and are famous for their mating habits—unlike most other birds, they are believed to find partners for life. Besides three different pairs of sarus in three different days, we also saw plenty of cormorants, egrets, grey and purple herons, pond herons, spot billed ducks, woolly-necked storks, painted storks, black headed and glossy ibis, moorhen, white breasted water hen, Eurasian coots, purple swamp hens. Among other resident forest birds were orange-headed thrush, rose ringed parakeets, common hoopoe, brown-headed and copper smith barbets. Some interesting and rare sight birds were black and yellow bittern and pin-tailed snipe. Among winter visitors, noteworthy sighting included northern shoveler, northern pintail, greylag geese, bar-headed geese, red crested and common pochard, gadwall, ferruginous duck, and garganey. Three types of kingfishers found there are – common, white breasted and pied kingfishers – we were delighted to sight all three. Among raptors, greater spotted eagle was in abundance, we also saw shikra, crested serpent eagle and booted eagle. But I was particularly excited with sighting a few spotted owlets, a pair of collard scops owl, a brown hawk owl and an Indian nightjar.

The sighting and photography of Indian nightjar was a 'lifer".

We wildlife photographers use this word almost universally and loosely whenever we see any flora or fauna for the very first time in life. Although I never understood why we can't simply say *"it was our first sighting in life"*. Dictionary meaning of this word is "a person serving a life sentence" or "a person who spends their life in a particular career". In both cases it sounds like bondage. Maybe the word symbolizes the bondage of fame photographers love to carry with them.

Nevertheless, this "lifer" sighting was made possible because of Shreeram's special connection with local nature guides Robin and Chhotu Afzal Khan. Along with two other photographers, they took us to a secret bushy patch of the forest at the edge of the fencing, where the nocturnal bird had been resting for a few days. Spotting and taking images of this nocturnal bird from touching distance is a fabulous experience for any nature explorer.

Among mammals, the population of three stripped palm squirrel, spotted deer, rhesus macaque and nil gai are in abundance in the park. In recent times, population of jackal and striped hyena have increased owing to sufficient scavenging opportunities. We spotted a male striped hyena and a couple of jackals. Another fascinating moment was capturing the image of a yawning juvenile python hiding in the bushes. Other reptile species we saw included a good number of flap-shelled turtle.

The crucial nature-based solution provided by the reserve is protecting Bharatpur from frequent floods. It also provides grazing grounds for village cattle. Managed ecosystem's contribution is undoubtedly crucial in ecotourism and biodiversity conservation in an agricultural country like India. Such manual intervention helps in enhancing and sustaining the biodiversity. These managed ecosystems have the potential to become a global ecotourism destination developed as an outcome of "ecosystem services"[6].

---

[6] The "ecosystem services" are illustrated as *"water storage, water purification, flood mitigation, erosion control, aquifer recharge, microclimate regulation, aesthetic enhancement of landscapes while simultaneously supporting significant recreational, social and cultural activities......",* in the preamble of a biodiversity conservation specific legislation of India, known as *Wetland (Conservation and Management) Rules, 2017.* This wetland related rule is originated as an outcome of ratifying a significant international convention related to environment and sustainability – *Ramsar Convention on Wetlands of International Importance Especially as Waterfowl Habitat,* which is an international treaty for the conservation and sustainable as well as wise use of wetlands, also known as the Convention on Wetlands.

The wetlands are not just ecotourism destinations for wildlife enthusiasts. They also provide "ecosystem services" to local community (for the purpose of fishing, agriculture etc.), in addition to serving as a sanctuary for critically endangered, endangered, and vulnerable species.

Neo-liberal sustainability was introduced by capitalism to create hegemony in environmental activism and as a result the commodity fetishism for tiger-centric pseudo ecotourism was born. However, I must add that the same neo-liberal sustainability coined the term nature-based solution, which can be used as an opportunity to shift the wildlife enthusiasts' attention from this pseudo ecotourism to an inclusive biodiversity tourism. This concept could be effective in dealing with "human-tiger" (or rather tourist-tiger) conflict in popular ecotourism destinations of this subcontinent.

In an article written by Annie Combs, titled *Nature-Based Solutions: The Key to Regenerative Tourism*, in the blog of *Solimar International*, published on 24th June 2022, the author states, *"Solimar International's Director of Conservation & Community Development, Chloe King, has published her White Paper: Climate Action through Regeneration: Unlocking the Power of Communities and Nature through Tourism.*

Chloe worked alongside Senior Sustainability Consultant, O'Shannon Burns and his organization named *Regenerative Travel and The Long Run,* on a year-long research project that sought to determine how tourism can be made into a more regenerative practice by embracing nature-based solutions. The paper identifies *Five Principles to Develop Effective Nature-Based Solutions* that highlight the connectedness between travel businesses, nature, and local communities.

The first principle emphasizes on developing nature-based solution through establishing a relationship between a travel business and local communities. This principle of Chole, is founded on a mutual understanding of the intrinsic value of nature and a duty to protect it for the greater good of both parties. According to Chole, the power of engaging with local community and transforming them as protectors of ecosystems has been recognized several times in successful ecotourism initiatives.

As I mentioned earlier, Dr. Ullas Karanth in his interview published in the electronic edition of *Frontline*, on 4th May 2023, resonated the same thought, *"the real potential of an enlightened wildlife tourism industry lies in working cooperatively with local farmers—on a profit-sharing basis—to switch land use around wildlife reserves from crops to wildlife habitat."*

The largest wintering ground for migratory birds in the Indian sub-continent, home to several threatened species of plants and animals, is one such great example of community engagement and transformation in creating an international ecotourism destination. Chilika Lake is the largest brackish water lagoon in Asia and the second largest coastal lagoon in the world, spread over the Puri, Khordha and Ganjam districts of Odisha state on the east coast of India, at the mouth of the Daya River, flowing into the Bay of Bengal, covering an area of over 1,100 square kilometres. The lake is an ecosystem with large fishery resources. It sustains more than 150,000 fisherfolks living in 132 villages on the shore and islands. The lagoon hosts over 160 species of birds in the peak migratory season. Birds from as far as the Caspian Sea, Lake Baikal, Aral Sea and other remote parts of Russia, Kirghiz steppes of Kazakhstan, central and southeast Asia, Ladakh and the Himalayas. These birds travel great distances; some of them possibly travelling as much as 12,000 kilometres to reach Chilika Lake.

Mangalajodi is one of the many villages located in and around the Chilika Lake. The village is located about five kilometres from Tangi in the district Khordha, sixty kilometres from Bhubaneshwar and situated in the northern side of Chilika. It is a freshwater zone with marshes, reed beds and rich birdlife. What sets Mangalajodi apart is that every winter thousands of migratory waterfowl descends upon its marshes, transforming the area into a carnival as they jostle about with resident birds.

According to an article written by Aditya Panda in the online version of *Conservation India*, journal titled, *Mangalajodi — A Village of Bird Protectors in Orissa*, *"up until the mid-90s, this winter carnival was often rudely interrupted by humans. As night fell on the noisy bird colonies, the sleepy villages surrounding the marsh would wake up. Dark shapes would lurk, gliding in canoes, crushing water-lily pods and lacing them with the deadly poison, Furatin. When dawn broke, hundreds of the birds would feast unknowingly on the deadly pods... canoe-loads of dead birds would thus be ready for meat markets far and near."*

Based on a booklet on Mangalajodi written by Chinmaya Bhujabal, *"poaching was causing irreparable damage to the avifauna of Mangalajodi. There were about 80 poachers in the village, proficient in various techniques in killing birds. These birds are regularly sold in the open market, at rates varying from Rs. 20/- to Rs. 60/- per bird, depending on the species and method of killing. A proficient poacher can earn anything between Rs. 10,000/- to Rs. 40,000/- in a year. There was a huge damage to the wetland habitat due to rampant poaching of waterbirds."*

Another related article written by Himanshu Nitnaware in *Thebetterindia.com* states, *"the grim picture has transformed over the years, as poachers themselves have become conservators. Hard to believe? The figures prove that from a population of 5,000 birds in the early 1990s, the number has steadily increased to over 5,00,000 in 2021. This change has come around owing to the efforts of Nanda Kishore Bhujabal, who strived for years to work closely with villagers and help change their mindset. Earlier a poacher himself, Nanda realised his wrong ways during the early years of his life, and this made him bring about a change in others. At present, 25 such ex-poachers work towards bird conservation and as tourist guides for visitors."*

Chinmaya Bhujabal, the son of Nanda Kishore, mentioned in the booklet on Mangalajodi, that in the winter of January 1996, Nanda Kishore along with a few others had formed the organization called *Wild Odisha*, had visited Mangalajodi village. This casual visit to view migratory waterfowl, revealed a whole new world. Chinmaya mentioned, *"It was late afternoon, and the whole place was resounding with gunfire. They saw many people moving around with guns and shooting, it was truly nightmarish!"* In 1999-2000, Nanda Kishore led the *Wild Odisha* team in Mangalajodi, and gained the confidence of poachers/hunters for controlling poaching. In December of 2000, *Sri Sri Mahavir Pakshi Surakhsya Samiti* of Mangalajodi was born, consisting of poachers and hunters. Poaching has been under control since then.

I witnessed the effect of this community centred approach of integrating nature-based solution in ecotourism, when I visited this marshy wetland and stayed at *Godwit Eco-Cottage* which conducts ecotourism activities in Mangalajodi through *Sri Sri Mahavir Pakshi Surakhsya Samiti*.

My first boat-ride in Mangalajodi started at 10:30 am with guide Ganesh. Each ride was typically for a duration of two and a half hours. Ganesh was particularly upset that day by the local peasants. The 44 km^2 marshy wetland of Mangalajodi is a grazing ground of buffalos. The cattle were shooing the birds away and adversely affecting his ecotourism activity.

With Mangalajodi's transformation from a poaching hell to a birds' paradise, the influx of world's ecotourists and wildlife photographers, like any other ecotourism destination, has raised the expectations from local nature guides. The prospects for capturing eye-level shots of birds in action were very high. From fighting of two birds, mating, hunting, feeding on prey or flying. The small country boat on the shallow water of wetland, takes tourists and photographers very close to these birds, making little noise. Such expectations, thus, appear "reasonable" to the wetland's human visitors.

In the four boat rides that I took during my visit, I saw fifty-two different species of migratory and resident birds including gadwall, spot billed duck, garganey, northern pintail, northern shoveler, ruddy shelduck, black-tailed godwit, black headed ibis, glossy ibis, Asian openbill stork, painted stork, small pratincole, whiskered tern, marsh sandpiper, wood sandpiper, spotted redshank, little stilt, and a few raptors such as peregrine falcon, eastern marsh harrier etc. The sky was overcast on both days with occasional light showers owing to the suddenly developed cyclonic storm, *Michaung*, in the Bay of Bengal. However, the days were not particularly warm, due to the cyclone. This also implied that the birds were, thus, less active. Despite the gloomy weather though, I could capture plenty of action shots of birds. A grey and purple heron snapping up a snake, a pond heron devouring a fish, an ibis hunting a frog, and plenty of in-flight shots of various waterfowls and raptors. Such is the enormity of Mangalajodi's photography and ecotourism potential.

Tourism at Mangalajodi was initiated in 2002 by *Wild Odisha* with the support of the *Chilika Development Authority*, and is today one of the primary sources of livelihood for the families of the erstwhile poachers. The Mangalajodi conservation and ecotourism model has demonstrated to the world that regulated, low-impact tourism has the potential to be a vital conservation tool as it helps win public support for wildlife conservation.

During one of my four boat rides, a guide Anand mentioned that he was previously a poacher. Now, as a nature guide, he may earn less than selling bird meat, but is content since he is no longer taking an innocent life.

Unfortunately, in this same state of India, another wetland of international and ecological importance failed to resonate with the local community and ecotourists/wildlife photographers in the same way.

Prior to visiting Mangalajodi, I briefly explored the Satkosia tiger reserve of Odisha. It is located at the border of Angul and Nayagarh district, covers an area of 988.30 km², and comprises the Satkosia Gorge Wildlife Sanctuary and the adjacent Baisipalli Wildlife Sanctuary. It is located where the Mahanadi River passes through a 22 km long gorge in the mountains of Eastern Ghats.

The ecotourism activities were even more casual in Satkosia than at Simlipal. After arriving at the all women-run *Tarava Eco-Camp*, I was informed that there were safari options available for a fee. Local villagers would organize it, and they expected payment in cash. The options included a boat safari on the Mahanadi River, day, and night safaris in the forests. However, the *Ecotour Odisha* website did not provide any information of these activities. While the website did mention guided nature trek and bird-watching, these were far from reality.

In Satkosia, I explored villages, village forest and patches of dense forest, in a local tuk-tuk driven by a local chap. The forest landscape was fragmented, much like Simlipal. However, the hour-long boat safari on the Mahanadi River was worth my while. I finally experienced some serious nature and wildlife exploration on the Simlipal-Satkosia trip. I saw a mugger crocodile, and seven different bird species such as Indian river tern, great thick knee, river lapwing, cormorant, egret, white browed wagtail, and pied kingfisher. The notable sighting, though, was a few red-crowned roofed turtles. The red-crowned roofed turtle or Bengal roof turtle (_Batagur kachuga_) is a species of freshwater turtle endemic to south Asia. Fewer than four hundred adult females are thought to remain in the wild, with the IUCN[7] rating this turtle as being "critically endangered".

Like Mangalajodi, the Satkosia Gorge has the potential to be a much sought after ecotourism destination for people from various parts of the world. However, in Satkosia, the local community was hardly involved actively in ecotourism activities. People who were superficially involved were not adequately trained in natural history. As a result, there was no influx of ecotourists and wildlife photographers to sight and shoot the critically endangered red-crowned roofed turtle.

By "wise use of wetlands" the International Institutions meant maintenance of wetland ecosystem for the benefit of wildlife as well as people dependent on them for their livelihood and survival. Pichavaram, Bharatpur, Mangalajodi and Chilika are near perfect examples of such wise use. Perhaps all wetlands of this subcontinent have some potential to provide a home to ecologically significant species, in addition to human wellbeing. They could be a patch of mangroves along coastal lines, a small village pond, a

---

[7] The International Union for Conservation of Nature (IUCN) is an international organization and global authority on the status of the natural world and the measures needed to safeguard it. IUCN is at the forefront of the global fight to save species from extinction.

canal flowing through a countryside, an urban recreation lake, estuaries, back water of a sea, or a vast salt lake on high-altitude mountains.

If we can rid ourselves of our obsession with a single species, we will be able to sight and shoot floral and faunal diversity in all of them.

Many nature and wildlife enthusiasts will agree with me that environmental awareness and authentic travelling experience are the key drivers for their ecotourism activity. Therefore, an ideal ecotourism which intent to meet the fundamental purposes of it, i.e., environmental awareness and authentic experience, should create opportunities to visit tea and coffee estates, agricultural fields, wastelands and wetlands.

I identify such ecotourism not just an alternative-wholistic ecotourism but also as an *inclusive ecotourism!*

CHAPTER TWELVE: Other Areas Are the New Hope

Wildlife photographer and photography trip organizer M. V. Shreeram of *Darter Photography* once mentioned, *"nature should not be a supplementary pursuit"*. While responding to my question on choosing wildlife photography as a profession in spite of being educated from *BITS, Pilani* and *IIM Bangalore*, Shreeram said, *"Premier institutes draw the nation's most talented individuals, capable of addressing many of society's problems. Nevertheless, upon graduation, there is a natural expectation from them to ascend to top executive roles within major corporations. This corporate rat race often relegates their ability, intent and aspirations to solve societal issues to the background. Besides their corporate responsibilities, everything else, including their passion for nature, becomes supplementary."*

Shreeram believed that given our dependence on nature, and the undeniable impact of all our actions on it, we should be very mindful of all our activities.

The pool of talent that made their way to premier institutes only to end up being trapped in the corporate rat race, do eventually realize their helplessness. Whether it is my childhood friend

Vedavyasa or famous Bengali novel's fictitious character, Prithu, they all identify themselves as victims of a commodified society that made them forsake their aspirations and passion.

In Guha's novel *Madhukari*, Prithu regrets being educated in modern science and technology. He attributes the development in science, technology, electricity, nuclear energy, wealth, and all other human-made elements of materialism for the perceived happiness, luxury, and arrogance of humankind. He reckons these are not genuine human inventions, but rather discoveries of what already existed in nature. Regrettably, these discoveries have instilled in the human a sense of pseudo supremacy leading to the thoughtless exploitation of nature.

But all is not lost. Not yet. Surprisingly, international communities struggling to implement sustainable development agenda by 2030, to ensure Earth's temperature does not rise beyond 1.5°C, has also introduced the term nature-based solution aligned with the concept of strategizing business built in harmony with nature, rather than in opposition to it.

Global Sustainability Leaders recognize that nature-based solution is the last resort to combat climate change, and I recognize it as the new hope to combat pseudo ecotourism.

Solimar International's Director of Conservation and Community Development, Chloe King, in her *White Paper: Climate Action through Regeneration: Unlocking the Power of Communities and Nature through Tourism*, explains, *"The first principle to develop nature-based solutions is centring community needs first. The most important piece of this principle is the ability to build a "collective path forward," which establishes a relationship between a travel business and local communities that is founded on a mutual understanding of the intrinsic value of nature and a duty to protect it for the greater good of both parties' interests."*

If local community and forest dwellers fail to see this relationship and do not recognize their responsibility to protect the forests, *aka* ecotourism destinations, then even tiger reserves may fall behind in the glorious success story of commercial ecotourism. Some of the northeast Indian tiger reserves are examples.

The tiger population in North-Eastern hills and the Brahmaputra landscape have witnessed marginal increase as per the *NTCA - Status of Tigers in India-2022* report. From 100 in this landscape in 2006, the tiger population in 2022 went up to 236. In 2018 tiger census, no tigers were recorded in two tiger reserves of this landscape – Buxa of north Bengal and Dampa of Mizoram. In 2022, although two tigers were photo captured in Buxa, Dampa still has no record of a tiger. In addition, no tiger was recorded in Kamlang tiger reserve of the state of Arunachal Pradesh.

An unexpected invitation from a social media friend Biswarup Ghosh, at the beginning of one winter, drew my attention to Buxa tiger reserve. Biswarup lives in Alipurduar, a city situated on the east bank of Kaljani River on the foothills of the eastern

Himalayas, the gateway to Bhutan and to the northeastern states of India. Biswarup has his own forest resort at Rajabhatkhawa, 21 basti, which is surrounded by forests and is a regular grazing ground for elephants.

At around 7:30 pm, after a drive of five hours from Bagdogra airport of West Bengal, we arrived at the resort, which is locally managed by Biswarup's older brother, Biswadeep. A sustainability consultant colleague of mine, accompanied me on this trip.

Padmanabhan Girinathan Nair *aka* Paddy, an ardent nature enthusiast, adventurer, sports person, a loving husband and a caring father of two, has been a consistent companion on many of my previous trips in the Western Ghats.

The sun bids farewell in haste, in the winter months of northeast India. That winter evening when we arrived at the resort it was pitch dark. The resort was located within the tiger reserve, and there were couple of other resorts and fragmented human habitats within the core area of Buxa tiger reserve. Indigenous communities of Rabha and Toto within the tiger reserve led to the presence of multiple rice and other vegetable cultivation fields, cattle grazing pasture and livestock sheds.

Staying in the core area of a tiger reserve is always adventurous. We met our local guides Reevu, Amiyo and resort manager Ashish. Ashish was responsible for catering to our food and other requirements for the next five days. We discussed the exploration plan with them, and soon after, they left the resort, cautioning us before leaving, to not explore outside at night, since the resort was surrounded by an elephant movement zone.

The following morning, at around seven, we walked towards the west side of the tiger reserve. The intent was to go on a bushwalk to get a feel of the forest, to spot the Oriental pied hornbill and to risk a potential encounter with a gaur or an elephant. Yes, risky indeed, but for our local guide Reevu, it appeared to be a regular activity and a form of recreation.

We walked for five hours in the core area of the tiger reserve, crossing different streams of local Dima River not less than eight to ten times. The entry point to the forest, also an elephant crossing point, was the backyard of our resort. After walking a kilometre or two through narrow muddy forest path covered with dense foliage, we spotted a couple of Oriental pied hornbills.

We meandered from one place to another, eventually reaching a clear area. We walked through the clear patch, and again crossed a few other streams of Dima, the banks of which were broken. By elephants, said Reevu, pointing to several elephant footprints on the mud, alongside the streams. While I struggled to cross muddy ditches and various streams with camera in hand, Paddy was more comfortable, walking effortlessly.

Son of a forest department veterinary doctor, Paddy grew up in closer proximity to nature than either

Vedavyasa or Shreeram. Decades before I started roaming the forests of this subcontinent holding a camera, he was spending time in the wild, with no objective of photography.

When one explores nature with the only intention of being part of it, the elements of nature are but facets of nature and not impediments on their journey. This is perhaps the real nature-based solution that ecotourism offers.

One morning, Paddy and I explored the local village and walked along the railway track which goes through Buxa tiger reserve. We ventured into the forest adjacent to the railway track. After an hour of roaming around, as we were exiting, we met a group of villagers walking towards the forest with sickles in hands. In a matter-of-fact tone, they instructed us to follow them if we were keen to see elephants

This statement suggested the presence of elephant(s) nearby. Panic stricken, I wanted to leave the forest at the earliest. Paddy was, however, busy shooting bright yellow and maroon striped Khasi common jester butterflies with his new camera and a 300 mm lens. Mesmerized by the beauty of butterflies and oblivious to the apparent elephant risk, he headed deep into the forest.

At first it might appear that he was unaware of how to assess wildlife risk. But clearly, my panic was an overreaction. Apart from the villagers' invitation to accompany them for elephant sighting, there were no other indications or traces of elephant activity.

Paddy had keenly noted it. Over thinking and over doing was not his style.

In spite of completing his post-graduation from University of Alabama (Tuscaloosa), in the state of Alabama, United States of America, and working for many years as a consultant in USA, he returned to India surrendering his green card. He was never overly ambitious in his professional life. Unlike Shreeram, he managed to steer clear of the corporate rat race without leaving the corporate realm, and unlike Vedavyasa, he did not cease his nature exploration to deal with any perceived imbalance between his profession and passion.

That perhaps explains why again, unlike Vedavyasa, he hasn't thought of abandoning his wife and children.

Life, to him, is a straight line, and he embraces it as it unfolds. Much like flattering the Khasi common jester in the elephant infested forest of Buxa tiger reserve. Avoiding needless complications in the name of fame and glory.

It is not Shreeram or Vedavyasa or me, but an ecotourist like Paddy who enjoys ecotourism most.

Chole King mentioned that a *"collective path"* must be built by centring community needs in ecotourism as the first principle to develop nature-based solution through ecotourism.

I insist that this "collective path" should be straight enough to demonstrate that the key characteristic trait desired of an ecotourist is simplicity.

During our bushwalk with Reevu, besides hornbill, we also found birds like mountain hawk eagle, open billed stork, chestnut headed bee-eater, tricolour long tailed shrike and chestnut tailed starling. Rufus tree pie and Asian pied starlings were in abundance.

Reevu grew up in the lap of Buxa tiger reserve. His father retired as the head forest guard. Reevu explained how encroachment by local tribes has disturbed the ecosystem of Buxa. Until 1993, there was regular news of tiger sighting in Buxa. Reevu's father saw tigers twice during his tenure with forest department. In the 1993 flood of north Bengal, towns like Alipurduar and Hamiltanganj on the banks of Kaljani River, were flooded due to leakage of the retaining wall of the dam. The river flowed into the town killing hundreds of people and animals. Since then, not a single tiger has been sighted in Buxa.

Reevu indicated that local forest dwellers' dependency on forest for cattle grazing, illegal logging, collection of shrimps and snails have caused lot of disturbances and degradation of forests. In many places, the severe shrimp collection activity has caused the adjoining land of the streams to becomes thickly covered in mud. Earlier in the day, we had struggled to move through such knee-deep mud. Clearly, it's not an ideal path for big cats. We saw local people collecting snails from streams and firewood from the forest. As the day progressed, the number of villagers – both men and women – venturing into the forest, increased significantly.

As we exited the forest around noon, Reevu pointed to a floating log on the water stream and revealed the mystery associated with it. He said that the floating log was a result of illegal tree felling. The local villagers were awaiting the rains, when the water level in the streams would rise, causing them to eventually merge with Dima River. The villagers would then push the logs into the river, and someone downstream would collect the logs. Reevu and Amiyo said that this happens under the watch of the forest department. Reevu claimed to have taken part in multiple tiger-census in Buxa, where he witnessed how forest officials created accounts of tiger sighting to allow Buxa to retain the status of tiger reserve and to continue receiving Project Tiger's fund to Buxa. They accumulate tiger scat from other places, or tamper the leopard's pugmark to make it look bigger so it resembles a tiger pugmark. Based on media report, Buxa's tiger population dipped from twenty to zero in three years (and of course raised to two in 2022). The figure of twenty was achieved through genetic analyses of tiger scat. The credibility of the analyses now appears suspect.

According to Azam Zaidi, Chief Wildlife Warden of West Bengal, as reported in an online Indian news daily, the tiger population has been decreasing in Buxa over the past few years for a number of reasons. The few key reasons among them include human intrusions, shortage of food and migration of tigers to other areas. Bengal Tigers are migrating to surrounding forests, which are more suitable for them, and gradually the control of Buxa is transitioning to the human, who now rules the forest of Buxa to meet his own needs. Nevertheless, the human is not at peace. If the national animal, tiger, is a victim of human greed, then the national heritage animal, the elephant, is the next challenge. Human-elephant conflict is an unresolved issue and a daily phenomenon in this area. Unfortunately, people have found "ecotourism" opportunity in this conflict as well.

Biswarup's key value proposition in selling his resort to me was a subtle promise of elephant sighting near his resort. He kept his word one evening at around half past eight, when we were at a nearby watchtower. The watchtower had been built by locals to observe elephant movement to protect their crops. That evening, we heard shouting from the direction of our resort. A young elephant stood just behind our resort. A lot of villagers gathered around, shouting, focussing high beam lights on the animal and bursting crackers to shoo it away. This continued for forty-five minutes before the elephant went away. The black elephant against the backdrop of a pitch-dark forest was nearly impossible to spot unless one picked up the noise due to its stomping on twigs or breaking of branches. The local people including forest department personnel shared with us the elephant's growing intelligence in managing human encounters. In an attempt to evade human attention, they had learnt to move silently, minimizing noise. The local villagers said that this particular elephant was a frequent visitor and was gradually losing fear of humans. They were concerned that the day wasn't far when he would attack and possibly injure or kill a villager.

This was not the only example of an ecotourism opportunity grabbed from the human-elephant conflict. Earlier in the evening we went on a gypsy safari in Buxa tiger reserve. The safari was guided by forest guide Lalit Thapa and driver Nitu Bhattacharya. We spotted wild boar, barking deer, spotted deer, and heard their alarm calls. Incidentally, this part of the forest had a good population of leopard. In the absence of Bengal Tigers, of course, leopards were the apex predators of Buxa Tiger Reserve.

The highlight of the safari was staying back in the forest after sunset, in the darkness, well beyond the official tourism hours, atop a watchtower near a salt pit created by the forest department for the animals. Around 5:30 pm, a huge parade of elephants appeared – matriarch, other females, young males and cubs. It was a full moon night, and quite mesmerising to see around twenty elephants in the moon lit forest. Their appearance was so silent that none of us realized their presence in such proximity until the light from the forest guards' torch gently illuminated their body. The whole idea of staying back in the forest after dusk was crafted by Nitu Bhattacharya, to pocket some additional money from us. On our way back, he bragged about his ability to take risk and break rules for conducting such "night safaris" in a tiger reserve. Apparently, a few months prior, a lady journalist of *Hindustan Times* from Calcutta submitted a news report alleging Nitu for conducting illegitimate night safaris. Nitu nonchalantly told us that forest department officials were well aware of such activities.

On our last morning at Buxa, Paddy and I decided to explore the village and the local market which are located near Rajabhatkhawa railway station. It was one of the main human-elephant conflict zones. There are multiple human habitats along the railway track and the track itself is responsible for numerous elephant deaths. The village market, which offers the essential amenities within a tiger reserve, is certainly a contributing factor in human animal conflict. The community dependency on forest and improper resettlement plan for forest dwellers by the government added a socio-economic dimension into this conflict. Reevu works as a volunteer with an

NGO, *Child Line*, which is involved in fighting child marriage, child labour and child trafficking. He shared his experiences on working as a volunteer at *Child Line*. Poverty and exploitation of local community residing in the forest, had left them with no alternative but to engage in soft poaching, illegal tree felling and collecting snails from the forest. A poor Toto or Rabha father is ready to sell his minor daughter to outsiders for a mere Indian rupee two thousand (approximately $25). The forlorn tribal girl most likely ends up in a brothel or massage parlour in Goa.

Our concept of environment conservation is anthropocentric; therefore, inadequate rehabilitation of forest dwellers would undoubtedly defeat the purpose of such conservation. As Ramchandra Guha mentions in *How Much Should a Person Consume?* *"For, in the poor and heavily populated countries of the South (Global South), protected areas cannot be managed with guns and guards. It is imperative here that we take full cognizance of the rights of the people who lived in, and often cared for, the forest before it became a national park or a World Heritage Site."* The forest of Buxa is a classic case in point.

With a heavy heart, Paddy and I headed towards our next destination in the North-Eastern hills and the Brahmaputra landscape of the subcontinental tiger habitat.

Pseudo Ecotourism

The first principle of regenerative ecotourism – the community first principle, and the core philosophy of nature-based solution – building ecotourism business strategy with the nature – fails in Buxa. The outcome is not just a depleting tiger population and degraded forests, but also a community deprived of their fundamental rights.

Ecotourism business disconnected from local community is detrimental to ecosystems. This disconnection fails to boost any initiative taken by conservationists to improve ecosystem integrity and biodiversity. In the long run nature-based solutions' core concept of building business in harmony with nature, and not in opposition to it, would be meaningless if ecotourism organizations do not involve community in their tourism activities.

As per Chloe King, the second and third principle of regenerative ecotourism is centred around improving ecosystem integrity and biodiversity. *"Tourism companies can use their financial resources to protect and regenerate ecosystems at risk, ensuring that the landscapes they profit from remain as beautiful as they are today when the next generation inherits their operations".* According to her, *"if every tourism company on Earth devoted a small percentage of profits to protecting their local wildlife, they could preserve the ecosystems that ecotourists love to see."*

However, connecting local community and improving ecosystem integrity as part of ecotourism business strategy is not as simple as King has mentioned in her white paper. The examples of such complexity are plenty in the North-Eastern hills and the Brahmaputra landscape.

Manas National Park of Assam state is a special forest of India with six national and international designations - World Heritage Site, National Park, Tiger Reserve, Biosphere Reserve, Elephant Reserve and Important Bird Area. As a result, this forest enjoys highest legal protection and strong legislative framework under the provisions of *Indian Wildlife (Protection) Act, 1972, Indian Forest Act, 1927,* and *Assam Forest Regulation 1891.* It is contiguous with the Royal Manas National Park in Bhutan. Evolutionarily, it is the entry point of tigers into India. It forms part of a large tiger conservation landscape, which includes Buxa-Nameri-Pakke-Namdapha tiger reserves, and shares international borders with two countries - Bhutan and Myanmar. For wildlife conservationists, Manas is the crown jewel in India's national parks, home to twenty-two of India's most threatened species including the Assam roofed turtle, hispid hare, golden langur, capped langur, Pygmy hog and Bengal florican.

A year after my Buxa trip, one winter I visited Manas and I saw plenty of capped langur in every part of the forest, despite its vulnerable status as per IUCN. In winter, these furry primates spend nearly 40% of the daytime feeding on leaves, flowers and fruits. The other interesting arboreal mammal of this forest is, of course, the Malayan giant squirrel. Spotting them was effortless.

During my six-day exploration in the Bansbari and Bhuyianpara ranges of the forest, I identified around 50 different bird species. Among birds of prey, Pallas's fish eagle, crested serpent eagle and honey buzzards were aplenty. The abundance of changeable hawk eagle in this northeast Indian Forest can be compared to the frequent sighting of crested serpent eagle in the forest of Western Ghats. However, the most unique raptor sighting during my exploration of this forest was a Jerdon's baza. Various dry riverbeds and flowing rivers cut across the forest. The bank of Beki River, a tributary of Manas, was a good spot to observe wetland birds. Besides red wattled, yellow wattled and river lapwings, cormorant, pond heron, purple heron, snipes, plovers and egret; open-billed storks, white storks, black storks and lesser adjutant storks were other frequently noticeable wetland birds. The golden hue of the grassland of Manas Forest at sunrise and sunset is certainly a photographers' delight. Different buntings, bush chats, shrikes, particularly tricolored long-tail shrikes, and grey-backed shrikes hopped and flew from one leaf of tall sedges to another. They can keep birdwatchers and photographers busy the entire day. Although my favourite finding was in the grassland of Bhuyianpara. It was of the smallest raptor found in this subcontinent – the collared falconet. The 18 cm long bird of prey is mostly found in northern and eastern Himalayan foothills. The local guide cum gypsy driver Tapan, said that he had seen a collard falconet preying on a fully-grown pond heron in Manas.

Other forest birds spotted in this large tiger reserve of Assam were sultan tit, white browed wagtail, scarlet minivet, golden oriole, Indo-Chinese roller, chestnut tailed starling, verditer flycatcher, scaly thrush, golden fronted leaf-bird, long-tailed broadbill, Asian fairy blue bird, great barbet, lineated barbet, blue-throated barbet among others. I have seen plenty of common, white-bellied and racket tailed drongo in various parts of the subcontinental forests. The spangled drongo, also known as hair crested drongo, spotted in Manas, though, was a completely new avian species that I photographed.

This "first sight" tag can also be attached to white throated bulbul, red-breasted parakeet, pin tailed, and wedge tailed green pigeon, which were gathered in flocks in almost every corner of the forest, and of course rufus necked hornbill. These are special birds of northeast India and eastern Himalayas.

Exploring in Manas was not about taking close-up shots of tigers, as in Central Indian or Western Ghats landscape (read Kabini and Bandipur). Despite being the largest tiger reserve of the North-East Hills and the Brahmaputra Plains, tiger density is comparatively low. The spotting of tigers becomes even more daunting due to the vast landscape and dense foliage. Nevertheless, tiger sighting in Manas is not as rare as it is in Nagarjunasagar and Amrabad of Eastern Ghats or Dandeli and Periyar of Western Ghats, where similar dense foliage is considered a barrier in spotting the animal. During our six-day visit, there was news of tiger sighting from another part of the forest. While we awaited the dhole on the bank of Rabbang River, some thirty gypsies full of tourists saw a male tiger in the Doimari zone of the forest.

Typically, photographers come to this forest not for tigers, but to capture its avian biodiversity and gigantic landscape in the backdrop of the enormous mountains of Royal Manas Bhutan. The boundless forest of Manas engulfs all the giant mammals of this subcontinental floodplain. Unicorn rhino, Asiatic elephant, gaur and water buffalo could emerge from any concealed part of the forest. Their massive heads can be seen through tall grasses from afar; or they may be spotted grazing, in pairs or with cubs, in salt pits dug by forest department, completely oblivious of spectators; they may also be sighted crossing the forest path, slowly and peacefully, far from your reach, against the picturesque background of Bhutanese mountains; or they could suddenly appear before you, gently walking towards you, compelling you to give them the right of way.

Manas is indeed the crown jewel among India's national parks, but the journey to achieve this status was marked with blood and sweat of conservation crusaders of this country. In general, northeast part of India is always known for political turmoil and unrest due to activities of several local factionist groups. It is also perceived that development of this part of the country is neglected and that the north eastern populace is largely ignored in mainstream developmental activities unlike the rest of India. In 2017, author Ananda Banerjee wrote an article titled, *"The resilience of Manas"*, published in the online edition of *Mint*. As per the article, soon after Manas received the status of UNESCO World Heritage Site in 1985, the forest was plunged into violence following an armed struggle demanding a Bodoland state carved out of Assam. From the late 1980s to early 2000s, this separatist movement took centre stage in Indian politics, and became a matter of concern for internal security. The forest of Manas turned into a hotbed of militancy that nearly wiped out the park's megafauna—tiger, rhino, elephant, wild buffalo and deer. Large-scale timber felling was reported but no official dared to venture even close to the park. This mindless plunder continued till the early 2000s. The situation began to change slowly from 2003, after the surrender of *Bodo Liberation Tiger Force (BLTF)*, and a peace agreement was drafted. A couple of years later, another militant group, the *National Democratic Front of Bodoland (NDFB)*, also signed a ceasefire agreement. It was only after the peace accord was in place, that the forest officials and conservationists could return to work and survey the park.

Famous Indian wildlife biologist, conservationist, and author of bestselling book *"Indian Mammals"*, Vivek Menon, was quoted in Banerjee's article. Executive Director and Chief Executive Officer of *Wildlife Trust of India (WTI)*, Vivek Menon says, *"The Manas National Park was almost completely stripped of its faunal and floral heritage during the period of civil unrest in the region. The park lost almost all its 100 or so rhinos, most of its swamp deer and wild buffaloes and a large number of elephants and tigers along with a myriad other creature during the peak of the poaching period. I was one of the few biologists who visited the park just after the dark years and I was stuck by its resilience and stark beauty despite the years of damage done to it".* Menon and his *WTI* team have done phenomenal work of connecting local community with conservation and have created awareness of their responsibility in protecting forests. Eventually with the help of the local community they improved the ecosystem integrity of Manas and successfully rehabilitated Asian elephants, clouded leopards, and Asiatic black bears in the forest. A large part of the restoration of the habitat and species relocation was made possible with support and funding from the *International Fund for Animal Welfare (IFAW)*. According to Menon, as mentioned in *"The resilience of Manas"*, *"When no one wanted to invest in this troubled landscape, IFAW's steadfast support to Manas for a decade is commendable."*

A few decades of persistent and unabated conservation work of many crusaders yielded a huge forest of 950 square kilometres. Involving local community is always essential in anthropocentric principle-based wildlife conservation. This value creation achieved by involving local community in forest protection was evident when I explored the forest. An example was our gunman Ajoy.

Ajoy, a proud Bodo, left no opportunity in telling us how Bodo culture is unique and rich, and how their language is different from Assamese, the state language of Assam. He studied in a school where the medium of instruction was Bodo. He was also conversant in a few other languages like Assamese, Hindi, Bengali, Nepali and a few tribal languages. In fact, his proficiency in spoken English language was not too bad. Because of his enthusiasm one afternoon, we had Bodo food for lunch in a local Bodo village at Kanchanbadi forest check post near the exit gate of Bhuiyanpara range. Besides rice, lentil, brinjal and spinach cooked in local style the main attraction on the menu was a Bodo chicken delicacy known as *Onla Khare*. Being a forest guard, on several occasions Ajoy had found himself in nerve-wracking situations in the forest. He witnessed, first-hand, an angry tusker stomping and crushing his friend to death.

A few days prior to my exploration, I saw video footage of a rhino chasing a safari gypsy. It was shot by a tourist in this park. Ajoy mentioned that he was in the gypsy chased by the rhino. He was the guard on duty, and he fired nine rounds of magazine into air, emptying his rifle, in an attempt to scare the rhino away. The rhino though was unafraid and continued chasing the gypsy until the vehicle sped away leaving the animal behind. This particular rhino was most commonly found in Latajhar area near Sarphuli check post of Bansbari range. A male rhino with a large horn, and lately infamous for its crazy chasing tendency.

Our team constituted of eleven people in two gypsies. On our first full day safari in Manas in Bansbari range, at the fag-end of the day one of our gypsies, in which I was plying, broke down in the Latajhar area. When the efforts of Tapan, Umesh and Ajoy to start the gypsy went in vain, the other gypsy, driven by Umesh, headed to our camp, *Smiling Tusker*, around thirty kilometres away, to drop a few of our team members at camp and return for the rest of us and the disabled gypsy. By the time the gypsy returned it was already dark. Without wasting any further time, we tied the disabled gypsy to the other, and headed towards the exit gate of the park. After a few kilometres of driving fast, we were compelled to slow down. There was a huge slow-moving lump of darkness ahead of us.

Through binoculars and telephoto lenses, we recognized it as a huge unicorn rhino of Manas. Ajoy identified it as the infamous gypsy chasing rhino – the "terror of Latajhar". Luckily the rhino was not facing us, neither did it feel our presence behind him. But as we slowed down, nearly fifty gypsies lined up behind us. The tourists in these vehicles screamed in fear. Many of them had seen the video or heard about the chasing incident from other fellow tourists.

After a while, another smaller lump of darkness appeared next to it. This time, vision through telephoto lenses confirmed that it was a wild boar. The rhino charged, a mock one, intimidating the wild boar to clear his path. We perceived this to be the trailer of the main show that would perhaps follow when he charged at us. This further increased our panic.

Of all the gypsies, we were the most vulnerable. Should the rhino decide to turn around and chase, the other gypsies could turn around or back track in reverse gear, a possibility not open to us, as we were towing a disabled gypsy. To our great relief, half an hour later, the rhino went down into the thicket from where the wild boar had emerged. It went further inside the dense forest, and once we received road clearance from Ajoy, we headed to our resort, with an exciting finish to the day's safari.

For a change, the central characters of these exciting stories of Manas were neither tigers nor leopards.

In spite of being the largest tiger reserve of Assam and northeast India, and one of the fabulous examples of tiger habitat restoration and cross border tiger conservation, Manas has emerged as a popular nature destination for its unique eastern Himalayan birds and magical landscape. Although tiger is the apex predator of this forest with a substantial population of leopards and occasional sighting of black leopards, unlike the tiger lands of Central India and Shivalik Hills, instead of the Big Cat, here the *Gentle Giants* (big herbivores like rhino, buffalo, gaur, and elephants) rule the heart of ecotourists and wildlife photographers. The purpose of wildlife conservation is achieved when the very core of it is based on the belief that the living environment should be respected wholistically. This "non-tiger centric" ecotourism in Manas is a key milestone towards this achievement.

Climate change has become a household term since 2015, when Global Sustainability Leaders and International Institutes gathered in Paris (for the Paris Convention or COP15). Since then, IUCN is also propagating and advising Nature-Based Solution (NBS) and one of its essential components - Other

Effective Area-based Conservation Measures or OECM[8].

Protected areas as in forests, wetlands, coastal and marine areas etc. which are protected by country specific regulations, are an important way to conserve nature. They sustain ecosystem functions and offer refuge to a diversity of species, and benefits people. Regulations prohibit developmental activities as well as cutting trees, clearing forests, diverting course of rivers, filling water bodies etc., in such areas. Therefore, ecosystem flourishes, boosting ecotourism. However, OECM areas are different from these protected areas. Protected areas are places that are dedicated to the conservation of biodiversity. They are cared for by individuals or groups who manage these areas (for instance, governing authorities like the forest department) with a conservation focussed outcome. But there are many places with potential to achieve long term *in situ* (the conservation of a species in its natural habitat and the maintenance and recovery of viable population of species in their original place) conservation of biodiversity that are outside of protected areas. These are ignored places where no formal conservation initiatives are implemented. As a result, no formal and, very often, even informal ecotourism, never develops in such

---

[8] *OECM: 'Other effective area-based conservation measures' (OECMs) are a new conservation approach, separate from protected areas, where conservation is achieved as a by-product of other managements. Examples of OECMs include set-asides within agricultural systems, conserved water catchments, locally managed marine areas, and other high conservation value areas.*

places. Thus, protection of threatened species in these OECM areas are never realized. The community dependent upon these places is unaware of the importance of these ecosystems, and gain nothing economically due to lack of ecotourism activities. These places are easy victims of materialism driven development.

I have previously mentioned stories of Chorla Ghats, tea/coffee estates of Munnar and Coorg, sand dunes outside Desert National Park, and village mangrove forests near wetlands of Pichavaram. These are some of the many examples of OECM areas with phenomenal ecotourism opportunities. However, when an OECM area lies adjacent to a tiger reserve, then it can be alarming for the local community if effective conservation measures and governance are not in place.

After visiting the largest tiger reserve of Assam, it was now time for the smallest one. Located around hundred and seventy-five kilometres away from Manas, the 79.28 square kilometres core area forest of Orang has around 30 tigers as per the *2022 National Tiger Estimation Report*. My last day in Manas was overcast and when I reached Orang the following afternoon, the weather persisted. Within half an hour of my first gypsy safari, it started drizzling. The rain lasted for about thirty minutes, following which the sky cleared up. Unlike Manas there was no provision for a full day safari. Although tourism starts at seven in the morning and continues till 4:30 or 5:00 pm, the safari gypsies are typically allowed to explore the forest for only two to two and a half hours at a stretch. The allocated two hours is all that is required to cover the designated safari route, including stopping at a watchtower to view a large waterbody.

Immediately upon entering the forest, I discovered the most annoying part of the gypsy safari in Orang. The forest department provides one gunman for every two gypsies. This implies that one gypsy will piggyback the other. The gypsy in which the gunman sits must be religiously followed by the second gypsy. This is annoying because if you are in the second gypsy then forget about photography and animal sighting, as your entire movement is controlled and restricted by the gypsy in front. If you are in the leading gypsy, then there are two possibilities. The first. There could be non-photographer ecotourists in the trailing gypsy and you, seated in the gypsy in front, are unsure about how much interest they have for wildlife or if they are visiting the park for mere amusement. Allow me to elaborate. I went on a total of four safaris in Orang (two in the morning between 7:00 to 9:30-10:00 am and two in the afternoon between 2:00 and 4:30 pm). On two trips, the tourists in the trailing gypsy were a group of elderly men and women, speaking aloud and at times getting overexcited upon sighting of a bird, which led to me missing my shots. On one occasion, a cuckoo shrike, and on another, changeable hawk eagle, both of who flew further away from a nearby branch, due to the sudden eruption of laughter or exclamation after seeing the bird. Besides, due to my frequent requests to stop along the forest route to spot birds or take images, they were bored and conveyed their wish to leave the forest early as they had other plans. Of course, I ignored the request and continued the safari.

The second possibility is that there may be wildlife enthusiasts and photographers in the trailing gypsy. Can you imagine their frustration and non-verbal cursing, as seated in the gypsy ahead you spoil their photo opportunity, and hinder the sighting of wildlife in favourable light and preferred angle? If you are anything like me, you would also feel guilty upon realizing that you had an advantage in stealing the precious moments from them, although you are not to blame. After all it's the stupid rule of the forest department that is to be blamed. On an afternoon safari I suffered this fate, along with a helpless middle-aged Bengali photographer couple.

This type of tourism policy is completely unfavourable even in protected areas, where ecotourism is well intended. I was fortunate enough to be seated in the leading gypsy in all four safaris. I owed it to Salam *Chacha*'s (*Chacha* is Hindi for Uncle) influence over the forest department staff who issued the permits for Orang. Salam *Chacha* is the father of Daud Abdullah, the owner of *Green Planet Resort* where I stayed for two nights. The resort was located within fifty meters of the entry gate of the park. Daud and Salam organized my entire trip. Accommodation in a basic wooden cottage, all meals, and a local guide

Hizbullah *aka* Pappu, who drove me around the forest.

All four safaris were identical. We followed the same route each time. Orang had only one tourism route. The gypsies are only allowed to drive forward along the route, like a monorail in an amusement park. You are allowed to stop briefly for photography but driving in reverse is either not allowed, or not practiced, unlike other tiger reserves of India. Therefore, even if there was an indication of tiger movement in the path once crossed, there was no way to go back and re-check. These are some of the potential causes for fewer tiger sightings in Orang despite having such high tiger density. Pappu mentioned that there were frequent incidents of territorial fight and death of tigers due to over spilling of tiger population of Orang. To avoid such territorial conflict most of the tigers, especially the subadult tigers prefer to stay near the boundary area of the forest rather than in the core forest. There are villages adjacent to the forest boundary. My resort was in one such village. Such proximity between human settlements and tiger reserve has increased tiger infiltration in these villages in recent past.

As a result, such villages, and the agricultural lands within, are turning into potential OECM areas. The areas which are not under any formal protection of forest department but are habitat of endangered fauna, thus having conservation/ecotourism potential.

During my first safari, forest guard Milon Jyoti Majumdar mentioned that the previous night an adult male tiger had entered a village nearby, named Nisalbari, and had killed a cow. The tiger was inside the village even the following day at 2 pm, and many forest guards were deployed in the village. This in turn led to shortage of guards to escort tourism gypsies. However, around 3:30 pm Milon received a phone call from his colleague with the news that the tiger escaped from the village and had re-entered the forest.

All evening, I heard the bellowing of alarm calls by hog deer. As I ate my dinner in the dimly lit resort at the fringe area of a tiger reserve, ear-piercing scream broke the silence. Salam *Chacha* declared, *"A hog deer is caught by a tiger!"* The poor animal was in the throes of death, crying in pain. Gradually the cries faded. The apex predator of this subcontinent was also perhaps finishing its meal in the deep forest of Orang just as I was, in my comfortable and cosy night-stay.

Salam *Chacha* also used to drive the safari gypsy in Orang before he built his resort. Therefore, he saw a lot of tigers, both inside and outside the forest. Sighting a tiger near the entry gate of the park or on the road next to his resort at night was not uncommon, he said. His wife, one evening, saw a tiger within ten meters of their resort as she carried some cooking accessories from the resort to their home. The tiger saw her as well and stared at her for a few minutes. She called *Chacha* on his mobile phone, and he quickly informed the forest guard posted at the entry gate. When the guard arrived at the place the tiger gradually retreated into the park, taking a narrow path further into the forest.

I heard similar stories of tigers sneaking into villages from a lady forest guard, Himani, and local tribal guard, Bolu. Himani mentioned that a month ago, a tiger killed one of her colleagues inside the forest near Ronghagorha check post, when he was patrolling on elephant back. Apparently, the tiger jumped onto the elephant. Bolu also showed me an astonishing clipping telecasted in local Assamese news channel a few days prior. The news clipping showed two tigers roaming through the streets of Mongoldoi sub-division of Dorrong district, located around forty-five kilometres from the tiger reserve.

Couple of weeks after my Orang trip I saw an *Instagram* post of a video clip in which a fully grown adult tiger was meandering on cattle grazing ground near Orang tiger reserve. The amazing part of this footage was a woman seen walking, engrossed in conversation on her mobile phone, completely indifferent to the predator. Pappu later confirmed that the incident had occurred in the village of Kosaribetuf, located towards the eastern side of the entry gate of the park, just half a kilometre away from the forest.

Forest area of Orang is small, but it has all the components of a northeast hill's forest that I witnessed in Manas. Grassland, dense foliage, water bodies and swampland. The wide wetland visible from the watchtower was full of water birds like mallard, lesser whistling ducks, darter, cormorants, egret, pond and purple heron, bronze winged jacana, black headed ibis, open billed stork. Around 40-50 migratory spot-billed pelicans, in the morning mist, were the highlights of my last day at Orang. Like Manas, the changeable hawk eagles were aplenty in Orang too. But unlike Manas, rose ringed parakeet was more in number, and I did not spot any red breasted parakeet. Also capped langurs were missing in this forest; instead, there were several groups of rhesus macaque jumping from one tree to another. I saw a rhino on both my afternoon safaris, submerged in the same water body. Pappu indicated that there are about 150 rhinos in Orang, which according to him, is significantly small, considering the forest area.

The agricultural land and village roads around Orang National Parks have the potential to protect natural habitats and corridors of tigers and its prey base of the park. Local villagers like Salam *Chacha* and his wife can be trained and recognized with the help of Government and Private actors (wildlife institutes, NGOs, and ecotourism organizations) to protect these areas. Not just pre-defined tourism route within the National Park, the adjacent agricultural lands and village roads lying outside of protected areas can also be transformed into destinations for wildlife photography and ecotourism if the local community is involved and benefits through such ecotourism activities.

IUCN mentioned in its online awareness building video on OECM, *"recognizing and supporting Protected Areas and OECMs across landscapes and seascapes promotes more equitable, diverse partnerships in global conservation efforts."*

Chloe King's fourth principle of regenerative ecotourism further strengthens the need for recognizing and supporting OECM by making sure that locals get the same attention as wealthy stakeholders when tourism companies make decisions. She mentioned, *"the ecotourism business should make sure that they foster relationships with local communities to create a long-term support system. They should also give communities access to the cultural and natural resources that they want to protect. Developing a sense of place and understanding through experience is the best way to keep every stakeholder motivated to continue developing a regenerative tourism model."*

Total involvement of community, thinking beyond protected areas and diverting attention from single species (read tiger centric) ecotourism and photography are keys to embrace nature-based solution in ecotourism and protect the depleting biodiversity, including tiger populations.

Pseudo Ecotourism

The craze for tiger-centric ecotourism was always under check in the northeast hills and that is why I consider this landscape as the peaceful abode of Bengal Tiger of this subcontinent. The tiger reserves of Assam, especially Kaziranga National Park and Tiger Reserve played a pivotal role in distracting tourists from tigers to other equally ecologically important and magnificent species of subcontinental forests.

Kaziranga is a tiger reserve of 625. 58 km² core area, with around 142 tigers, as per *NTCA 2022 Tiger estimation report*. But the flagship species of this park is the rhino. The national park hosts two-thirds of the world's great one-horned rhinoceroses. Tourists and photographers visit this park to see the big guys - the giants of the floodplains – Asiatic elephant, water buffalo and one-horned rhino. Perhaps this is why tourism-induced pressure to increase tiger population does not exist here. This pressure is the greatest threat in Central Indian Landscape.

I visited Kaziranga along with ten other wildlife photographers as part of a photography bootcamp.

We went on six safaris, but did not see a single tiger. Of the six, three were in Central Zone. Although, allocating 50% of our safaris to Central Zone was based on recent news of frequent tiger sighting in that zone, I was pleasantly surprised to see that none of the participants in our bootcamp was visibly disappointed, upon non-sighting of the animal. In Central India or Western Ghats, non-sighting of the animal even in one safari typically leads to eruption of dissatisfactory feelings among participants. Many are vocal about it as well. This floodplain of gentle giants has so much to offer wildlife photographers and natural history enthusiasts alike, that "tiger-tourism" can take a back seat.

Besides its recent tiger sighting records, the Central Zone is rather less happening when compared to Eastern and Western Zones. The Eastern Zone is a delight for nature enthusiasts. Herds of rhino, elephant, and buffalo in a vast landscape of mixed grassland and broad-leaved trees against the background of Brahmaputra riverbed tells the story of phenomenal forests of lower Himalayan northeast India. I had my first ever sighting of smooth coated otter in one of the wetlands in this zone. The pair was swimming in water and rolling on forest floor. I also sighted the northern and grey-headed lapwing – the two-winter migratory avian species of eastern Himalayas for the first time. The youngest participant in our group, eighteen-year-old Vibhu, made a list of avian species we spotted during our bootcamp. The list had 119 birds including rare sight Himalayan and northeast Indian species - swamp francolin, green-billed malkoha, Asian barred owlet, slender-billed vulture, Himalayan griffon, grey-headed canary flycatcher, and Himalayan bulbul to name a few. The most astonishing sighting was greater adjutant stork. Greater adjutant was once abundant across southern Asia, mainly in India and extending east to Borneo. Now it is restricted to a much smaller range with only three breeding populations - two in India, with the largest colony in Assam, a smaller one around Bhagalpur (Bihar); and another breeding population in Cambodia. The bird with an average height of 4 feet 6 inches is declared endangered by IUCN due to loss of nesting and feeding habitat through the draining of wetlands, pollution, and other disturbances, together with hunting and egg collection in the past. The world population was estimated at less than 1,000 individuals in 2008. In Bengal and Assam, the bird is known as *Hargila*, said to be derived from the Sanskrit roots *har* for "bone" and *gila* - "to swallow"- which describes the bird as a "bone swallower".

The Western Zone of Kaziranga, on the other hand is a dreamland for photographers. The zone is full of swamplands. Rhinos in early morning mist and buffalos against the backdrop of Karbi hills in the dim light of late evening, create magical moments for wildlife photographers. Spotting a rhino, in this zone of the forest is much more regular than what I witnessed in Manas and Orang. That gives even more opportunities to experiment with images of these stunning creatures. Their skin that almost looks like a suit of armour reminds you of prehistoric creatures, which must have roamed the Earth centuries ago. The visual of Karbi hills tells people that the name floodplains given to this land is for specific reasons. During the annual monsoon flood, the water level of Brahmaputra could rise up to eighty-six meters, thus forcing the animals to climb up the hills to save their lives.

If you are not distracted by the commodity fetishism influenced tiger chasing game, then you learn phenomenal natural history associated with every landscape of this subcontinent.

Chloe King's final principle emphasizes the importance of collaboration for regenerative tourism. In her opinion, *"the ecotourism organizations should serve as a bridge between communities and the government to enhance social and ecological regeneration"*. Here, government's involvement is quite crucial, especially in the complex geo-political landscape of northeast India. Northeast landscape of India is situated alongside international borders with Nepal, Bhutan, People's Republic of

China (China occupied Tibet), Myanmar, and Bangladesh, and is connected to peninsular India through a narrow strategic stretch, Siliguri Corridor. As the landscape shares 90% of its boundary with neighbouring countries, it is one of the most important geo-strategic locations of the country. Therefore, without government involvement, it may be difficult to fully understand the effects of a regenerative tourism operation (which involves local community and also focuses on areas outside protected forest areas) on both human and natural communities, in northeast India, the landscape - home to more than 200 ethnic and indigenous communities. This cultural plurality adds a different dynamic in the natural resource diversity of North-East and Brahmaputra flood plains landscapes.

Based on *2022 NTCA tiger status report of India*, tigers were photo-captured for the first time in Buxa Tiger Reserve, Neora Valley National Park, and Mahananda Wildlife Sanctuary in West Bengal. As per the report a tiger was also photo-captured in the Namdapha Tiger Reserve of Arunachal Pradesh. The report also mentions that tiger reserves and protected areas in Arunachal Pradesh are connected through large, forested tracts and a few reserve forests situated along the interstate border between Arunachal Pradesh and Assam. This landscape is further connected to Intanki National Park in Nagaland and Dampa Tiger Reserves in Mizoram through some weak linkages of degraded forest. Several indigenous forest communities dependent on bush meat and forest resources for subsistence inhabit this landscape; hence, the prey base is almost depleted in many of the forests. In addition, due to its strategic location, several highways are planned in Arunachal Pradesh to provide faster access to international border areas. Fragmentation of habitat by this rapid infrastructure development would eventually destroy the weak linkages between the tiger habitats and might lead to the local extinction of tigers in this landscape. Substantial poaching for the illegal trade of tiger body parts and ungulates constantly threatens the tiger population in this landscape. Since the landscape shares porous international borders in many parts with neighbouring Southeast Asian countries, it is comparatively easy for poachers to operate in this landscape. In the recent past, the skin and body parts of two tigers were seized from Dibang Valley in Arunachal Pradesh and Itakhola on the Assam-Arunachal Pradesh border. Direct exploitation of tigers from this already low population, coupled with habitat fragmentation and biotic pressure, could eventually deplete the tiger population in this landscape.

The institute responsible for tiger conservation in India itself recognizes these facts behind depleting tiger population in the Dibang-Kamlang-Namdapha block of tiger landscape in Arunachal Pradesh. The state has three tiger reserves - Pakke, Kamlang, Namdapha and one wildlife sanctuary - Dibang. As per 2022 tiger status survey, only nine tigers were photo-captured in this state.

However, the status of Arunachal's tiger population does not tell the real story of its phenomenal biodiversity resources. This state is an ecological wonder that remains largely unexplored. The tropical rain forest of the Namdapha National Park, one of India's largest protected area, throbs with a dizzying array of flora and fauna, many of which are lesser known, hidden gems of the wild.

One winter-season, few years after my Buxa, Manas, Orang and Kaziranaga explorations, I embarked on an intense biodiversity exploration in the approximately 400 kilometres stretch consisting of Diban camp of Namdapha and its surrounding areas including Haldibari, Highand and Kamala Valley camp, Dheing Patkai National Park and Maguri beel as well as adjacent grasslands of Dibru Saikhowa National Park. I was accompanied by a reputed bird watching guide from the northeast, Palash Phukan.

I was also joined by another experienced bird photographer from Pune, Suyog Ghodke. A typical bird photographer, he came with a target list of birds in pocket and an expectation to tick them all off on a trip that he had paid for. A stark contrast to Paddy.

Obviously, such "target chasing" puts a lot of stress on the guide and fellow photographers, much like any corporate job. However, Palash seemed experienced in dealing with such photographers. Initially I was annoyed by Suyog's hyperactive photography approach, but later it helped me to follow a structured photography schedule. as Suyog's list helped us chart out a plan for the trip.

Early in the morning we started for Namdapha National Park and Tiger reserve. On the way we stopped at various village forests, ponds and water streams for bird watching. Some noteworthy sightings were - greater necklaced laughingthrush and red headed trogon near exit gate of Dehing; Oriental pied hornbill feeding on banana and coconut tree in a village; pied falconet perching on a tree top and occasionally snooping for butterflies, in a village just before the entry gate of Namdapha; and few black capped and white crowned forktails near a water stream outside the regulated boundary of Namdapha. We arrived at Deban Forest camp of Namdapha at around 4:00 pm. In this part of India, sun goes down by 4:00 pm. In the evening between 6:00 pm and 8:30 pm we went on a night-walk within the tiger reserve to search for slow loris. We stayed in Deban camp for three nights and every night we searched for that nocturnal animal. With no luck. Instead, each night we saw red giant flying squirrel feeding on tree bark within our campus.

The following morning at six, we went on a moderate trek in the Haldi Bari area of the tiger reserve. It was a three-hour hike from our forest camp, and included crossing Nua Dehing river through a precariously constructed hanging bridge made of bamboo, climbing a steep hillock, and walking through dense foliage. The day was sunny, and the forest resounded with the iconic call of hoolock gibbons. This reserve is unique, not just for its lofty stature as the third largest of its kind in India but also due to the strikingly varied altitudinal range of its landscape. Ranging from 200 metres to an astounding 4,500 metres, it provides the tiger and numerous other species with an environment of unparalleled diversity. Before we returned to our camp at noon, we spotted and captured quite a few rare birds. Some of them were slaty bellied tesia, white tailed flycatcher, streaked wren-babbler, white throated bulbul, rufus backed sibia, long-tailed broadbill, Durian redstart, and eye-browed wren-babbler. In the afternoon, we again explored the road that goes through the buffer zone of Namdapha towards Vijaya Nagar, where India ends, and Myanmar begins. Oriental hobby, rufous-gorgeted flycatcher, dark breasted rose finch, little forktail were some notable sightings. Our day ended with much delight as we sighted the elusive Oriental bay owl, which we had been trying to spot from day one.

We spent the following day walking along the road passing through the tiger reserve towards the India-Myanmar international border. We left our camp at 6:00 am and returned at 5:00 pm. Between Deban camp and Kamala Valley camp we spotted and identified birds including white-bellied erpornis, snowy throated wren babbler, brown crowned scimitar babbler, greater rufous headed parrot bill, white hooded babbler, hill prinia, black throated sunbird, white-rumped munia, Nepal fulvetta, pale-billed parrot bill, white browed piculet, whistling warbler, grey headed canary flycatcher, black chinned yuhina, long-tailed sibia, and mountain imperial pigeon.

As per forest department's norm, a local forest guide, Assam Mussang, accompanied us for two days in Namdapha. He told us that tourists are allowed only in selected routes in the buffer zone of this tiger reserve. Rest of the forest is not suitable for walking. The possibility of driving a car or jeep, is thus, nil. There is thus, no ecotourism activity in most of the buffer zone, and the entire core zone of Namdapha. Only the forest department staff and researchers visit to study and to install camera traps. Even forest patrolling is limited in a major part of this forest due to accessibility issues. This is perhaps why NTCA sounded helpless in their 2022 tiger status report while explaining depleting tiger and its prey base population in Arunachal Pradesh. Assam Mussang mentioned that Kodwai zone is part of buffer and core, where maximum number of tiger pugmarks and camera trap images were recorded. His comment aligned with NTCA's 2022 status report of recording one tiger in Namdapha.

The day was sunny and the snow-capped Dapha bum, the highest point of Namdapha, was visible from our exploration track. Despite depleting tiger population, Namdapha stands tall with its array of magnificent biodiversity. As the new era of humankind is marked by climate change and biodiversity loss, Namdapha is indeed a hope, and a sanctuary for countless non-human life forms. When we returned to camp at the end of the day, we saw the resident red giant flying squirrel busily feeding on tree bark. This is how my last night in India's last tiger reserve ended. With a message. *"To transform into a splendid ecotourism destination, raining of tigers is not imperative. The forest has much more to offer than just tigers."*

On our last morning, at six, we checked out from Deban camp and drove towards Miao, the border town between Arunachal Pradesh and Assam. On the way we engaged in some bird watching and again visited the water streams flowing through Namdapha. We put a lot of effort to sight Blyth's kingfisher (guided by Suyog's check list) but with no luck. The other birds spotted were golden crested myna, pintail green pigeon, yellow bellied fantail, barred buttonquail, crested kingfisher, pale headed woodpecker, wreathed hornbill, and plumbous water redstart. Besides flying squirrel, in the last few days we also saw other mammal species such as Himalayan striped squirrel, Malayan giant squirrel, Assamese macaque, crab eating mongoose and ruddy mongoose.

On this trip I saw around 100 different birds and about eighty percent of them for the first time in my life, most of which were spotted outside the protected areas of Namdapha. Precisely why it was one of my memorable biodiversity and photography trips in India.

Although I have said it before, that forests of Arunachal have much more to offer than tigers and elephants, one cannot deny that to protect this exquisite biodiversity, tigers and elephants are required too. Otherwise, human greed will eventually annihilate the biodiversity abundance of this "Land of the Rising Sun".

Nonetheless, because of depleting tiger population of Namdapha, its glory of diverse natural resources and biodiversity should not be eclipsed. If the surrounding areas of this landscape, including villages, waterbodies, hillocks, spice gardens of local Lisu tribes, and community forests, are recognized as OECM areas, it would support an effective long-term conservation.

Ecotourism organizations, NGOs, local community, and forest department also need to collaborate to boost regenerative ecotourism, so that local NGO volunteer Reevu of Buxa, knowledgeable nature guide Tapan of Manas, village resort owner Salam *Chacha* of Orang, and renowned local bird expert Palash of Namdapha can engagingly work together with brave Bodo forest gurad Ajoy, energetic lady forest guard Himani, and experienced forest department staff Assam Mussang to bring the best of this northeast Indian landscape to avid bird watchers as well as general ecotourists.

And as ecotourists, my readers have a choice to be either Suyog or Paddy.

CHAPTER THIRTEEN: The Climate that is Changing.

Award winning wildlife photographer M. V. Shreeram believes it is not fair to compare the complexities across various genre of wildlife photography. Photography of a venomous pit viper may be physically challenging as it may require you to be around thick bushes of a monsoon clad rain forest, on a dark night. But to photograph a tiger you must first find the ferocious beast in its natural habitat. He said, *"People make multiple trips to tiger reserves to get their best shots of the majestic animal. You may spot a tiger on your first safari in a tiger reserve, but it may have just allowed you a glimpse of it. The next time, perhaps it walked up to your gypsy, even waiting for some time, but it is possible the lighting or the angle wasn't favourable to capture your best shots. Yet another time, the settings may have been perfect, but other safari gypsies in the background of the tiger didn't allow you a clean frame of image."*

Clearly, tiger shooting also has its own challenges and the perfectionist tiger photographers may make multiple visits to a single tiger reserve to get their desirable images. Therefore, they do lot of planning for each tiger photography trip. The most important part of this planning is the prediction of weather before they embark on the trip. The sighting of the animal for photography requires favourable light and that is possible only on a good sunny day. This is why winter in Indian subcontinent is one of the preferred seasons for ecotourists and wildlife photographers, especially if the target species is the Bengal Tiger. But what if all your pre-tiger tourism planning goes for a toss due to sudden changes in weather?

I experienced this first-hand at Ranthambore, one winter season. Most of my safaris were washed out by unexpected heavy downpour. Another winter, much before my trip to Ranthambore, I travelled to Dudhwa National Park. This is a national park in the Terai belt of marshy grasslands of Northern Uttar Pradesh state of India. It stretches over an area of 490.3 km^2, with a buffer zone of 190 km^2, located on the Indo-Nepal border in the Lakhimpur Kheri District and has buffers of reserved forest areas on the northern and southern sides. It represents one of the few remaining areas of the diverse and productive Terai ecosystem, supporting many endangered species, obligate species of tall wet grasslands and species of restricted distribution.

After an overnight stay in the city of Nawabi culture and Tunde Kababs, Lucknow, I was picked up by driver Sailendra, at seven in the morning. The entire Indo-Gangetic plain including states of Punjab, Haryana, Delhi, and Uttar Pradesh was shivering in an unusual mid-winter cold wave. After a journey of five hours from Lucknow, I arrived at *Oriole cottage* of Forest Department resort located inside Dudhwa National Park and tiger reserve. The early morning fog delayed us by an hour.

The previous night I received news about the fog situation in Dudhwa and Lucknow from my local guide Sonu, *aka* Liladhar, who resides within the forest department campus and aside from his regular job as a nature guide with the forest department, he also runs an NGO to equip forest guards, guides, and drivers with knowledge of flora and fauna, and provide them necessary resources, like torch lights, warm clothes etc.

In my telephonic conversation with Sonu, the morning safaris in Dudhwa had become less eventful (less sightings of big mammals like elephants, rhinoceros and of course Bengal Tigers), because of fog and cold weather in the last couple of days. I arrived on a gloomy afternoon, and it seemed there would be no sunlight for the rest of the day. At least it appeared so until I started my jeep safari scheduled that afternoon at half past two, when temperature was around $14^{O}C$. In addition, the open safari gypsy exposed us to the chilly breeze, and was not particularly comfortable. In the hazy background, we saw herds of barasingha or swamp deer, comprising both male and female and few lesser adjutant storks. The swamp deer herds were grazing in marshy land;

some of them submerged in marsh and few young stags mock fighting.

Around a month before my Dudhwa trip, I came across a heart-breaking news published in the *Times of India*. A female tiger, locally named as Beldanda, lost her five cubs the previous year. On 12th of November that year, she again lost a cub out of a new litter of four. All the cubs were apparently killed by a male tiger sighted in her territory of Kishanpur Wildlife Sanctuary, part of the tiger reserve. As per the news report, the director of Dudhwa, Mr. Sanjay Pathak said, *"Beldanda female might have mated with him to save her cubs, in what is known as false mating. But eventually failed to trick the mighty male."* According to Pathak, there are around seventeen tigers in Kishanpur and for every male, cubs are a threat – once they grow up, they could challenge them for territory. I was reminded of T12, *aka Maya* of Tadoba, and her strategy for saving cubs through *false mating."*

This incident reported in the national English daily, reminded me of a touching statement made by renowned wildlife biologist, Dr. Ravi Chellum in a nature and wildlife related seminar in Bangalore in August 2019. He said, *"If we measure the success of wildlife conservation by merely counting the increased number of species, then we are short-sighted."* The Number of tigers has seen an exponential rise in Tadoba and Dudhwa. In fact, among the Indian forests, Tadoba is known as the *"maternity centre"* of Bengal Tigers. However, this has triggered several other problems. One of them is forcing female tigers to engage in false mating in an attempt to save their cubs. Moreover, the Dudhwa incident is a clear indicator that such attempts by the female tiger do not always succeed.

During my Dudhwa trip, one day, on our way towards Banke Lake within the tiger reserve, we saw fresh pugmarks of a female tiger. I wondered if it was Beldanda female. Sonu said that the following day we were to visit Kishanpur Wildlife Sanctuary area of the tiger reserve, which is her territory.

Some interesting bird species I spotted that afternoon were common quail, jungle owlet, red and grey jungle fowl, common bush chat, a female white rumped shama, erythromolous long tailed shrike, common hoopoe, and nesting of lesser adjutant stork. Few spotted deer and wild boar crossed our path a few times, grazing here and there in the forest undergrowth. The forest resort itself was invaded by a good number of rhesus macaque.

Following morning I woke up to a temperature of 5°C. The previous afternoon the ISO setting in my Nikon D7500 camera was 6400. This ensures entry of a lot of light through the camera aperture to enable a sharp photo being taken, as there was insufficient natural light. This, I hope, gives you an idea of visibility levels in Dudhwa. We entered the forest at 6:45 am, and slowly light began to improve. The previous day we explored zone one, mainly around Guleri zone. That day we roamed along the bank of Suheli River, where we again spotted fresh pugmarks of a male tiger moistened by early morning dew. With some hope we followed the track. We tracked it for some time along the forest path, but at a junction, the pugmark disappeared in dense forest. We decided to wait for a while, should the tiger choose to come out, or if any alarm call is let out as indication of his movement. An orange-headed thrush was hopping around on the forest undergrowth, a brown-headed barbet flew away and a changeable hawk eagle circled the sky. As we waited, we had hot, steamy black tea that Sonu had carried in his thermo-flask. We arrived near a wetland; a grey-headed fish eagle was sitting patiently on the ground. Flocks of red avadavat hopped and flew around in tall grassland. The remaining hour of our morning safari was spent spotting and watching barasigha herds through a hazy curtain of fog prevailing in the forest of Terai. We left the forest at around 10 am. Post lunch, at around 1 o'clock, we started our journey towards Kishanpur Wildlife Sanctuary, located thirty-five kilometres away from our forest rest house. It took us an hour to arrive at the entry point of the sanctuary, through sugarcane fields and local villages.

Sonu mentioned that the 204 km^2 forest area of Kishanpur Wildlife Sanctuary consists of approximately twenty-three tigers. This is too high for a healthy tiger density. The forest was once famous for sighting of the Beldanda female and her cubs. However, the department decided to close Beldanda's area along with the adjoining areas to tourists, to ensure protection of the tigress. The tigress had given birth to a new litter, and was busy in nurturing them. This was during COVID 19 lockdown. Thus, in post lock down Dudhwa, the chances of sighting her was slim. This was probably a noticeable difference between the management of Tadoba and Dudhwa. Both forests were known to have unhealthy tiger population density, but Dudhwa forest department had decided to close down a few areas in the tourist zone, sacrificing revenue for the sake of protection of tigers. Whereas in Tadoba the tourist zone was created in a way that increased the chance of sighting tigers with cubs.

The following morning, I woke up to the sound of heavy rainfall, but when I stepped out of my cottage, I did not find a single drop of water on the ground. It was the pitter-patter of dewdrops falling over leaves and branches of the teak forest around my cottage. At seven in the morning, as we started on our safari, I noticed that it was colder than the previous day and the fog was denser than ever. As our search for Beldanada female the day prior, had yielded nothing, we were now headed towards a different zone - Sathia zone, known for elephant movement.

From the entry point on we were welcomed with fresh elephant poop on moist ground accompanied with fresh footprints. However, in such cold and hazy weather it was difficult to spot anything. We saw streak throated and a lesser flame back woodpecker flying and climbing tree trunks. After an hour and a half, we returned to zone one of Dudhwa. Again, we saw fresh footprints and dung of elephants, an indication of early morning movement of the animals along the cold forest path. Later near the waterbody, I was delighted to sight a black necked stork and a stork billed kingfisher. In Sathia zone, as we were returning, we saw fresh elephant dung on the track of our gypsy tyre. Certainly, the animal had been there after we had visited the area, and then moved towards a different direction. Nonetheless, amidst the cold and fog in Terai Forest, I completed another "unsuccessful tiger exploration" in the Indian subcontinent.

The Terai winter fog has been getting worse every year because of a combination of factors like industrial pollution and smog, the spread of winter irrigation that raises the concentration of water vapour in the air, and climate change. The sun does not shine for weeks on end — a phenomenon that stretches right across the Indo-Gangetic plains. This condition may not be to the liking of most wildlife photographers and nature explorers, but generally, my experience in any forest in any part of the world, in any climatic condition has always been satisfactory. The main reason behind this is that after my initial explorations, I stopped venturing into a forest with a target species in mind. Now I always find something new and interesting to see in the forest. I must admit, though, that although I got a different perspective of the Terai Forest in winter, the biodiversity of this region can be better appreciated in spring, much like I had experienced earlier in Corbett National Park.

On 27th November 2018, the Programme Director of Global Tourism company *Dolma Eco-Tourism* posted an article in *LinkedIn* on *Effects of Climate Change in Tourism*. The article mentions, *'From the last few decades, there has been a growing concern about climate change all over the world. With the growing urbanization, industrial development and the pollution produced by them have made a great negative impact on the climate, which has resulted in climate change. With every passing day, climate change is becoming a more pressing topic to the world community. Melting of snow in the Himalayas, more drought and heat waves, rising temperature are few effects of climate change. As of now, Earth's climate is changing faster than at any point in the whole history of modern civilization, primarily as a result of human activities."* He specifically points out, *"The changes and disturbance caused by climate change have also made a very significant effect on the tourism industry. Tourism is directly related to the environment and environment is directly affected by climate change, so climate change and tourism have a very clear and depending relationship."*

This changing climate is adversely impacting the ecotourism potential in tourism destinations in cold climate areas, such as the Himalayan regions. Dudhwa is just one such example, where the only source of income for the eco-tour guides and the forest department is showing big mammals to ecotourists and creating photography opportunities for them. The unpredictable Indo-Gangetic winter weather during peak tourism season is unfavourably impacting these opportunities.

Based on *Dolma Eco-Tour's LinkedIn* posting, among the nations in the subcontinent, Nepal is the worst victim of the consequences of climate change with regard to ecotourism. Various studies have been conducted in different regions of Nepal relating to climate change and tourism. Nepal is a hub for trekking and mountaineering, and tourism is the prime source of revenue for the locals of the Himalayan regions. Not just the Himalayan regions, Nepal as a nation is dependent on tourism as a primary source of income. Wildlife, including tiger tourism, draws a lot of wildlife photographers and ecotourists to Nepal. Like Dudhwa, this Terai habitat of Bengal Tiger is also susceptible to adverse effects of climate change.

However, ecotourism, although a victim of climate change, plays a critical role in mitigating and adapting to the effects of climate change. Supporting the local community who are affected by various impacts of climate change such as flood, drought, sea level rise, loss of crop, spread of disease, loss of income etc., through ecotourism could both mitigate and adapt to the effects of a rapidly changing climate. Such efforts not only help to reduce the impacts of climate change, but they also provide economic benefits to local communities and help to build resilience in the face of a rapidly changing climate. We can correlate this with the very first principle of regenerative ecotourism which embraces nature-based solution.

In fact, Nepal the arguably worst victim of climate change among all subcontinental nations, in the sphere of ecotourism, has demonstrated the effect of community involvement to cope with this menace. Located in the shadow of the Himalayas, the Terai Arc belt stretches from Nepal's Bagmati River in the east to India's Yamuna River in the west covering an area of 51,000 km². In the Nepal segment of this landscape, the tiger population has risen by nearly 20% between 2014 and 2018. Based on an article written by Pragati Shahi on 3rd January 2019, in the online edition of *The Record*, published from Kathmandu, the driving force of this success was described as *"coordinated efforts among police, community members, and conservationists have been fruitful"*.

In the article, a former chief conservation officer of Bardiya National Park, Mr. Ramesh Thapa particularly emphasized the community's role in this success, *"the willingness of the local community to help protect wildlife by managing the key wildlife corridors, allowing for smooth wildlife movement, was a key factor."* I witnessed this community wildlife interaction and its impact on ecotourism in three tiger reserves of Nepal, which together comprise around 83% of the country's overall Bengal Tiger population. One spring, when I reached Kathmandu, the result of 4th cycle of tiger estimation had been announced by the Nepal Government. As per the announcement, from 235 in 2018, Nepal increased its tiger population to 355, a 51% increase in four years. Of the 355 adult tigers, around 295 of them are in Parsa, Chitwan and Bardiya national parks.

As per plan, the following morning at seven, I started from Thamel area of Kathmandu, and arriving after a six-hour drive at Birajgunj, the closest town to Parsa, where my local guide Raunak lives. When I met Raunak, I was surprised to see that he had gathered five of his friends to accompany us. Certainly not a pleasant surprise. My intention was to explore and camp inside the forest in solitude to maximize my chances of wildlife encounter. However, I was left with no option and we began our hour-long drive from Birajgunj to Suwarnapur gate of Parsa. On the way Raunak mentioned, *"Four-five days ago there was uncertainty about staying in the community forest of Parsa and camping inside, as a tiger entered a village to pray upon livestock. Luckily the tiger was caught couple of days ago by the forest department. Now there is no concern in staying in the forest."*

Incidentally Raunak had arranged my stay in a community homestay at Todi village inside the buffer zone community forest, adjacent to the core area of Parsa national park. Such community homestays in the vicinity of Parsa national park are examples of how wildlife tourism and ecotourism represent interesting opportunities for local communities to boost their income-generating potential whilst also safeguarding the conservation of the species. The Todi village is mostly inhabited by the Tamang community and showcases distinct Tamang culture while offering nature-based experiences to tourists.

At around 4 pm after eating a delicious Tamang snack (puffed rice and fried egg), consuming local Nepali beer and smoking locally grown weeds, we entered the core area of the forest for our evening safari in a seven-seater open top Bolero. Soon I realized, that neither Raunak, nor his friends had any idea or interest in wildlife. All they were interested in was drinking and smoking. They were on a picnic in Parsa at my expense. The other intent was pilgrimage. Like many Indian tiger reserves and national parks, Parsa is home to a Hindu Shiva temple, *Dudheswar Mahadev*, within the core zone. Throngs of local Nepali folk visit the temple daily, defeating entirely the purpose of conservation and ecotourism.

We stayed inside the forest for about three hours; smoking weed and drinking beer. Some of my companions took bath in a water stream near a designated camping area, named Ghodemasan, the area I was to camp the next day. Despite such disinterested and noisy companions, I did spot a few birds like Indian roller, rufus treepie, velvet-fronted nuthatch, spotted dove, and plenty of chestnut headed bee-eaters. As we exited at dusk, we saw a nightjar on the road and a spotted owlet flying away. We also sighted a pair of jackals near the exit, at the boundary with the community village. On entering the forest in day light, we saw plenty of rhesus macaque, Terai grey langur and Indian pea fowl. No herbivores until then. This was how I began my tiger habitat exploration in Terai landscape outside India.

The night camping within Parsa, was as lacklustre as it was the previous evening, in terms of wildlife sighting. After spending twenty-four hours in a tiger habitat on foreign soil, and with no thrilling stories to narrate to a spellbound audience, we left our camp at six the following morning. *En route* we saw a burking deer, a sambar deer, a few spotted deer, and a wild boar. At the end of the forest, we again saw a pair of jackals. There was a serpent eagle, plenty of drongos, tree-pies and a lineated barbet on various tree branches. The mammals and even birds were very shy in Parsa. They ran away or flew higher, even on sighting our vehicle from afar. An indication of a not-so-developed ecotourism in this part of forest. Clearly the forest fauna was not familiar with human and their vehicles.

My Parsa experience was very similar to Simlipal and Satkosia. Local community is engaged in ecotourism but not empowered with adequate knowledge.

We exited the forest and headed for Sauraha, where Chitwan national park is located. When I reached Sauraha, after a three-hour drive from Birajgunj, I discovered a very contrasting image of ecotourism. The whole area was designed to cater to the needs of international tourists. There were hundreds of resorts offering various eco adventure facilities including Bolero safari, local Tharu village tour, jungle trekking, kayaking in Rapti river and many more. Sauraha also had plenty of eateries, pubs, shops, ATM and tourist information centres. The area was crowded with Western tourists. I checked in at *Chitwan Tiger Camp* owned by Neeraj Thapa. He charted out my exploration plan for the upcoming two days. The resort was located on the bank of Rapti river, on the opposite side to where the national park is situated. Rapti river forms the northern boundary of the park.

The following morning, we crossed the river on a kayak and arrived at the entry point of the park where our open-top Bolero was waiting. Neeraj appointed a nature guide with thirty years of experience to me. Balaram Choudhury, a local Tharu tribal. I enjoyed the most memorable day of my entire wildlife exploration tenure. Within fifteen minutes of entering the forest, we saw a subadult tiger through tall elephant grasses. His big tender head and cautious innocent eyes were visible to us. It was my first tiger sighting outside India.

As per the most recent (2022) tiger census, there were 128 tigers in 952 km^2 national park of Chitwan. The highest tiger population in any tiger reserve of Nepal. Not sighting a tiger in one of the 13 tiger range countries where tiger conservation was apparently most successful, would have then, been a shame. Over the next ten hours, we saw around 11 species of mammals, 44 species of birds and a few mugger crocodiles. Rhino sighting was quite phenomenal in Chitwan as in the scorching heat of the early summer afternoon, they submerged themselves in various water bodies. Other interesting big mammal sightings were gaurs and elephants. In a sharp contrast to Indian tiger reserves, especially the central Indian ones, in Chitwan, people were more emotionally connected with elephants than tigers.

In the last hour of our safari, as we turned into a forest path, we saw another Bolero waiting at the bend of the path. A few western tourists and photographers waved at us.

As we reached closer, one gentleman whispered, *"Dhrube was seen on the forest path"*.

My guide, Balaram, looked alert and nervous. He decided not to proceed further. It was natural for me to assume that *Dhrube* was a tiger.

The following moment a huge tusker slowly appeared in front of us, walking in the opposite direction. In Chitwan, it's the elephants that have human names, not the tigers. Dhrube and Ronaldo were two such tuskers. Both, infamous for human killing. According to Balaram, Ronaldo had killed at least sixteen humans till date. Whereas Dhrube, in the last month alone, had killed fifteen people. All his victims were Tharu villagers who lost their forest patch to the national park, but still entered the forest to collect herbs and firewood. While exiting the forest we got a glimpse of Ronaldo too, through large trees.

Among the 44 bird species that we spotted, some remarkable species were puffed throated babbler, grey headed fish eagle, great hornbill, spangled drongo, grey capped pygmy woodpecker, Himalayan flame back woodpecker, red turtle dove, emerald dove, black redstart etc. The following day, on our Chitwan core area exploration, we went on a thirty-minute kayaking in Rapti river, followed by a three-hour trek in the buffer zone, where with guide Vishnu, I saw 16 more species of birds, including hill myna, woolly necked stork, stork billed kingfisher and rare grey headed woodpecker. This was possible only because my guides Balaram and Vishnu were not chasing the tiger or any other targeted species. We spotted whatever came our way, without creating any disturbances in the natural environment of the tiger reserve.

A nature guide belonging to the local community understands their forests much better than any outsider wildlife tour operator or photographer. They are also more compassionate about all living forms that belong to the forest, as their livelihoods depend on them. As a result, they are well equipped to conduct an inclusive ecotourism, if they are empowered adequately. My exploration through Chitwan is a case in point.

"Tourism and development can be an industry spearheading the tangible solution (to battle climate change)" said by John Pagano, group CEO of *Red Sea Global*, a tourism development company of Saudi Arabia, in his article titled, *"Battling climate change with regenerative tourism"*, published in *Business Reporter*.

The development to meet the materialistic need of humankind seems inevitable, so as climate change as an outcome of this "development". Therefore, integrating these two (tourism and development) to empower local community is the key to become resilient to climate change. Dudhwa and Parsa, although involved locals in ecotourism, but the empowerment effort was feeble. But Chitwan showed me a great example of this empowerment and thus I believe, in challenging days ahead, Chitwan would emerge out as more climate change resilient, in Terai Arc of this subcontinent.

However, in the same Terai Arc of Nepal, is another famous tiger reserve where I had a bitter-sweet experience, where the local guides were not given the full freedom to conduct ecotourism.

Bardiya National Park has the second largest tiger population in Nepal after Chitwan. The 968 km^2 forest is the largest and most undisturbed national park in Nepal, located at the eastern bank of the Karnali River and bisected by the Babai River in the Bardiya district. As per the 2022 tiger census the park has 125 Bengal Tigers. Thakurdwara, the village where the park is located is not as touristy as Sauraha in terms of availability of modern amenities (read development), but it attracts a large number of wildlife photographers and ecotourists. On visiting the park, I realized that, as always, the main reason for it was that a high possibility of tiger sighting in the park. Tiger sighting possibility in Bardiya is considered the highest among all tiger reserves of Nepal. Availability of several human made waterholes is the primary reason. Therefore, of all the parks and sanctuaries of Nepal, Bardiya is the most preferred destination for wildlife tour operators from India and other nations. It is understandable then, that such a reputation of the park brings unprecedented stress on local nature guides, similar to what we experience in some of the Central Indian tiger reserves.

I was part of a photography bootcamp in Bardiya organized by an Indian photography tour company. Once there, we did a two-hour long night safari in the community forest of Dalla, where we saw a lot of Indian hares, spotted deer, a jungle owlet and long tailed nightjar. Spotted deer bellowed alarm calls relentlessly. Over the next three days we went on three full day safaris in an open-top gypsy in various zones of Bardiya, with guide Deepak Rajbanshi, driver Ranjit, tour leader Soumyajit and two other elderly fellow photographers, from Calcutta and Coimbatore respectively.

In the first hour of the first full day safari, we spotted a subadult leopard on a fallen tree trunk. The moment it saw our gypsy, it got off the trunk, and hid behind it. No photo opportunity there. At around 1:45 pm, as we were finishing our lunch on the bank of Karnali River, a female tiger appeared from a faraway thicket and crossed the river slowly, disappearing into another thicket. Through the day we heard plenty of alarm calls of spotted deer and pea fowl. In Bardiya, we entered the forest at around 6:45 am and exited at 6:30 pm. A good twelve hours of thorough forest exploration including couple of breaks for breakfast and lunch.

On day two, just after breakfast, from the Lamkohli watch tower we saw another female tiger appearing through the bushes and then proceeded to cross the forest path below the tower. After taking a few shots of the tigress from the watchtower, we ran down to a forest path where we were expecting her to cross. There was no time to get the gypsy out as that would have delayed us. However, she made us wait for a long time near the crossing point, and finally crossed when there were a couple of vehicles on the other side too. The day ended with sighting a parade of ten elephants crossing the forest path.

Day three started quite dramatically. We stopped near a grassland after hearing frequent alarm calls from a nearby thicket. There were a few other gypsies as well. Everyone eagerly awaited the tiger, hoping he would come out in the open. Instead, a herd of swamp deer came out. They were alert and staring in the direction of the alarm call. Within a few minutes a huge tusker appeared from the thicket and walked along the edge of the forest. People were confused about where to pay attention, and then everybody looked at the sky. A thundering sound of flapping wingspan erupted over head. An adult great hornbill flew across. When the hornbill disappeared into the horizon, a troop of Nepali army marched into the scene. They were patrolling the forest.

All this happened in rapid succession, but there was no sign of the big cat. We took our breakfast break and waited for a couple more hours and then followed a different track, in the direction of new alarm calls. The entire day there were frequent alarm calls from different parts of the forest, and we followed these alarm calls, waiting for a few hours occasionally, before heading out in the direction of another alarm call. But did not see any tiger.

In three days, I saw 12 mammals including two tigers, and around 40 bird species. Whereas, in Chitwan, in a day and a half, I saw around 11 mammals including a tiger and around 60 bird species. That way Chitwan could be considered as more satisfactory, however we should not forget that the constant tiger sighting pressure from Soumyajit and other two fellow photographers did not give much opportunity to Deepak and Ranjit to stop for birds or any other less glamorous species. Nepal's extraordinary feat of more than doubling its tiger population in the past ten years, bringing them back from the brink of extinction, also doubled up the tiger sighting expectations from ecotourists, photographers, and tour operators. Exactly what has happened in India in the past ten years.

Shreeram once said to the people desperate to see tigers on a wildlife safari, *"There is a good recipe for life to be learnt from our beloved tiger. Most often we see a tiger just sleeping. When it is thirsty, it makes its way to the waterbody and has a drink. When it is hungry, it tries to hunt. It is never restless accumulating anything for future. In fact, no other life form in nature does that."*

We tiger loving ecotourists have this essential lesson to learn from our demigod, the Bengal Tiger. This lesson can teach us compassion for every non-human life form in nature and help in contributing to build an inclusive deep ecology-based ecotourism. Moreover, in the long run, this realization will, while engaging in any ecotourism activity, make us happier. It is indeed, this happiness, that the ecotourists seek in response to all living and societal crises.

Pseudo Ecotourism

There is another tiny Himalayan tiger range country of this subcontinent, which until recent time was not open to Global community. The country that is regarded as an epitome of happiness – the Kingdom of Happiness, has realized this essential lesson through a spiritual belief. Mythology has it, that the spiritual belief was spread in this country by a monk on tiger-back.

Among the four Bengal Tiger range countries of this subcontinent, Bhutan is considered special among environmentalists and ecotourists. Bhutan is the first carbon negative country (that is, it absorbs more carbon than it emits) in the world, absorbing six million tons of carbon every year. The Constitution of Bhutan places a high premium on conservation of its natural environment, mandating the country to maintain at least 60% of its land under forest cover for all time to come. The ecotourism companies in Bhutan claim that more than 70% of land in Bhutan is under forest cover. When I travelled across the length and breadth of this country one winter, I had no reason to disbelieve this claim.

I landed in Paro, then travelled further north to Thimphu and via Dochchu La arrived at Punakha. I then went further up to Phobjika wetland. Then I ascended further to 3800 meters, and crossed Thrumshing La. There after I started descending towards the south and crossed Tingtibhi, Panbang and Gelephu, all of which lie on the international border between India and Bhutan. After that I moved again towards the northwest direction and crossed Tama La, Tsirang, Wangdue and finally went on an excursion at Chele La, at an altitude of 4000 meters. I spent on an average twelve hours a day on field, 50% of which was involved in trekking and bushwalk through forests of various categories. It was alpine-subalpine of northern Bhutan to montane-submontane of central and western Bhutan to tropical-subtropical of southern foot hills of the country. I did this exploration in varied climatic conditions, where minimum temperatures ranged from 10°C in Southern foot hills to -6°C in Great Himalayan landscape of Bhutan. I was overwhelmed, as with the help of my local nature guide Sonam Tshering, I could spot and shoot around 270 bird and 10 mammalian species. 48% of these sightings, were for the first time in my life. Almost every day in these three weeks I saw at least one new bird or mammal. The top few mention worthy bird species I spotted are, white-bellied heron, rufus necked hornbill, beautiful nuthatch, black necked crane, Ward's trogon, Himalayan monal, rufus throated wren babbler, fire tailed myzornis, yellow rumped honey guide, rufus faced warbler, and blood pheasant. The top mammals are golden langur and Himalayan yellow throated marten. Many of them are very region restricted species. Especially golden langur, long considered sacred by many Himalayan people, also known as Gee's golden langur, is an endangered species as per IUCN. It is an Old-World monkey found in a small region of western Assam and in the neighbouring foothills of the Black Mountains of Bhutan (between Jigme Singye Wangchuk and Royal Manas National Park).

This remarkable and overwhelming exploration through the great Himalayan, inner Himalayan and southern foothills of Bhutan unfolded during what is considered inarguably as off season. According to my guide Sonam, the peak seasons of biodiversity exploration in Bhutan are spring and autumn, during which time one can easily spot between 300 to 400 faunal species. Most importantly, the phenomenal ecotourism prospect of this country, one of the four tiger range countries of this subcontinent, does not depend upon a single species called the Bengal Tiger.

The question that arises is: How has Bhutan managed to avoid succumbing to commodified, single-species-centric ecotourism, while the other three countries struggle to do so?

I believe the answer lies in Bhutan's iconic concept of integrating *mindfulness* and *sustainability* in their way of life.

In my Paro bound Druk Air flight from Delhi, I flipped through a few pages of Druk Air's inflight magazine *Tashi Delek (A Dzongkha phrase which meanes - have a good day or life; Dzongkha is a Sino-Tibetan language that is the official and national language of Bhutan. It is written using the Tibetan script)*. An article by Dr. Ritu Verma, an anthropologist and researcher, titled, *"The Mindful and Sustainable Nation: Compassion and Loving-Kindness"*, published in the magazine mentions, *"Now, more than at any other time in history, the need for mindful reflection and sustainable action has never been more pressing. As the world reels from multiple crises – climate, environmental, social, economic, and political conflict – travellers are increasingly seeking antidotes in the form of moments, spaces and experience of calm and peace, informed by age-old wisdom."*

In her article the author also opines, *"In response to these calls for regenerative travel, experiences, the terms mindfulness and sustainability have become common in popular language and social media circles. Entire hospitality business, online-apps and travel companies have been created, or are taking up the idea of promoting or facilitating these concepts, which are closely inter-linked to ideas of compassion and loving kindness."* The philosophy of Buddhism put forward the idea of compassion and loving-kindness. Dr. Verma explained, *"a shift in mental attitude towards compassion allows for acts of kindness to follow and that is loving-kindness. On the other hand, compassion is the ability to feel concern for the suffering of others, no matter who they are, or what they are – human or non-human."*

This inclusivity and equality of human and non-human is the core principle of *bio-spherical egalitarianism*. Here in Bhutan Buddhism goes hand in hand with Deep Ecology, thus giving birth to the concept of regenerative ecotourism which does not commodify nature or any of her inhabitants. This philosophy resonated in my guide Sonam as evident from the ecotourism offerings he made to me.

Ecotourism in Bhutan is certainly not single-species-centric. Nevertheless, the Bengal Tiger is not ignored in spiritually and ecologically conscious Bhutan, which has a special relationship with the Bengal Tiger. As early as the eighth century, this majestic cat was associated with the divine. The famous Indian saint Guru Padmasambhava (known as Guru Rinpoche in Bhutan) who brought Buddhism to Bhutan is said to have ridden a flying tigress in course of preaching Buddhism and subduing demons in the seventh century. Thus, tiger conservation in Bhutan has a deep religious connection and sentiment. Based on a report, *Distribution and Habitat Use of Tigers in Bhutan*, published by *Nature Conservation Division, Department of Forests and Park Services of Government of Bhutan*, the current strongholds of tiger habitat in Bhutan includes Royal Manas National Park, Jigme Singye Wangchuck National Park, Phrumsengla National Park, Jomotshangkha Wildlife Sanctuary, Zhemgang Division, Bumthang Division, Sarpang Division, Wangdue Division and Tsirang Division. During my visit to Bhutan, I explored all habitats except Jomotshangkha. However, like Namdapha of northeast India, in Bhutan the core areas of the forests are beyond the reach of tourism and also unsuitable for gypsy ride or even bushwalk. I consider this as a clear indication of Bhutan's ecotourism fraternity's intent towards wholistic tourism, as opposed to a species-based tourism.

India, Nepal and Bangladesh have to learn this essential lesson from the smallest country of this subcontinental tiger landscape.

Adopting the concept of nature-based solution in the sustainability landscape of one of 17 mega-diverse countries, India, the home to 7.6% of all mammalian, 12.6% of all avian, 6.2% of all reptilian, 4.4% of all amphibian and 11.7% of all fish, is absolutely crucial. Particularly when the 73 species of India - including 9 species of mammals, 18 species of birds, 26 species of reptiles, and 20 species of amphibians - according to IUCN criteria, are critically endangered.

Ironically, adopting nature-based solutions is at times in direct conflict with the sustainable development agenda of the state, as we have seen in the case of Great Indian Bustards that are a victim of windmill installation projects to meet the country's renewable energy targets. The victims of such conflicts are often those critically endangered faunal species and the local human community.

The most sustainability-conscious country of the world, Bhutan, is also not beyond such anthropogenic dilemma.

I mentioned earlier that Bhutan has high regards among environmentalists and ecotourists for putting sustainability as its core value. The biological corridors of Bhutan are one such example, that represents a bold and innovative vision unsurpassed by any other nation on Earth. Thus, Bhutan can be rightly pointed out as a world leader in attempting to use corridors as a cost-effective, reliable strategy to conserve meta-populations of wide-ranging species, promote gene flow for all species, and allow species to adapt to climate change.

In Bhutan, I spent a few days in one such biological corridor known as biological corridor three or Gelephu biological corridor. It is located exactly between the Jigme Singye Wangchuck National Park – Royal Manas National Park in the northeast to Pibsoo Wildlife Sanctuary in the southwest under Sarpang Dzongkhag (Division), adorned with tropical forest of abundant hardwood trees. It enjoys hot rainy summer and cold winter seasons. The diversity of the flora and fauna is rich. This 407.6 km^2 area with elevation range of 329–2,647 meters, is the habitat of near threatened Himalayan goral, Asiatic golden cat, marbled cat, Assamese macaque, Malayan giant squirrel and endangered golden langur, Asiatic elephant, Bengal Tiger and dhole.

Besides the corridor between the two national parks, we also visited other areas like Gelephu sewerage pond, the grassland and tropical shrubs forests around an adjacent river called Moukhola, a community teak forest in the Gelephu town, and nearby forests in Fishery Road and Gelephu Main Road. All potential OECM, as in these areas, we saw around 50 bird species including Siberian stonechat, green crowned warbler, dusky warbler, wreathed hornbill, large billed leaf warbler, white throated fantail, grey breasted prinia, oriental honey buzzard, black napped monarch, large cuckoo shrike, red breasted parakeet etc. During a night walk in Fishery Road and Gelephu main road we enjoyed a clear view of brown boobook and spotted owlet.

As our exploration in Gelephu winded down, Sonam revealed that this was probably the last time he was conducting a bird watching tour at Gelephu and we were perhaps the last few photographers lucky enough to be there. The Government of Bhutan has initiated construction of a *Mindfulness City*, and very soon all bird watching spots of Gelephu will be engulfed by this construction activity. During the 116th National Day of Bhutan, His Majesty King Jigme Khesar Namgyel Wangchuck introduced the master plan for this prospective economic centre in the country. It is an envisioned master plan that draws from Bhutanese culture, Gross National Happiness principles, and spiritual heritage. An international airport, railroads, a hydroelectric dam, public areas, and architectural features representing the nine domains of Gross National Happiness are all included in the master plan. In fact, during my visit, I saw piling of construction equipment and initiation of road building near Moukhola river as well as timber felling in the community teak forest, which was a habitat to a good population of collard owlet and red-breasted parakeets among many other birds.

There is one other critical ecological aspect which poses threat to Bhutan's age-old concept of mindfulness and sustainability. That is the concern over significant habitat loss of critically endangered white-bellied heron. The white-bellied heron also known as the imperial heron or great white-bellied heron, is a large heron species living in the foothills of the eastern Himalayas in northeast India and Bhutan to northern Myanmar. It inhabits undisturbed rivers and wetlands. Currently, the global population is estimated at less than 300 mature individuals and it is threatened by habitat loss and human disturbance.

When I was driving from Tsirang to Thimphu via Wangdue, we drove along a twelve kilometres long stretch of river body. Starting from northwest of Tsirang, the east of the river is Puna Tsang Chu, and north of its tributary is Burichu. Previously Puna Tsang Chu was known as a critical habitat for white-bellied heron. During our exploration we did not see any of them, and Sonam mentioned that the increased population in Punakha valley and the hydro-electric project are the main reasons of habitat destruction for this critically endangered bird.

Eventually we saw one adult heron further east of the river. Few days later when we were between Wangdue and Tsirang, again, we saw another adult heron somewhere near Burichu. After driving a few kilometres, we saw that the entire terrain of wetland habitat had been transformed into a massive construction project site containing huge equipment and bunkers. The once-pristine forest road was covered with unprecedented amount of construction dust. The white-bellied heron spotting site had sadly transformed into a construction labour camp site.

Apparently, it was a hydroelectric project that had been kicked off sixteen years prior, funded by Government of India. I saw many project offices and labour camps of various Indian construction companies such as BHEL, GCC, Jaypee and L&T. The project which was supposed to be completed in five years was far from completion as on 2024.

An undergrad student of the Royal University of Bhutan, Tashi Wangdi, in his graduation thesis on *"Land use change effect on habitat and white-bellied heron population by hydropower project along Puna Tsang Chu"* mentions, *"Puna Tsang Chu basin is increasingly disturbed and degraded by increasing developmental activities and human population. The maximum recorded population of white-bellied heron was 30 in 2008 to 2009 and in 2014 it has declined to 22. Considering the significant loss of population with the commencement of hydro-power project, it is concluded that such project can be a threat to critically endangered white-bellied heron."*

Sonam once told me, during a conversation over dinner, that his country produces enough electricity to meet basic needs of its citizens. It is only the greed of humans which is creating demand for more and more hydroelectric power plants. In the days that I spent with him, he sounded worried about the future of sensitive and crucial ecosystems of Bhutan. He was worried about the future of communities dependent upon these ecosystems. More importantly he was worried about his future as an ecotour operator and nature guide. The effect of climate change has resulted in the drying of many glaciers of Bhutan. These glaciers were the sole source of many rivers. The ongoing hydropower projects are aggravating this climate crisis even further.

Eventually the Kingdom of Happiness is revealing its inclination to human's worst enemy – *Commodity Fetishism*. Just saying *Tashi Delek* may not suffice anymore.

CHAPTER FOURTEEN: When Human Culture Merges with Non-Human Nature

At the very end of Buddhadeb Guha's novel *Madhukari*, Prithu realized that *"Work is love made visible....and if you can't work with love but only with distaste, it is better that you should leave your work and sit at the gate of the temple and take alms of those who work with joy. (The Prophet by Kahlil Gibran)"*

If the urban affluent folks solely embrace wildlife photography and ecotourism as a means to escape their dissatisfaction with work, then such wildlife photography and ecotourism may eventually become substitutes for enjoyment that should have been derived from their professions. Gradually such wildlife photography and ecotourism will come to be treated as a target oriented supplementary pursuit. In the long run such supplementary pursuit is likely to create more stress than joy. The result of this, is evident in the various tiger tourism destinations of this subcontinent. Not to make nature a supplementary pursuit is the principle to be embraced in life.

Not just the non-human, there are fellow humans who have shown us the path to include nature in everything we do, rather than just considering her as an escapade from the monotony of urban life. I have seen how Prithu's realization of *"work is love made visible"* resonates in the daily life of indigenous people.

The authors of the book titled, *In Tribes of Koraput*, published by the *Council of Analytical Tribal Studies*, Koraput, mention, *"Some of the scholars have mentioned that the tribals are the men of the moment; they do not think of tomorrow. On deep analysis it may be found that this is mainly because, since historical times they had to fully depend upon nature to fulfil their basic needs/minimum wants. Secondly, they now have extremely poor access to resources, and they are very primitive in technology. Within these severe limitations, they too try to maximize satisfaction by using the scarce means in productive way."*

For indigenous people of this subcontinent, nature is neither an escapade nor a supplementary pursuit. Shreeram said, *"Nature should not be a supplementary pursuit"*. I must say that ecotourism should also not be a supplementary pursuit. Neither should it be an easy way to achieve fame and glory, that transforms it into a single-species-centric commodified pseudo ecotourism.

The indigenous people of this subcontinent have challenged all efforts to convert nature into a supplementary pursuit since time immemorial.

The strongest criticism of Neo-liberal Sustainability is based on the principles of Deep Ecology. The Norwegian philosopher and environmentalist Arne Nares introduced this concept in 1973, through his original deep ecology paper, titled as *"The shallow and the deep, long-range ecology movement: A summary"*. Naess referred to *"bio-spherical egalitarianism-in principle"*, which he explained as, *"the right of all forms [of life] to live is a universal right which cannot be quantified. No single species of living being has more of this particular right to live and unfold than any other species."* *(Ref: Naess, Arne (1989). Ecology, community, and lifestyle: outline of an ecosophy, Translated by D. Rothenberg. Cambridge: Cambridge University Press. pp. 166, 187).*

In 1985, Bill Devall (emeritus professor of sociology at *Humboldt State University*, Arcata, California) and George Sessions (chairman of the philosophy department at *Sierra College* in Rocklin, California) summed up their understanding of the concept of deep ecology with the following eight points: *(Ref: Devall, Bill; Sessions, George (1985). Deep Ecology. Gibbs M. Smith. p. 70).*

I. The well-being of human and nonhuman life on Earth is of intrinsic value irrespective of its value to humans.

II. The diversity of life-forms is part of this value.

III. Humans have no right to reduce this diversity except to satisfy vital human needs.

IV. The flourishing of human and nonhuman life is compatible with a substantial decrease in human

population.
V. Humans have interfered with nature to a critical level already, and interference is worsening.
VI. Policies must be changed, affecting current economic, technological, and ideological structures.
VII. This ideological change should focus on an appreciation of the quality of life rather than adhering to an increasingly high standard of living.
VIII. All those who agree with the above tenets have an obligation to implement them.

The modern world believes that environmentalism or environmental activism started with these principles. But 500 years prior, in medieval India a philosophy gave birth to a tradition that embraced the fundamental principles of bio-spherical egalitarianism based deep ecology. In 1485, the Bishnoi tradition was born in the hands of Guru Jambeshwar, a Rajput chieftain of Marwar, in western Rajasthan. He formulated twenty-nine commandments that a Bishnoi is expected to follow until death. Of these, six are extraordinary – they cover environmental protection and compassion for all living creatures. The Bishnois are commanded to provide shelter to abandoned animals and prohibited from felling trees. They follow a system of sharing resources with the wildlife around them.

In an article titled *"The Bishnois, India's original environmentalists, who inspired the Chipko movement"*, published in the online journal *Ecologies.in*, on 28th

May 2017, author Ishrath Humairah mentions, *"The Bishnois are considered as the first environmentalists of India. They are born nature lovers. They have, for centuries, married eco-conservation with their faith, making it one of the most ecologically relevant orders of today. Long before the world came to know about the environmental crises, Bishnois have been cognizant of man's relationship with nature and the importance to maintain its delicate balance. It is remarkable that these issues were thought about, half a century ago by Bishnoi visionaries. No other religious order has given this level of importance to environment value, protection, and care."*

In 1730, in the remote village of Khejarli in western Rajasthan, 363 Bishnoi men, women, and children sacrificed their lives trying to protect hundreds of Khejri trees that the king's men had come to fell to fuel the cement lime kilns for the king's palace. The ancient creed has been translated into modern activism. One of the more well-known cases that catapulted them to fame was when the community dragged Bollywood actor Salman Khan to court for allegedly killing two blackbucks during a movie shoot near Jodhpur in 1998. The community followed the case with dogged conviction for twenty years, until, in 2018, Khan was sentenced by a local court. As Ishrath mentioned in his article published in *Ecologise.in*, *"If not for the Bishnois, the Black Buck and Chinkara, which come under Section 9 of the Wildlife Protection Act, supposedly getting the highest degree of protection by the state, would have had vanished like other species. Salman Khan or Mansur Ali Khan of Pataudi – the Bishnois spare nobody."*

Although the influence of Guru Jambeshwar and 1730's Khejarli massacre and sacrifice of 363 Bishnoi men and women were almost forgotten, the 1998 chasing of the Bollywood celebrity reminded the entire nation of the significance of the Bishnoi way of life. In today's Rajasthan, it is now an ecotourism attraction. Located around thirty kilometres from the city of Jodhpur, around 23187 km^2 area of conservation reserve forest is now under the protection of Bishnois. The sanctuary is home to black bucks, chinkara, nil gai and various other herbivores and variety of birds, particularly migratory Demoiselle crane.

In the beginning of one winter season, I stayed in one such villages located within the conservation reserve. Manoj Bishnoi's father owns a 3.75-acre land that was eventually converted into a village homestay to meet the demand of commercial ecotourism once Bishnois became famous after the 1998 black buck killing incident. Manoj now runs this place where one can experience Bishnoi-life by staying in their traditional hut made from material gathered locally. During my stay I was treated to Bishnoi food comprising of the famous *sangri khadi*, *bajra roti*, lentil, *khichdi*, garlic-tomato *chutney*, *ghee* and jaggery. Early morning, I went on a gypsy safari in the conservation reserve known as Gudha Vishnoiyan Conservation Reserve, arranged by an organization known as *Guda Bishnoi Village Safari*, run by two brothers Bhagirath and Mahender Bishnoi. Bhagirath, Mahender and Manoj are cousins and together they have been running this ecotourism activity for eight years. During the two hours of wildlife safari in the conservation reserve, with Mahender as guide, we spotted hundreds of males, females, and young black bucks, a few chinkaras, wild boars, and a few female nil gai etc. Among birds we saw Indian peafowl, black drongo, long-tailed shrike, house sparrow, red vented and black-eared bulbul, white breasted kingfisher, few species of lark, cormorant, couple of spoonbill storks, lesser grebe, and folks of Demoiselle crane. The migratory birds visit this place during winter. There are waterbodies near Bishnoi villages, and local villagers feed these birds as part of their Bishnoi tradition of protecting nature and all life forms.

After the conservation reserve, we visited a few Bishnoi settlements to see how traditionally they make their living. Besides being shepherds, their other means of livelihood are pottery, block printing and weaving. Of course, the agenda of including this visit in the ecotourism package was purely commercial. The tourists were expected to not just see their artwork, but also to spread the word of their work to the outer world and promote their products to encourage as well as support their livelihood. In the era of digital intervention in fashion and handicrafts, these artisans who make everything with their bare hands, are on the brink of extinction.

As per Ishrath's article, *"The Bishnois are rightfully called the first environmentalists of India. They have given more to nature in comparison to what the entire country would have contributed so far. In spite of living in the arid desert regions for centuries they have been following the dictates of their religious principles."*

Not just protecting and conserving endangered wildlife, which are a delight for ecotourists and wildlife photographers, they made their settlements in the most ecofriendly manner. They do not fell trees. They only collect dead wood. Even a carpenter waits patiently for the tree to fall. Wild foliage grows on their agricultural land and farmers are known to demarcate a portion of their cultivable land for animals like nil gais, chinkaras and black bucks to feed on. To minimize the use of green trees, they use cow dung cakes as fuel for cooking. Potter Rezzak, whose house I visited, uses only mud and a spinning wheel to create his marvellous artwork. Block printer Haider Ali uses only vegetable colour for printing, and weaver Om Prakash uses only camel hair, cotton, and coconut fibre to weave carpets. Thus, no fossil fuel is burned to generate electricity in any form, no chemicals are discharged to contaminate land or water, no emission to pollute air, and no depletion of natural resources. Bishnois do not need to break their heads to learn the complex *"Circular Economy"* to reuse and recycle plastic or electronic wastes. They do not generate any of them.

Ishrath mentions in his article, *"To unite people on a common platform, Guru Jambeswar Ji advised 29 principles to become a Bishnoi. The word 'Bishnoi' stands for BISH (which means 20), and NOI (mean 9) derived from these 29 principles out of which 6 principles are dedicated to environmental protection and compassion for all living beings. Of the 6 tenets that focus on protecting nature, the two most profound ones are:*

1.   Jeev Daya Palani – Be compassionate to all living beings.

2.   Runkh Lila Nahi Ghave – Do not cut green trees.

Though these rules have been made centuries back, they still hold good and are more than relevant to the environmental problems faced in today's world."

Notably, *"Jeev Daya Palani – Be compassionate to all living beings"* sums up the first two principles of modern day's Deep Ecology principle and *"Runkh Lila Nahi Ghave – Do not cut green trees"* is the underlying thought of the third principle.

If you still think "Deep Ecology" and "Bio-spherical Egalitarianism" are utopianism, then you are yet to experience the "Bishnoi way of life".

However, as I mentioned at the beginning of this book, there is a hegemony created by the Capitalist World to counter Deep Ecology and all forms of radical environmentalism. Therefore, Neo-liberal Sustainability was born.

On 3rd January 2024, Chief Executive Officer at Global Waste Management company, *Re Sustainability* and my mentor Masood Mallick published a short article in *LinkedIn*, titled, *"SUSTAINABILITY - A NARRATIVE HIJACKED…"*. In that article, he mentions, *"We are in deep trouble environmentally – and things are actually moving from bad to worse! Across our oceans, our forests, our cities, our communities... we are facing an environmental crisis of a proportion that is unprecedented in history!"*

Masood mentioned in his article, how a *green utopia* has been created in the name of sustainability, which presents a misguided narrative through *"images of lush organic farms, gleaming wind turbines, smiling children... and the mandatory pair of hands holding a very green globe..."*. He firmly conveys that *"beneath this glossy veneer of social media campaigns and influencer posts, a troubling reality lurks. On-ground facts are very different."* One classic example is modern society's ecstasy over electric vehicles to meet their sustainability aspiration. Masood has enlightened all these aspirers with the fact backed by *"real science"*, *"your new "green" electric car.... likely has a higher carbon footprint, than your old diesel jalopy... and this, by the way, is true for most electric vehicles sold in India today!"*

Sustainability initiatives far from being supported by real science would not meet any Global Leaders' aspiration of combating climate change by 2030. In fact, Masood mentions in his article, that as per a recent *WRI report (State of Climate Action Report 2023)*, we are not on track to realize the 2030 targets for the indicators related to sectoral climate action assessed, across power, buildings, industry transport, forests and land, food and agriculture, technological carbon removal, and climate finance. *"Ironically – the one indicator that is on track to meet its 2030 target as per this (WRI) report – is the growth in sales of Electric Vehicles!!!*

And this, while the annual rate of deforestation was equivalent to 15 football fields per minute in 2022."

The urban affluent folks captivated by this green utopia, are failing to see this environmental crisis. The pseudo environmentalism (the Neo-liberal Sustainability strategy) of Capitalist Corporations created enough commoditized sustainability solutions for them to be distracted from any deep ecological solution (termed as radical environmentalism by these Corporations).

But the indigenous people across this subcontinent are not deceived by them.

A decade ago, on 18th April 2013, the Dongria Kondhs, a particularly vulnerable tribal group from Rayagada in Odisha won a historic legal battle in the Supreme Court of India. In the *Orissa Mining Corporation Ltd vs Ministry of Environment & Forest case*, the court recognised their cultural, religious, and spiritual rights on the Niyamgiri Hill, over *Vedanta Company*'s claim to exploit the hills for bauxite. The

Vedanta-OMC joint venture wanted to mine bauxite in the Niyamgiri Hills and faced stiff resistance from the Dongria Kondhs, as they not only inhabited the Niyamgiri hills, but also worshipped Niyam Raja, the supreme god of the Niyamgiri forest and sustained themselves on the resources of the Niyamgiri forests, by practicing horticulture and shifting cultivation. The Corporations (*Vedanta-OMC*) wanted to create an open-cast mine there, violating Niyam Dongar, disrupting its rivers, and ending the Dongria Kondh's status as a distinct group. When the case was adjudicated by the Supreme Court of India, the apex court recognized the cultural, religious, and spiritual rights of the tribe on the hills. The referendum issued by Supreme Court, resulted in the establishment of a rare registration of the Dongria Kondhs' claim for sovereignty, self-determination, and territorial autonomy. It is also considered as India's first environmental referendum in which Dongria Kondhs won a landmark legal battle against *Vedanta Company*'s plans to exploit the Niyamgiri Hill for bauxite.

If Bishnois were the pioneers in radical environmentalism, then 500 years later Dongria Kondhs continued the same legacy of challenging Capitalist Economy's exploitation of nature in the name of development. Ironically *Vedanta* as an organization is committed to *"transforming the planet"*. Their *"comprehensive Environmental and Social Governance (ESG) vision"* promises *"building a sustainable future for an empowered nation by addressing its social and environmental needs."* They claim that they *"proactively engage to incorporate sustainability in all their practices."* This is what could be termed as *"SUSTAINABILITY - A NARRATIVE HIJACKED..."!*

There are many indigenous people in various remote and isolated forest villages who have silently lived their lives in a deep ecological way, centuries before the term "nature based solution" was coined. One such indigenous community who also stunned the world by their sustainable ways of living is a small tribe in Arunachal Pradesh. Their wet rice cultivation system and their agricultural system are extensive even without the use of any farm animals or machines. So is their sustainable social forestry system. *UNESCO* has proposed their valley to be included as a World Heritage Site for its "extremely high productivity" and "unique" way of preserving the ecology.

For five days in a winter season, after my stay at Bishnoi village and visiting several indigenous communities of Odisha, I went to Ziro Valley, which is home to the tribal group called the Apatanis. One amongst the very few tribes in the world that worships only nature (*Donyi- Polo* or Sun & Moon). Ziro is a small, picturesque valley tucked away in the lower Subansiri district of Arunachal Pradesh. In the villages of Hong, Hari and Modang, I interacted with around fifteen octogenarian Apatani men and women. Couple of them are village priests known as *Saman* and perform rituals and medical diagnosis on a need basis. These octogenarian folks are unique because of their women folks' tattoos and nose plugs. My homestay host, a middle aged Apatani man and a schoolteacher by profession, told me that hundreds of years ago Apatani valley was invaded by another indigenous tribe called Nyishi. Nyishi men found Apatani women very pretty and abducted them. Therefore, to protect themselves from Nyishi men, young Apatani girls started nose plugging to appear ugly.

I heard similar stories in Koraput and Rayagada of Odisha when I met Lanja Saura and Gadaba. Lanja Saura women have their own unique way of ear piercing and Gadaba women wear heavy bangles around their necks. Apparently, these are efforts by women to appear ugly to men from other tribes, to avoid abduction. However, I noticed that these traditions are no longer followed by the younger generations among these indigenous groups. Even many women from older generations have opted to remove their nose or ear plugs and heavy bangles from their necks.

The book *In Tribes of Koraput*, mentions that, *"these tribal people show utmost respect to these trees and their sacred groves and never cut down even a branch of it. This shows that the tribals are tree worshippers and this aspect of culture among the tribals can be systematically encouraged. It will definitely help in preservation of ecology and nature in tribal areas. The sacred groves also reflect biodiversity and if preserved will attract ethno-tourism."*

In various remote and isolated villages of Odisha and in Ziro, I witnessed this emerging trend of ethno-tourism as quite a few national and international tourists were found to be roaming around with their cameras. Not just sacred groves and forests, photography of women with tattoos, nose plugs, dangling earlobes with heavy earrings and bangles around neck are probably the key photo-tourism attractions for urban affluent folks. Especially, as these traditions are dying, the urge for documenting them at the earliest is also growing. My local ethno-tourism guide of Odisha, Jayant told me that there are only two living old Gadaba women who still wear such bangles around their neck.

An inclusive ecotourism should not just focus on unique features of people, place, habitat, flora, and faunal species, it should promote the importance of various indigenous ecological practices that are effective in combatting climate change. Such ecotourism is based on the concept of nature-based solution. Such ecotourism is Deep Ecology based tourism, and a response to Neo-Liberal Sustainability based commoditized Pseudo-Ecotourism.

During my trip to Ziro Valley, a lesser-known book, authored by Apatani scholar Dani Kacha caught my attention. In his book, *"Paddy-Cum-Fish-Culture In Ziro Valley"*, he mentions, *"a unique land and water resource utilization system known as 'paddy-cum-fish-culture' was developed by the energetic early settlers in the Ziro valley. They used to build up dams and dug channels in the valley bottom to an unbroken series of rice field. Ever since the Apatanis established themselves in their present habitation, rice cultivation on irrigated terrace fields has been the main base of their economy. It has been necessitated due to the limited land resource of the Apatanis in the valley. The physical, socio-cultural and economic factors of the area have played vital role to make the valley distinct from the rest of the districts."*

In his book, Dani explained the concept of paddy cum fish culture, which I witnessed being practiced among Apatanis firsthand. *"In rainy season wild fish migrate to the crop fields from rivers and other water bodies through excess water flow and flood. These fish are trapped in the paddy fields and grow there for some month. After rainy season when water dries up in the paddy fields, farmers use to collect them from their crop fields. Thus, cultivators earn considerable revenue by collecting these fish from their crop fields by selling them in market. There cultivation field are supported by strong bunds for preventing leakage of water and retaining it to the desired depth and also to prevent the escaping of cultivated fishes during floods water run-off."* The fish excreta increase the availability of nitrogen, phosphorous, calcium and magnesium in paddy water and hence it increases rice yield.

These traditional agroecosystems are intricately linked with nature and are well fitted to local environmental conditions for socio-economic and cultural needs of the people of the valley. These are sustainable, self-sufficient, and efficient due to the strong organization and sharing of ecological knowledge such as crop soil interaction, nutrition management, soil, and water conservations among the farmers engaged in agriculture in the Ziro valley. The perfect real-life demonstration of nature-based solution implemented by humans to protect environment. Ecotourism organizations should not shy away from including this in their tourism itinerary.

Such ecotourism will play a pivotal role in eradicating all disillusions about sustainability and help humankind in re-focussing on real science-based solutions for climate change.

I wrote this book with an aspiration to see every school going child encouraged to participate in ecotourism as part of their basic education, and every higher educational institution teaching ethical, deep ecology-based ecotourism, embracing the concept of nature-based solution.

I wrote this book with an aspiration to see an inclusive deep ecology-based ecotourism in practice in every ecotourism destination by every ecotourist, wildlife and nature enthusiast, and photographer.

I wrote this book with an aspiration to see every ecosystem of the planet – mountains, hillocks, deserts, grassland, barren field, wetlands, forests, agricultural field, tea and coffee estates, villages, and ponds – wherever there is potential to protect threatened species, inside or outside protected areas - included in the ecotourism business by ecotourism organizations.

I also wrote this book with an aspiration to see every forest dweller, indigenous person, village farmer and fisherfolk of every ecosystem included in the ecotourism business and recognized for equal benefit sharing, generated from such ecosystem services and ecotourism business.

More than two decades ago, I started pursuing my career as a sustainability consultant with a certain ideology. But in the process of chasing materialistic demands of the corporate clients I served, I forgot about the ideology and fell into the trap of the mundane professional life. As Masood mentioned in his *LinkedIn* article, I too was busy in drawing feel-good pictures of *"lush organic farms, gleaming wind turbines, smiling children... and the mandatory pair of hands holding a very green globe..."*, to meet the demands of Corporations. The nature exploration, which I had started a decade ago reminded me of the ideology and I rediscovered the passion I had for my profession. The passion for abating the possibility of *"an unprecedented environmental crisis"*.

Witnessing the merging of human culture with non-human nature completed the merger of my passion with my profession once again.

Nature and the Ecotourism are no longer mere supplementary pursuits for me.

I never met Vedavyasa after our Nameri trip. After many years I heard from a close friend that he was in Gabon, a country on the Atlantic coast of Central Africa, with one of the most varied and important fauna reserves.

In Gabon, besides his regular job as an electrical engineer, he joined *Field Guide Association of Southern Africa*. In-between his regular work, whenever he finds time, he takes his guests around to show forests and animals.

He left urban life and now lives in raw nature, waking up in the morning to a huge African rock python or a deadly Gabon viper lying in his front yard. Some days he sees pug marks of the golden cat on wet sand in the backyard of his office cum home, situated in the deep African rainforest. On another day as he enjoys his meal consisting of the meat of African water buffalo, a woodland kingfisher with its bright blue back and white neck, rapidly flutters through the fence around his cottage. Perhaps, the bird is cautioning all other living creatures about the human intruder, in its loud trill call which sounds like a nail run down the teeth of a comb. In peak rainy season, he encounters new types of insects. Some of them sting causing swelling, some others cause eczema or sores on the skin, that might lead to severe fever and hallucination.

Living in proximity with nature almost like other non-human life forms is not just a mere escapade for him. It is no longer a substitute for enjoyment from his profession. He has no reason to chase fame and glory any more. Eventually he *"found far more answers in the woods than he ever did in the city!"* I am glad he did.

The Epilogue

A Survival Story in the "Shadow of the Bengal Tiger"

Why does the urban affluent class, surrounded by extreme form of materialism, believe that surviving in nature, in a raw-dense forest, the territory ruled by the mighty Bengal Tiger – would add fame and glory to their already "successful material lifestyle"?

Is it true that despite all-out efforts in integrating economics and environment, as a last desperate attempt to save this planet, in the innermost recesses of our soul we believe that it is not "anthropocentric ecology" but "deep ecology" which reinforces the core foundation of our survival-success on this planet?

The urban affluence is sustained by market economy and to respond to the need of market economy we have relentlessly commodified nature. To achieve this commodification, we integrated ecology and economy and named the cocktail conservation approach as "sustainable development".

Clearly, we do not adequately trust the "sustenance" of "sustainable development". Therefore, as a community, we support "sustainable development" in public; and as an individual, secretly we look for every opportunity to live life based on the philosophy of "deep ecology".

When we successfully survive the "deep ecology" based lifestyle for a short time, we return to live the life of "sustainable development" to join the larger community in response to the needs of market economy. We sing glorious songs of our survival in "deep ecology" based lifestyle and proclaim our proximity to nature. We do so just to surrender ourselves again to the usual materialistic lifestyle, to live in comfort. Afterall, we have been conditioned so.

For a sizeable population of urban nature lovers, this is the pattern of their life. Living a self-contradictory life and making every effort for self-consolation in an attempt to shield themselves from the ruthless reality of materialistic lifestyle.

The seventy-two-hour survival story of eight men and women of urban affluent class, in the buffer zone of Bandhavgarh tiger reserve, at the onset of monsoon, was all about this conflict between "deep ecology" and "sustainable development".

These eight men and women, known as "survivors in making" were put together inside the dense forest of Bandhavgarh National Park and tiger reserve, by an India based organization known as *Jungle Survival Academy (JSA)*. The organization, with the help of local traditional forest dwellers, and ex-Indian Army service men designed a seventy-two-hour survival course to enable non-forest dwellers to fight fears of forest, as well as to live a dream, that of being in the wilderness of the Bandhavgarh Jungles in Madhya Pradesh. The idea was to enable the urban folks to experience the wild, to explore the unexplored and to challenge their inner self to survive in an unknown terrain with few resources. As proclaimed by the *Jungle Survival Academy*, they bring to us (non-forest dwellers), one of its kind survival courses to test our spirit and to make our adrenaline rush to fight and survive in the wild.

The most interesting part is that they document this entire survival challenge, and the "survivors in making" were chased by the camera crew during the entire course.

Before I proceed with this survival story, allow me to introduce the eight individuals who were selected for this challenge.

Soma Ghosh from Lucknow. A radio jockey and presenter who works for a State Government influenced FM channel of Lucknow city. A lady in her late thirties or early forties, separated from her husband and living with parents, looking for a meaningful and exciting life. She finds participating in adventure sports a great way of adding colour to her life. She has participated in bungee jumping, river rafting etc. and participating in a jungle survival challenge, she says, in her own words, *"would add another feather to my cap"*. Soma arrived at the forest with contrasting bright clothing, a bagful of cosmetics and other make up accessories. On several instances during our stay in the jungle, she applied cosmetics right in the middle of the forest, in the shade of a tree.

Akash Shrotriya from Bhopal. A guy in his early thirties. I never understood why he was there and what his expectations were. Apparently, he runs his own NGO which is involved in community welfare and wildlife awareness programmes. He contradicted himself several times, on and off camera. To his credit, he was one of the fittest 'survivors in making' and always critical of JSA and its instructors (off camera of course).

Ojas Mehta from Surat. A businessman by profession and a bodybuilder cum model cum Netflix TV series actor by hobby. Like most of the body builders he looks strong and capable of taking any challenge, and was very particular about dietary preferences. Through this course, he missed his high protein diet and regular hydration plan, and was quite vocal about it. Ojas is also an ex-cricket player who play for the state of Gujarat in Ranji trophy. He is well connected with top-notch Indian national cricketers and Bollywood movie stars. His primary objective was to create adequate video footages of his survival activities in wilderness. He surprised us all when he revealed his age to be 49 years. He looks no more than 35.

Neha from Delhi. A 29-year-old marketing professional with a multinational company, and a

Yoga instructor and trekker by hobby. She is fit, strong and up to any challenge but again like most fitness enthusiasts, very particular about diet. She loves talking about herself and reminded us very often how much she missed her three meals a day. Like Soma, she came with a mind-set of participating in an adventure sport, but with the right kind of mental and physical preparation.

Mahim from Noida. A Corporate Trainer by profession, but that's not his real identity. He was the most royal amongst all "survivors in making", revealed over time, as the challenges became tougher. Despite his honest attempt to remain modest and polite, his discomfort due to the hardships of living in wilderness became gradually apparent. He is a descendent of the King of Patiala, and his royal lifestyle made him vulnerable in raw nature. Like Akash, I was not too sure about Mahim's purpose for being part of this course. I initially assumed it was because of Neha. They appeared to me, to be a couple. They adorned similar clothes and shoes, and travelled and stayed together. In fact, during introduction, Neha mentioned that they were together. But gradually they went into a denial mode, and learnt that although Mahim was single, Neha had married six months ago.

Rishabh Goel from Delhi. The youngest in the group. Another businessperson who runs a few departmental stores and manages a family run business to feed 18 members of his family. He was the one amongst all the participants who was more candid about his reasons for being there. He had a bad accident some time ago and consequently went into depression. Once he recovered from his injury, he started looking for something, which would help in regaining his lost confidence to take challenges. And thus, he ventured into the middle of this tiger reserve.

Dr. Prakash Arya from Gandhinagar. A pediatrician by profession and pianist by hobby. The most grounded and down to earth person amongst us. Probably the most suitable candidate for the challenge with a strong survival instinct. Over time, we realized that surviving in the wild came effortlessly and naturally to him. He was probably there to re-assess his already tried and tested ability to survive in raw nature.

Last but not the least, this confused storyteller who is caught between "eco-centrism" and "anthropocentrism". The man who makes his living by practicing "sustainable development" but wants to adopt the principles of "deep ecology" in his life. I wanted to participate in this course to get an opportunity to stay as close as possible to the *shadow of the Bengal Tiger*. Not that I had not explored tiger territory before, but as a hobbyist wildlife photographer, I was always privileged to avail support services on demand, which made my survival as comfortable as it could be on any nature holiday. Ecotourism is designed in such a way that ecotourists never get an opportunity to complain about the facilities provided to them.

From that perspective, this seventy-two-hour survival course was quite indifferent about "anthropocentric" requirements and behaviors. Therefore, I decided it would be interesting to observe the struggle and behavior of other participants in raw nature. Participants who came from different spheres of life, particularly those built upon hard-core materialism.

One Indian monsoon morning, operational manager of JSA, Mukul picked me up from a rural bus stand of Bagdara village, located around ten kilometres from the base camp where our survival journey would begin. While driving me there, a three-time jungle survivor and Himalayan trekker himself, Mukul told me that due to prolonged COVID19 pandemic induced lockdown, people movement had reduced significantly in the villages and on the roads in the fringe area of the buffer zone of the tiger reserve. This has increased the free movement of other animals including tigers. Presently tiger sighting near waterbodies at the edge of the forest or in the corridor between the core and buffer zones of the forest is more frequent. Along with excitement, this piece of information also brings necessary caution for the "survivors in making", as possibility of close encounter with tigers, in that patch of forest, is now higher than pre-pandemic era.

Therefore, at the beginning of our course, our instructors - ex-service personnel Colonel Iqbal

Mehta and ex special force commander Shambhu *aka* Ustad ji, spent some time educating us about animals' tracks and signs, and ways to escape any animal attacks.

When we started from basecamp, we were provided with some basic survival tools like knife, axe, head-torch, and a whistle. After entering the forest, our first task was preparing a spear from a bamboo tree with the help of the knife and axe. Both Iqbal and Ustad ji explained and demonstrated how to make and use improvised weapons from raw green hard bamboo. Dislodging a bamboo shoot from the thick stump of bamboo tree needed a lot of strength and energy. Although it was monsoon season, the rain was delayed. Therefore, we quickly dehydrated in the scorching heat. I noticed Soma and Mahim giving up quickly and looking for aid from others to complete the task.

Besides two instructors, we also had a local septuagenarian forest dweller with us, Harshad Dada. With Ustad ji's and his help we each made a spear that would both protect us from animal attack and also help during our hiking, in addition to removing thorny branches of small trees that may obscure our path.

We started hiking, and were soon dehydrated due to excessive sweating. We filled our water bottles before we pushed off from the base camp, but I noticed that the water level in my 1-liter bottle was alarmingly low. When I asked for any water sources nearby, as if I wasn't sufficiently alarmed already, Ustad ji replied, *"due to less rainfall, all waterbodies in this forest patch are dry. Therefore, we must wait till we reach our next camping point. We should get there by dusk."*

From my marathon running experience, I know that my sweat rate is high, with a tendency of cramps due to excessive dehydration. This thought worried me further, and I decided to walk as slowly as possible but at the same time keeping a constant distance from the last person of the group. Another way of avoiding any possible predator attack is to walk in a group.

Eight of us, with three nature survival teachers, were not just hiking. Rather we were engaged in the most important aspect of surviving in the forest. We were foraging, looking for naturally available resources, under the guidance of local forest dwelling tribal man, Dada.

Dada was helping us to identify edible leaves, tubers, and fungi. We gathered them and collected it in a bag. It was to be our lunch and dinner for the day. Tubers of plants locally known as *shatavari* (*Asparagus racemosus*) and *moori*; leaves of a shrub locally known as *moker* and a circular fungus locally known as *koru* constituted our collection for the day.

Around 2 pm, we stopped at a place to cook. We were given ration of rice and black gram (locally known as *Urad dal*). We carefully used water to wash some portion of the rice and lentil, both mixed together. We then added leaves of *moker* into it. We chewed on tubers of *shatavari* and *moori*, sucking the juice while hiking to keep our lips and tongue moist in an attempt to cope with thirst. *Koru* we saved for evening supper.

Lighting fire by creating friction between dry tree branches was the toughest task. Even ex special force commander Ustad ji, was almost on the verge of giving up. Although the rain was irregular in early monsoon, it was enough to make the branches and leaves wet and moist. Thus, lighting of fire appeared to be a never-ending process. After immense struggle, the fire was lit, and we boiled all the edible stuff together. However, thirty to forty-five minutes of boiling was not enough, resulting in half cooked rice. We did not add enough water to rice. We did so, to save water for drinking as we still had to survive another two-three hour before we found a waterbody.

We were all hungry, so we ate and patted our own backs for whatever we had managed to cook. Only Mahim and Ojas were visibly upset with the outcome. But they ate quietly.

The last few hours of the day were all about surviving thirst. All our bottles were empty by then and we were not even close to a waterbody. We literally dragged ourselves by throwing ourselves onto our bamboo sticks. Walking through dense forest was not new to me. I have done it in the forest of Western Ghats and North-East India. But the rainforests provide a good canopy cover. On the other hand, the forest of Central India is dry and moist deciduous in nature. There are tall trees, but the canopy is not big enough to protect from the harsh sunlight. Our energy drained rapidly. Less intake of food and water made our movement slower.

We were desperate for water. We reached a place where the forest floor was covered with dry leaves. Ustad ji picked up a leaf, smelled it and poured something from it into his mouth. It was rainwater that had accumulated in dry leaves. He told us, *"If you are desperate to quench your thirst then this is the only option available to you. Walk slowly and come closer so that you don't step on the leaves containing rainwater."*

We all gradually gathered and drank the water. Mahim and Akash refrained from drinking it. Mahim later said that he could not imagine drinking water like that, therefore, he thought it was all right to stay thirsty and dehydrated.

Iqbal warned, *"Smell the water first before you gulp it"*. Any foul smell from accumulated water in ditches, or leaves indicates that the water is not potable. There is no other way of measuring potability of water in wilderness.

By 7 pm, it was dark, and we arrived at the camping site, where we had to pitch the tent. Ojas and Mahim expected someone to receive them with tea and snacks at the site. When they expressed this expectation, the camera crew laughed sarcastically.

Once we pitched our tents, Soma put on her evening make up, did her hair, and slipped into her evening dress. Rest of us dispersed into the forest to collect dry wood to light a bonfire. Another difficult hour trying to light the fire to cook, and another dismal outcome as far as the quality of cooking was concerned.

Ojas was more content this time and accepted the outcome as a natural process in wilderness. Mahim became grumpier and criticized the idea of putting *koru* (fungi) in food. He declared it was rubbery and not at all tasty.

Not a leaf stirred the entire night, and it was difficult to sleep in the tent. Fortunately, we had individual tents; therefore, it was possible to strip down to nothing in an effort to escape from sweating like a pig. Early morning, we were greeted to a light shower, but that just worsened the situation.

I got out of my tent at six; the surrounding grassland was still wet and moist. We had survived in this tiger terrain for twenty-four hours and we had forty-eight more hours to go.

At eight in the morning, we started hiking through the forest. We spent the day learning unarmed combat, and making ropes with the leaves of *moori*. We needed a lot of rope to tie and carry thick wood for the bonfire and more importantly for making shelter.

Foraging continued besides all these activities. Besides our regular *moori*, *shatavari* and *moker*, we added fungi to our menu, known as *"deema ki piri"* or fungus grown on termite tower (*Termitomyces sp*. Or Termite Hill mushroom). The white globulous head at the top of a slender white body popped out from termite towers. We happily collected the mushrooms in hope of eating a better meal than the previous two.

Rope making and foraging took more time than the previous day. Meanwhile as we walked, Dada sensed movement of some animal. We sat quietly on a plain grassland for a while, and took a detour until he found it safe to move. As we crossed a ditch full of sand, both Dada and Iqbal drew our attention towards fresh pugmark of a female adult tiger. The tigress clearly walked along the ditch and according to Iqbal it was perhaps in the morning, suggesting that the tigress must still be around the area. Apparently, this area was used frequently by a female and her cub as a corridor between the core and buffer zones of Bandhavgarh tiger reserve.

Iqbal looked at us and said, *"Some story to tell others once you survive next forty hours".*

Experience of tiger encounter in wild, even if it is not the tiger itself but the sign of its presence around you– sign of debuckling on tree trunk, pugmarks on soil – all count as "some story to tell others". Everybody - wildlife enthusiast, nature lover, adventure sports person or jungle survivor alike – wants to tell this story to others. The story, that makes one stand out from others; the story, that makes one brave and cool; the story that makes one a glorious survivor in the forest that is ruled by the majestic beast of this subcontinent.

That statement from Iqbal at that moment in the buffer zone of Bandhavgarh National Park was sufficient to establish the glory of Bengal Tiger in the subcontinental forest. If one can survive with him in his territory, without any harm, then one has lived few hours of his/her life embracing principles of "deep ecology".

Dusk had fallen, and we hadn't had the time to cook our lunch. Almost twenty-four hours since our last meal. We had learnt to survive thirst by then. Our body and mind were conditioned to live twenty-four hours in the hot summer on 1 liter of water.

As light was diminishing quickly, we ramped up our shelter making and cooking arrangements. We divided ourselves into two groups, each taking charge of one of these two key tasks. Afterall, we had to spend the night in the forest, where tiger movement was already confirmed.

The previous day, we had been given a cooking vessel, but today to make it more challenging, it was taken away. Therefore, in the absence of a civilized cooking utensil, the remaining rice, black gram, leaves of *moori* and *deema ki piri* were all mixed, washed, and wrapped in leaves. The leaf bundle was placed over dry branches inside a rectangular hole dug into the ground with the help of axe and knife. With a lot of patience and effort, the fire was finally lit and the mixed edible stuff began to bake with the aid of dry wood charcoal. As usual, we were running short of water. We had to survive on a treetop, where the makeshift night shelter or *machan* was made with bamboo sticks and rope made from leaves of *moori* plant. Therefore, we dared not spend too much water in cooking.

In the darkness, it would not be a wise idea to venture out for drinking water, especially when predator movement around us was suspected.

The end result was having to eat for the third consecutive time, half cooked or barely cooked meal.

Rishabh, Ojas and Mahim decided not to eat anything. Soma, Doctor, Neha, and Akash ate to the best of their best capacity. I hogged the food to fill my stomach. I wanted a good night's sleep.

Mahim was on empty stomach for almost thirty-six hours by then. To top it, there were spiders near our cooking area. He said he hated spiders as they spoiled his garden plants in the balcony. In addition, he also had Arachnophobia. He was just very disgruntled.

In the *machan,* once our camera crew and instructors left us in the wilderness to survive the rest of the night, the possibility of a coup started brewing under the leadership of the Prince of Patiala. Mahim's royal legacy just refused to accept such ill treatment caused by "uncivilized food" and "unhygienic living conditions". Neha and Ojas supported him softly as both of them were genuinely missing their rigid diet regime. As a result, packets of glucose biscuits arrived at the *machan* to serve his majesty and his hoi polloi.

Yet again, the pseudo affection for nature by urban affluent class was exposed; once again urban folk's inability to cope with challenges thrown by wilderness was visible; once again the urban lifestyle's lack of faith towards complete dependency on nature was revealed; once again human's preference to live as per their own convenient lifestyle over the way of life offered by nature was proven; and yet again "sustainability development" won against "deep ecology".

Next morning, to my surprise Mahim said he was not hungry. He was just clearly trying to make a point that he deserved food palpable to "civilized" people. The human life forms will always remain entangled in this web of complexity of so-called civilization and keep all other non-human life forms at bay. Hence, it defeats the purpose of all human defined conservation concepts- like cohabitation, eco-resilience, eco-restoration among many others.

Each of our abilities to survive in the forest like other non-human life forms was significantly challenged. Nevertheless, we all survived forty-eight long hours in the wilderness of a tiger reserve of Central India.

The next twenty-four hours really broke us completely, both mentally and physically. The climate was even more hostile due to rising temperatures. Few rounds of shower during daytime increased the humidity further, making our life more miserable. For three continuous days, we were in same clothes and undergarments. Everything was soaking wet in our own sweat, attracting a lot of insects to sit on the open parts of our body, thus triggering fierce itching all over.

We had to manage with lesser supply of water, and again it was yet another day without food. We spent the day learning how to tie different knots, which may come handy during climbing, material lifting and rescuing; we learnt slithering with the help of a rope from 30 feet tall treetop; we learnt how to collect rainwater and filter it with charcoal; and how to make improvised traps to capture animals. Ustad ji was a real artist of all these techniques and taught us with a lot of patience. We were mesmerized with Ustad ji's military art and Dada's local knowledge. These activities did not give us enough time to light a fire and cook food; however, we made time to forage for the night.

Ojas and I were marginally happier than others as we collected enough forest fruits called *bael*. *Aegle marmelos*, commonly known as *bael*, also Bengal quince, golden apple, Japanese bitter orange, stone apple, or wood apple, is a species of tree native to the Indian subcontinent and Southeast Asia. It is present in India, Bangladesh, Sri Lanka, Nepal, Thailand, and Malaysia as a naturalized species. This was the only edible fruit lying on the forest floor in abundance.

I remember during my childhood my father used to run after me with his concoction made from this horrid tasting fruit to cure my constipation. Who was to expect that a day would come, when I would consume this fruit as if it was panacea from heaven.

As night fell, many of us thought it was enough of survival and their body was no longer able to take the toll any further. Soma, Neha, and Mahim decided to leave. Ojas and Akash were in a dilemma. Although Akash was visibly tired, he claimed repeatedly, that he had lived through tougher situations. However, Ojas was quite honest in confessing that he had not gone through such hardship ever in his life. He comes from a background where he does not even need to carry his gym kitbag and protein shake on his own. But here in this forest he was going through these hardships with a smile on his face. As much of a smile that he could muster, that is. Despite his celebrity status he was quite a down to earth person.

Eventually both decided to stay back in the *machan* for the last night of our survival course.

The usual cooking process started for the night. Ojas lost his patience and decided to stay hungry. But Ustad ji told us boldly, *"You have to cook for me, I don't care whether you stay hungry or not!"*

The message was loud and clear to everybody, so we cooked food the same way as previous night and much to our surprise, the food was adequately boiled and quite palpable. It was just rice and *moori* leaves, but the most delicious meal we cooked during our survival course.

The next morning Rishabh, Dr. Prakash Arya, Ojas, Akash and I exited the forest after completing seventy-two hours of jungle survival in the tiger territory of a Central Indian landscape.

We all ventured into this forest with different objectives, but we all had one common ground. We all believed that we humans are incomplete without any connection with non-human life forms, regardless of how much we underestimate and disregard them. We agreed that ability to live in nature like any other living species, does not diminish us, rather magnifies our fame and glory as human beings.

All eight of us would indulge again in our regular life and respond to the needs of materialism. Nevertheless, my journey to embrace "deep ecology" has begun.

Few of the Images I took during various explorations in the subcontinental forests

Image 1: First tiger sighting at Tadoba

Image 2: Conflict over dominance at Corbett

Image 3: Tiger crossing river at Sundarbans (India)

Image 4: Human is part of tiger's food pyramid

Image 5: A fisherman of Sundarbans (India)

Image 6: Snarling by an annoyed tigress at Ranthambhore

Image 7: Love making at Tadoba

Image 8: Tiger tourism of Bandhavgarh

Image 9: A Coorg yellow bush frog at sacred grove

Image 10: A large-scaled pit viper at tea estate of Munnar

Image 11: Great Indian Bustard & windmills at DNP

Image 12: White bellied heron at Bhutan

Image 13: Black buck in Bishnoi village

Image 14: Dongria Kondh, the protectors of Niyamgiri Hill

Image 15: A rice-fish cultivation field of Apatani village

Image 16: "Lying down to get better perspective"

Acknowledgements

Firstly, I extend my heartfelt gratitude to the forest dwellers, the diligent forest guards, knowledgeable nature guides, safari-gypsy drivers, and boatmen I interacted with over the last decade while exploring various forests, sanctuaries, national parks, wetlands, deserts and other ecotourism destinations across the subcontinent. I am also thankful to fellow ecotourists, wildlife photographers, ecotour operators, eco-resort managers and staff, as well as tour leaders and mentors who have enriched my experiences and shaped my perspective on ecotourism and wildlife photography in this subcontinent.

The work of this book would have not been completed without the dedication and encouragement of my friend Brinda Nair. Brinda is a scholar of Cultural Studies from Christ University, Bangalore, with a masters in English literature (UGC-NET qualified), a theatre artist (associated with Bangalore Little Theatre), a management consultant (with degrees from BITS Pilani, and an MBA from Drexel University, USA). Brinda graciously edited my manuscript thoroughly and provided feedback to close the open loops in my narrative. Additionally, her husband Paddy, who is also my former colleague and a frequent companion on my nature-explorations, offered his technical expertise as a sustainability professional and took the burden of multiple readings of my manuscript. I am really grateful to them for their unwavering support and assistance.

I am grateful to my publisher, Zuri, and her dedicated team at Ukiyoto Publishing, for providing me the opportunity to publish with them and for their invaluable support and guidance.

My sincere gratitude to my employer ERM, and all my colleagues for their continued support during my extended sabbatical to complete the manuscript of this book. My special thanks to ERM's Southeast Asia Managing Partner, WeiChee Liew, for recommending and facilitating my sabbatical leave, ensuring I had the necessary approvals that allowed me to dedicate my time peacefully to this book.

I am fortunate to have friends and well-wishers who graciously read the manuscript prior to publication, offering valuable feedback and providing endorsements for the book. I appreciate the comments from and acknowledge the support of R. P. Nair, Pooja Uthappa, Gauri Noolkar-Oak, Anupam Bhattacharyya, Chubzang Tangbi, Tara Ramanujan, Parvathi Shajil, Raghu K Nair and Dr. Arun Venkataraman.

I am thankful to my photography mentors and ecotour team leaders – M.V. Shreeram, Manish Lakhani, Harsha Narasimhamurthy, Debashish Banerjee, Santosh Krishnamurthy, Phillip Ross,

Alfred Jacob, Tamanud Mitra, Soumyajit Nandy and Mohit Aggarwal.

I extend my deepest regards to some of the most exceptional natural history teachers in this subcontinent who have been my on-field ecology coaches and naturalists over the past decade – Gauri Shankar and Prashanth of Agumbe, Nirmal Kulkanri of Chorla, Foridi Numan of Bangladesh, Mirza Zulfiqur Rahman of Ziro valley, Nabi of Corbett Park, Lara Shering of Spiti, Reevu of Buxa, Rahul Gurung of Latpanchar, Anand Prasad of Tal Chhapar, Shambu *aka* Ustad ji of Jungle Survival Academy, Musa Khan of DNP, Palash Phukan of Namdapha, Sonam Tsering of Bhutan, Jayanta of Dulcimer-Odisha, Bhagirath and Mahender Bishnoi of Jodhpur, Shwetha and Akhil of Amrabad, Malik of Nagarjunasagar, Bahow Uddin of Drass, Konchok Dogmo of Ladakh, Sonu Liladhar of Dudhwa, Deepak Rajbanshi of Nepal, Ashy and Ajo Eldhose of Thattekad, Vikram Shill of Andaman, and Bijoy Kumar Das of Bhitorkonika.

This book could never have been written if I had not met these wonderful people.

I also thank my old friend Sankar Singha. The seed for this book was sown during my stay at Sankar's office guesthouse in the Baridhara area of Dhaka, while I was unexpectedly stranded due to an unfortunate train incident. In hindsight, perhaps, it wasn't unfortunate.

Lastly, I thank the forest departments, wildlife boards, tourism departments and tribal welfare authorities of India, Bangladesh, Nepal and Bhutan, for their efforts in fostering tourism opportunities in this subcontinent.

Bibliography

Anand vikamshi, S. S. (2023). *Birds of Old Magazine House*. Maharashtra: Anshasu Publications.

Arbabi, S. (2011). *The Complete Guide to Nature Photography*. New York: Amphoto Books.

(n.d.). *Bangladesh Tiger Action Plan 2009-2017 and 2018-2027*. Bangladesh Forest Department and Ministry of Environment and Forest.

Bhattacharyya, S. (n.d.). *A history of the social ecology of Sundarbans the colonial period*.

Bhujabal, C. (2019). *Mangalajodi - Bird Heaven*. Bhubaneshwar: Wild Orissa.

Bhushan, B. (2016). *Birds of Ramayana*. Pune: Vishwakarma Publications.

Bhutan. (n.d.). Lonely Planet.

Bhutan Himalayan Kingdom. (1979). Thimphu: The Royal Government of the Kingdom of Bhutan.

Carson, R. (2002). *Silent Spring*. Boston, New York: Mariner Book.

Chaoji, A. (2016). The Mighty Forests. *Maharashtra Unlimited, 5*(1).

Corbett, J. (1994). *Man Eaters of Kumaon*. New Delhi: Oxford India Press.

Corbett, J. (2016). *The Man-Eating Leopard of Rudraprayag.* New Delhi: Rupa Publications.

Daniel, J. C. (2018). *The Book of Indian Reptiles and Amphibians.* Mumbai: Bombay Natural History Society.

Dhamankar, A. (2014). *Trailing the Tiger.* Mumbai: Inking Innovations.

Dimitriyv, Y. (1984). *Man and Animals.* Moscow: Raduga Publishers.

Division, N. C. (2019). *Distribution and Habitat use of Tigers in Bhutan.* Department of Forests and Park Sevices, Ministry of Agriculture and Forests.

Foundation, M. S. (2010). *Pichavaram Mangrove Wetland : Situation Analysis.* IUCN.

Ghosh, A. (2019). *The Hungry Tide.* Noida: Harper Collins Publishers.

Guha, B. (1986). *Madhukari (Art of Honey-gathering) - Bengali.* Calcutta: Ananda Publishers.

Guha, R. (2006). *How Much Should a Person Consume?: Thinking through the Environment .* Delhi: UC Press.

Higgins, P. (2010). Eradicating Ecocide.

Hushangabadkar, P. (2022). Dog that doesn't bark. *Tadoba Diaries January 2022*(Issue 2).

John Seidensticker, E. D. (2010). *Tiger range collapse and recovery.*

K.K.Mohanti, P. J. (2021). *Tribes of Koraput.* Koraput: Council of Analytical Tribal Studies.

Kacha, D. (2017). *Paddy-cum-Fish Culture in Ziro Valley : Arunachal Pradesh*. Ziro Valley: Partridge.

Karanth, K. U. (2023). *Among Tigers: Fighting to Bring Back Asia's Big Cats*. Chicago: Chicago Review Press Incorporated.

Karanth, K. U. (August December 2003). Tiger Ecoloy and Conservation in the Indian Subcontinent. *100*(2&3).

Khullar, R. (2006). *Flowring Trees Shrubs & Climbers of India, Pakistan, Sri Lanla, Bhutan and Nepal*. New Delhi: Timeless Books.

Kipling, R. (2016). *The Jungle Book*. Kolkata: Projapoti.

Krishen, P. (2013). *Jungle Trees of Central India*. New Delhi: Punguin Books.

Mallon, T. M. (2016). Snow Leopards. *Biodiversity of the World : Conservation from Genes to Landscapes*.

Md M Rahman, M. M. (2010). The causes of deterioration of Sundarban Mangrove forest ecosystems of Bangladesh: Conservation and Sustainable Management issues. *2*(3).

Menon, V. (2014). *Indian Mammals A field guide*. Gurugram: Hachette Book Publishers India.

Ministry of Environment, F. a. (2018). *Status of Tigers in India*.

Mongomery, S. (2016). *Spell of the Tiger*. New Delhi: Aleph Book Company.

Muggenthaler, E. v. (2000). *Secrets hidden in a tiger's paralyzing roar.* AMERICAN INSTITUTE OF PHYSICS.

N. Krishna Kumar, P. U. (2013). *Flowering Plants of Sholas and Grasslands of the Nilgiris.* Coimbatore: Institute of Forest Genetics and Tree Breeding.

NEILSON, L. T. (2014). The Neoliberalisation of Sustainability. *Volume 13*.

Numan, F. (2017). *Amader Sundarban (Our Sundarban: A book about world largest mangrove forest Sundarban) - Bengali.* Dhaka, Bangladesh: Adorn Publication.

PA Sebastian, K. P. (2009). *Spiders of India.* Hyderabad: Universities Press.

(2023). *Project Tiger Achievement Book : 50 years of Tiger Conservation in India.* National Tiger Conservation Authority.

Ramgaonkar, D. J. (2022). More Space to Tigers. *Tadoba Diaries January 2022*(Issue 2).

Ranjini Murali, P. J. (n.d.). *Fungus Among Us : An exploration of fungi in the Anamalai hills.* Mysore: Nature Conservation Foundation.

Rawal, J. (2016). Editorial. *Maharashtra Unlimited, 5*(2).

(2006). *Report of Task Force on Grassland and Deserts.* New Delhi: Government of India, Planning Commission.

Richard Grimmett, C. I. (2014). *Birds of the Indian Subcontinent.* Oxford India Press.

Richard Grimmrtt, C. I. (2019). *Birds of Bhutan and the Eastern Himalayas*. London: Helm.

(2019). *STATUS OF TIGER HABITATS IN HIGH ALTITUDE ECOSYSTEMS OF BHUTAN, INDIA AND NEPAL (SITUATION ANALYSIS)*. GTF, Wildlife Institute of India, National Trust for Nature Conservation, Nepal and WWF.

(2022). *Status of Tigers 2022*. New Delhi: National Tiger Conservation Authority, India & Wildlife Institute of India.

(2022). *Status of Tigers and Prey in Nepal 2022*. Kathmandu: Department of National Parks and Wildlife conservation & Department of Forests and Soil Conservation.

(2010). *The St. Petersburg Declaration on Tiger Conservation*. Russia.

Vedavyasarao, D. (2017). *Hampi : The World Heritage Site*. Hampi: Sri Venkateshwara Book Centre.

Verma, D. R. (2024). The Mindful and Sustainable Nation : Compassion and Loving-Kindness. *Tashi Delek, XXV*(1).

Visuddha, L. (2021). The quest to see the Pallas's cat. *02 Jungwa*.

Wiseman, J. ". (1986). *SAS Survival Handbook*. London: Harper Collins.

About the Author

Arnab Basu

Arnab Basu, is a sustainability consultant, an environmental writer and a wildlife enthusiast. He has more than two decades of experience in advisory work on sustainability, nature-based solution, and environmental law. He did his graduation in Botany from University of Calcutta and post-graduation in Environment Management from Indian Institute of Social Welfare & Business Management (IISWBM), Calcutta. He also holds a post graduate diploma in Environmental Law from National Law School of India University (NLSIU), Bangalore.

As a wildlife enthusiast he has travelled across more than two-hundred eco-tourism destinations of eight countries in three continents. These include Western Himalayas of India and Eastern Himalayas of Bhutan and North-East India; Western Ghats; Central India and Eastern Ghats; Sub-Himalayan Terai region of India and Nepal; Mangroves of India, and Bangladesh; Tundra region of Scottish Highland; Rain Forest of Sumatra; Desert of Kutch and Western India; and Savannah of South Africa.

www.ingramcontent.com/pod-product-compliance
Lightning Source LLC
LaVergne TN
LVHW091538070526
838199LV00002B/121